Sophocles
Plays : One

The Theban Plays:

Oedipus the King, Oedipus at Colonus, Antigone

Collectively known as The Theban Plays, *Oedipus the King*, *Oedipus at Colonus* and *Antigone* stand at the fountainhead of world drama. They are presented in this volume in a new translation, accurate yet poetic and playable, by the playwright Don Taylor, who also directed them for a BBC-TV production broadcast in autumn 1986. The cast included Michael Pennington as Oedipus, Juliet Stevenson as Antigone and John Gielgud as Teiresias.

Sophocles was born at Colonus, just outside Athens, the son of a prosperous arms manufacturer. He first won a prize for tragedy in 468 BC, defeating the veteran Aeschylus amid scenes of great excitement. Altogether he is said to have composed some 123 plays. His long life spanned the rise and decline of the Athenian Empire and he held several public offices, both military and civil. As a priest of a minor deity he welcomed the cult of Asclepius to Athens in 420 BC, and for this he was honoured as a hero after his death. He was the leader of a fellowship of the Muses, or literary circle, and wrote a prose treatise On the Chorus, *now lost. He was content to spend all his life at Athens, and is reputed to have refused several invitations to royal courts. When he died, Aristophanes testifies that his genial charm was greatly missed.*

The translator, Don Taylor, was born in London in 1936. He graduated from Oxford University and spent a short time in the theatre before joining BBC TV. He became a leading drama director and worked exclusively on new plays, including early work by David Mercer, Hugh Whitemore and David Turner. He became a freelance in 1964, and since then has directed plays for television and theatre. His first stage play was presented at the Edinburgh Traverse Theatre in 1967 and he has continued to write many plays for TV, among them Dad, Flayed, When the Actors Come, In Hiding *and* The Testament of John, *and for the theatre including* The Roses of Eyam, The Exorcism *and* Brotherhood. *Including works for radio, he has written more than fifty plays and films, including three verse plays.*

SOPHOCLES

The Theban Plays

Oedipus the King
Oedipus at Colonus
Antigone

Translated and introduced by
Don Taylor

Methuen Drama

METHUEN WORLD CLASSICS

This edition first published in Great Britain in 1986
by Methuen London Ltd.

Reprinted in 1991 (twice) by Methuen Drama
an imprint of Reed Consumer Books Ltd
Michelin House, 81 Fulham Road, London SW3 6RB
and Auckland, Melbourne, Singapore and Toronto
and distributed in the United States of America by HEB Inc.,
361 Hanover Street, Portsmouth, New Hampshire 03801 3959

Reprinted 1992
Reissued with a new cover design 1993
Reprinted 1993

Copyright © 1986 Introduction and translation by Don Taylor

British Library Cataloguing in Publication Data
Sophocles
    The Theban plays.— (World dramatists)
    I. Title   II. Taylor, Don   III. Series
    IV. Sophocles. Oedipus Rex. *English*
    Oedipus the King   V. Sophocles. Oedipus
    Coloneus. *English* Oedipus at Colonus
    VI. Sophocles. Antigone. *English* Antigone
    882'.01   PA4414.A2

ISBN 0-413-42460-X

The front cover shows *La Mémoire* by René Magritte and is reproduced
by courtesy of the Collection de L'etat Belge. Copyright © ADAGP,
Paris and DACS, London 1992.

Printed in Great Britain
by Cox & Wyman Ltd, Reading, Berkshire

CAUTION

CONTENTS

INTRODUCTION
Sophocles, our Contemporary

Sophocles has probably been the most continuously popular dramatist in world literature. In the year 468 BC, when he was in his late twenties, he beat the reigning playwriting champion, Aeschylus, in the dramatic festival at Athens, and from that day to this – partly due to the fact that Aristotle, writing many years after his death, took *Oedipus the King* as his model tragedy – Sophocles' reputation as one of the two or three supreme masters of the dramatist's art has never suffered a decline. The Middle Ages lost sight of him, as they did of all Greek Art, but with the Renaissance, and the rediscovery of the few scraps of Greek drama that had survived, he returned, with his playwright's crown quite untarnished. No one, except Homer himself, has reigned so completely and for so long.

Is that, in itself, any good reason for reading and performing his plays? Do we value works of art merely for longevity, or even because generations of men and women have regarded them as the benchmark of excellence? The spirit of our particular age questions all such judgements. If there is a canon of literature, and an implied hierarchy of writers, by whose judgement is such a canon constructed? In the late twentieth century, there are no universally accepted systems of value, indeed, the world is now divided into two opposing camps, whose intellectual, philosophical and spiritual values confront each other as uncompromisingly as their nuclear weapons do. Traditional literary values are everywhere under attack as writers conscious of the cultural and political variety of the world ask the subversive questions 'by whose system of values do you decide that this writer is better than that one? Whose interests does this writer serve in his works? What ideological systems, consciously or unconsciously, do his writings reinforce?' It is the continuing task of poets, playwrights, directors and critics to try to define the standards by which we decide what is good or bad in art, in behaviour, or in different forms of human society. If, as practitioners, we feel instinctively that Sophocles contains something which is in every sense a matter of superlatives, we must give full rein to that instinct: but we have imposed upon us also, by that very act of assertion, the absolute necessity of trying to define that excellence, of stating quite clearly why this generation needs to hear what he has to say.

Sophocles, after all, wrote nearly 2,500 years ago for a society that had only recently emerged from the age of robber chieftains and piracy, and where the memory of human sacrifice was not a distant one. That society had confronted for the first time the task of living in organised urban political communities, and had conceived the idea of democracy. But it had signally failed to practise it with much success or for very long, and was in any case economically founded on an unenfranchised slave class. The culture which produced him achieved perhaps greater marvels of intellectual, spiritual and artistic insight, in a shorter time and in a smaller geographical area, than any culture before or since: but it was encumbered with a State religion that was out of date to many of the men of its own age. Even Homer, at the dawn of European culture, though he may be strict on the necessity of paying the gods the sacrifices and rites which are their due, pictures them in action in such a way as to provoke something less than respect. Euripides, Sophocles' contemporary, recognises that Dionysus and Aphrodite symbolise forces in human life of immense creative and destructive power: but he regards the idea of the gods' actual existence as divine creatures either as a ridiculous joke, or a moral insult to the human race. Can a man of such an age really have much to say to us, in a time when religion in all but the Islamic world has ceased to have much moral or intellectual force? We live under a two-pronged threat of destruction either from nuclear winter or ecological collapse, and we have discovered in ourselves, in the present century at least, a slavering brute who delights in organised murder, torture and repression to an extent which would probably have horrified sensitive men of any previous generation, even accustomed as they were to seeing brutalities publicly enacted which we see only on our television screens. What social or spiritual advice can this poet of the City State give to us, as he sees our divided world on the brink of destruction? Perhaps we should admit that Sophocles is just literary history, a nostalgic look back to the hopeful days at the beginning of the story, when the enacting of Oedipus' relation to the malign intricacies of destiny could have greater meaning than it can for us, under the threat of infinitely more total and more destructive myths.

It's not my intention to attempt to fly in the rarified atmospheres of literary theory, where only Eagletons dare. The new post-structuralist critics are easy to laugh at, and they seem to have set themselves the ambition of making literary criticism totally self-regarding and quite unreadable; but they do have more than a ha'porth of concrete truth to all their intolerable deal of theorising. Works of art are not timeless, as the mandarin critics of an earlier generation would have had us believe: if they were, they would be a great deal less interesting to us than they are. They are products of unique individuals in unrepeatable circumstances, and each generation that re-experiences them is equally unique and unrepeatable. The texts themselves are part of a continuous process of change, even though the marks on the paper stay the same. We cannot experience the Sophocles plays as a fifth-century Athenian experienced them. We have seen Shakespeare and Racine and Ibsen and Shaw and Chekhov, and we have lived through the Holocaust and the Stalinist terror, so that *Antigone* – to take the most obvious example – means something quite different to us to what it meant for the Idealists and Romantics of the nineteenth century, let alone for Sophocles himself. As T S Eliot said of his own poetry, if a meaning can be found in a poem, it is there, regardless of whether the author consciously put it there or not. But though value systems, and the judgements which arise from them, are always changing with the economic and political systems which produce them, certain blocks of feeling seem to be common to humanity, in all cultures, and from the earliest times of which we have record. All human beings experience joy, fear, terror, religious awe, love, hatred, delight in physical nature, and the desire to be masters of their own destinies; and all human beings go through the same brutally simple process of birth, living and death. Works of art which dramatise or otherwise picture these basic human states are likely to be of interest to all of us, because they are speaking about subjects we all know about. What writers say about these states may indeed be qualified by their economic and political circumstances, just as how we read them is qualified by ours, but the dilemmas we both confront remain essentially the same. We have more in common than divides us, and those fences too can be removed with a little historical knowledge and imagination.

It isn't, however, just a matter of shared experience. We are creatures of imagination, who live in a world of metaphor as well as fact, and the supreme metaphor the human race has created to illuminate its dilemmas is the metaphor of art, the idea that the experience that we all share can be shaped into patterns that we regard as significant, and beautiful in themselves, and that in the very act of shaping, of beautification, the very deepest significance is located. We all know that this is a lie, the sublime untruth that all our enjoyment and insight is erected upon. Our experience is random and disordered, and over the centuries has stubbornly resisted our attempts to bring it into comprehensible order. But we all accept artistic creation as the most joyous of all metaphors, so that our experience can be read in terms other than it is, for the enlightenment and pleasure of us all. Religious art is the most tremendous of metaphors, and over the centuries the most sublime works have been built upon it. Tragedy is another. In the witnessing of the destruction of an admirable human being, we see in metaphorical form the destiny of every one of us. We are all headed for the same defeat and darkness, and like Oedipus, we try to make our passing as memorable and worthwhile as we can.

What makes us value artefacts from the past is the fusion of these two elements, shared experience, and our need for metaphor, into a perfectly realised form, so that the experience and the metaphorical shape are qutie indivisible and express each other. That is why we can love works of art even though we don't share the opinions of the artist who made them. Very few of us would share Milton's theology or Wordsworth's politics, but that doesn't stop us from valuing *Paradise Lost*, *Samson Agonistes* and *The Prelude* as supreme works of art, full of meaning and insight for us in our own twentieth-century lives. Soap operas prove the point dialectically. Their worthlessness is principally because they are without a sense of artistic shaping, and consequently lack any validity as metaphor. They are mere dialogue and story, to no purpose, a form of dramatic behaviourism, and the compulsion which many people feel in them is the curiosity value of overheard gossip at a bus stop or on a crossed line. Sophocles is the supreme shaper, a writer in whose work formal artistry is taken to such peaks of balance and instinctive design, that in that respect at least, hardly any dramatic artist can match him. Let those readers who think of form in art as a badge of hierarchical repression stop reading here, because they will receive no further nourishment.

How can we re-experience Sophocles at a distance of nearly 2,500 years? Almost all critics except a few in recent years have tried to experience him as a literary text, taking their cue from the first literary critic, Aristotle, who declared that he could experience the tragedy more keenly from the text than in the theatre. Generations of literary men, delighted to distance themselves from the vulgarities of the public playhouses, have seized upon his example, and tried to read the Greeks, Shakespeare, and all the poetic dramatists, as though they were written to be experienced in the contemplative serenity of the study. But Aristotle, we know, was reacting to the savage assault of his master, Plato, upon the theatre and all its works. Any of us who have any practical experience of plays and play-making, at whatever level, know that a text is the merest indication of what goes on in a theatre. Most of the problems discussed over thousands of pages of learned and thoughtful analysis, problems of structure and character and tone, simply evaporate on the rehearsal-room floor. To try to discuss what the playwright meant, merely from studying the text, is to invite misapprehension, and too often a fundamental error is made at the beginning, because the wrong questions are asked. We are not concerned, unless we think of ourselves merely as cultural historians, solely to find out what a play was about then, but how it works now. We know very little worth knowing about how Greek plays worked or what meanings were perceived in them in fifth-century Athens, and statements about performance practice or audience perception are always dangerous, because they are mostly based on flimsy superstructures of guesswork: theories of the use and function of masks derived from a few vase paintings, most of them several hundred years later than the period we are concerned with; statements about dance and music, when not a fragment of choreography nor one complete score has survived. Even the secondary material is inadequate. There is nowhere in classical literature an eye-witness account of the performance of any of the Greek texts we have, and from the actual period when the great playwrights were alive and working there is nothing at all. In this situation, the critic's most useful task is to examine how these plays work for us, today, and to use what little historical information we possess as a tool in this examination. The plays must be considered as living artefacts, not archaeological fragments.

Some of the present generation of Greek scholars – Oliver Taplin, for instance – are trying to push the balance in this direction. Certainly it is worthwhile reminding us that Greek choruses ought to be a musical experience, and that a great deal of the dramatic energy of a Greek play comes from the contrast between musical and purely dramatic passages. Certainly it is equally worthwhile to remind us that movement is of crucial importance, and that choreography need not simply mean dance steps but the whole sweep and pattern of the staging; and anyone who approaches the production of Aeschylus without realising that he had a pronounced taste for the spectacular, is likely to go well adrift. There is a great deal of Grand Opera in Greek tragedy. It has more to do with *Tosca* than *Waiting for Godot*. Bleak, text-orientated, psychological productions, verging towards naturalism, will never unlock the secrets hidden in these scripts. A little bit of theatrical vulgarity, thundersheets, great swirls of movement, cries of pain and sudden unexpected reversals are part of the recipe. This was popular art, if ever any theatre was. What other playwrights can boast of having played to houses of at least fifteen thousand per performance, or can have been pretty sure that the whole population of the city will have seen their work? The productions were partly subsidised by the State, and the poor were given an allowance in compensation for loss of earnings to enable them to attend. Important people, visiting diplomats, priests, kings or merchants, were given privileged positions near the front. 'Chance would be a fine thing', mutters the modern theatre playwright, contemplating his usually sparse audience of bourgeois intellectuals, students and tourists.

Beyond these considerations there is a further mystery to be explored, which reveals the most about the way these plays, or indeed any plays, work, and that is the mystery of the triangular relationship between a text, an actor and an audience. This mystery is part of the freemasonry of the theatre, and cannot really be experienced outside the discipline of rehearsing and performing a play. This is, I know, not a helpful thing to say. Not everybody who wants to understand theatre can get the opportunity, or would even wish, to be involved in a performance. But the blank fact remains, and nothing useful can be said about what goes on on a stage without recognising the situation.

In a theatre, three forms of human experience confront each other, and, if the performance is going well, are held in a kind of creative tension. The playwright brings all the experience of his own life, and all the skill and insight he has acquired in his craft, which he has formalised into a script. The actor meets the playwright in the rehearsal room, and he too brings with him a whole life experience, quite different from the playwright's, as well as the skill of his own demanding discipline. The director, assisted by the designer, the lighting designer, the costumier, creates the circumstances in which these two experiences and skills can meet and interact. The director is not the creator, neither is the designer nor the lighting man; but the contribution of these people is vital, particularly that of the director, who, if he is skilled and subtle at his own work, can create the ideal circumstances in which the meeting of playwright and actor can occur. That meeting is a subtle, strange, indefinable business. Sometimes, in spite of the most careful preparation by talented people, it stubbornly refuses to happen. When it does happen it is unforgettable, what we go to the theatre for.

When it does happen, when the experiences and skills of playwright and actor meet; what they create between them is a third experience, a combination of the other two, but essentially unlike either. Every playwright has had the experience on the first morning of rehearsal of facing the living actor who is to give life to his imaginary creation, and thinking, 'Oh no, he's hopelessly wrong!' During rehearsal too, he will see ideas arising he hadn't foreseen, moments working rather differently from the way he had imagined. Finally, if he is lucky, he will see a performance of real life, essentially unlike his imagination, because real life, with all its brutal physical immediacy, always is. The playwright comes eventually to relish this process as his richest reward and subtlest pleasure, till his reaction isn't 'Oh God here's another actor who is going to spoil my beautiful imaginary creation,' but rather 'I can't wait to see what new things this actor will find within the pattern I have created.' Each actor brings quite different qualities to any role, and will find in it his own dimensions, making the character more direct, more arrogant, more reserved, more passionate, depending on his own personality: indeed, on each occasion an actor plays a part, the character will be subtly changed, depending on how the actor is feeling that night, and how the audience is behaving. Of course, there is a core of meaning which is entirely the playwright's, and which the actor can't change. *Macbeth* is always going to demonstrate to us the corruption of ambition by power; *Hamlet*, the moral implications of revenge; *Antigone*, the relationship between public and private morality. But within those broad categories, the poet's chosen subject matter, the actor's instinctive choices are going to be as crucial as a painter's choice of colour tones. Anyone who has seen a performance in the making, or developing during a run, or even the same part played by many actors, knows that a playwright's meaning is crucially changed by the preoccupations of the actor who embodies that meaning. What we are talking about is an art, living creation at the moment of action, not a mechanical process: an art, what's more, which is always a co-operation of many talents learning to work together towards a common end. There is no room for lonely geniuses in the theatre. It is the supreme social art.

The third side of the triangle is the audience. It too brings its life experience with which to confront and measure what the actors and the playwright are doing, and everything that happens on a stage is subtly qualified and changed by its presence. My own play, *The Exorcism*, which is an attack on the affluence of the early seventies in the form of a ghost story, was performed in Poland, in Polish, in 1976. My portrayal of conspicuous consumption, clearly critically meant for an English audience, had a quite different effect on a Polish one. They took great pleasure in the drinks, the food, the expensive clothes and furnishings of my characters. Having had no opportunity to experience such things for themselves, there was on their part a yearning to participate, not a puritanical distaste; so that when the reversal came in the play, and my affluents were brought low, the effect on my Polish audience was powerful, but in a quite different way from what it had been on my English one. My meaning had been changed by their participation, and I had had demonstrated to me, in a clear and unavoidable form, one of the central truths of the theatre.

Which brings me back to the Greeks, and the point of my digression. The greatest of the vulgar errors committed by those who read the Greeks as literature rather than imagining them as theatre is the pronouncement, on the basis of reading alone, or the recollection of a few evenings in the theatre, that a specific text is 'about' this or that. Any text of any play is about many different things, depending upon who is playing it, where, to whom, and in what circumstances. The story and the words may remain the same, but what appear in the study to be major themes can disappear in public performance, and other elements, unspoken, but clearly sensed by the actors, can sometimes brood over a performance and give it new meanings; and events occurring outside the theatre, in real life, can equally throw a new slant on what is being performed within it. Those people who saw Leonard Rossiter's performance in *The Resistible Rise of Arturo Ui* at the Edingburgh Festival in 1968, during the very days when Czechoslovakia was being invaded, will never forget Rossiter's delivery of the final words, as he took off his make-up and said 'and now the bitch is on heat again'. For those people, Brecht's words, Rossiter's performance, and History, will always remain a single indivisible experience, a gloss on Brecht's text he never imagined, but would surely have approved of. My own remarks upon the three translations contained in this volume make no claims to general validity, other than as a report upon what happened in a certain set of circumstances. What I have to say about these plays grows directly from my experience of directing them, with the people whose names are mentioned at the beginning of each text, and though its scope may be limited, the reader can be quite sure it is based on concrete experience. I don't come out of my study bearing these tablets of the law. They were carved in the rehearsal room, and the results of their application are there for all to see on videotape.

Having said that, I had of course done my homework. Any play from the past must initially be approached in an historical way, so as to learn all that can be reasonably known about how and in what circumstances the play was originally made. It is no part of my intention to encourage the ignoramus school of direction, which announces in its arrogance that all it needs is the text and the certainty of its own genius. There is much that professional scholars can tell us about Greek drama, historical and archaeological material that we would be very unwise to ignore. Whatever hard facts or well-attested traditions about these plays we can discover must be assimilated, before the process of reading or production begins. That discipline can't bring these plays to life, and wrongly applied it can ensure that they remain dead, but it is an important part of the process.

Who was Sophocles? In terms of hard fact, sources verifiable by archaeological inscription or reliable historical text, we know hardly anything about him at all. He was born at Colonus, a pleasant and rural suburb of Athens, probably in the year 495–494 BC. He won the leading prize at the principal dramatic festival in Athens on many occasions, though he only managed second place with *Oedipus the King*. He served as Hellenotamias in 443–442, and was chairman of the board of what was in effect the treasury of the Athenian Empire in a difficult year when the appointment was no poet's sinecure; and he was appointed one of ten generals to command the Samian expedition in the war of 441–438. A strictly historical conscience demands that we say that's just about all we can rely on. However, there is more material than that, most of it not very reliable, but, to put it at no higher level, great fun; and since it does come down to us from the ancient world, though from Hellenistic sources gathered together generations after his death, it must be considered.

The ancient life of Sophocles is not a biography in any modern sense, merely a collection of fairly scrappy anecdotes. These tell us that Sophocles was an Athenian of noble birth, not a tradesman, otherwise he would never have held a generalship alongside the likes of Pericles. They tell us too that he was well educated, raised in comfortable cicumstances, and celebrated as much for his life and personality as as for his playwriting. As a boy he won crowns for both wrestling and music, and after the victory of Salamis, when he was in his teens, sang naked to the lyre as part of the victory celebrations. As a playwright, he learned his craft from Aeschylus, introduced the third actor, didn't like performing himself because his voice was too weak, changed the number of the chorus from twelve to fifteen, and won twenty victories in the major Athenian festival, the Dionysia, as well as coming second many times. He loved Athens, and refused to leave it, though often lured abroad by kings who knew of his poetic fame, and he was a pious and religious man, who held several offices of the priesthood. He was elected general when he was nearing seventy, proof of his continuing popularity in Athens, but was considered to be a greater poet than strategist. A story is told of his persuading a beautiful young slave boy to kiss him, and saying, 'At least I have sufficient strategy to accomplish that, whatever Pericles says.' Aristophanes says in *The Frogs* that he was very easygoing and everyone liked him, and in *Peace* that he was old and debauched, and would go to sea on a raft to make money. In old age, he is said to have had a family argument with his son Iophon, who wanted his property and accused him of being senile, and to have written *Oedipus at Colonus* at the age of ninety to prove otherwise. Phrynicus however says that his life was happy, and he enjoyed all his faculties till the end. He died, according to the ancient biographer, either by choking on an underripe grape pip, or by running out of breath in the midst of a recitation of the *Antigone*.

None of this is to be relied on; indeed, Mary Lefkowitz in her book *Lives of the Greek Poets* makes a good case for its virtual worthlessness. Compiled hundreds of years after the poet's death, almost every detail of the life can be shown to be either a simple mirror image of something in the poet's own work, or what she calls representative rather than historical material: the sort of life the poet of the Theban plays ought to have had, rather than the life he actually lived. Thus the religious man can be projected from the attitude to the gods in the Oedipus plays, and learning from Aeschylus and introducing the third actor – Aeschylus uses a third actor too, but may well have been following Sophocles – can be seen as representing his place in a dramatic tradition rather than an actual fact. The noble birth, the youthful genius, the extraordinary death, these are all the accepted attributes of a remarkable man. The story of the argument with his son is the clearest example of all, being an obvious reflection of *Oedipus at Colonus*.

When we come to the question of the Greek theatre as Sophocles knew it, we are on firmer ground, if only for the fact that the theatre of Dionysus in Athens, where most of the Greeks plays we have were premièred, still exists; though even there we must remind ourselves that we are looking at a Roman reconstruction, and that the theatre Pericles built, and the pre-Periclean theatre of Aeschylus and early Sophocles, were probably much less substantial, more flexible theatrical instruments. One thing we can be certain about is that the presentation of plays in fifth-century Athens had very little in common with our own ritual of going to the theatre. Our theatregoing is, and has been for many centuries, almost since the very beginnings in western Europe, part of a pattern of entertainment. It's something we do largely in the evening, indoors, for fun, and though it is certainly often serious in intention, it has no formally accepted social or religious relevance. The classical Greek theatre included both these aspects.

Scholars are not agreed on the matter of how tragedy, literally, 'a song about a Goat' – the goat sent out of the city in ancient ritual, taking with it the burden of the city's sins, familiar in Hebrew mythology – came into existence. The traditional view is that the legendary actor, Thespis, developed it from the sung choruses that were a part of religious ritual celebrations, in the mid-sixth century BC. According to this version, Thespis isolated himself from the chorus, and wrote a solo part, thus creating the essence of dramatic conflict, a dialogue between a single character and the chorus. This idea seems likely: all actors look for the opportunity of isolating themselves from the chorus and writing themselves solo parts. But at least one modern scholar has argued convincingly that as Homer describes the singing of his bard Demodocus being accompanied by young men dancing and singing, the two aspects of solo and choral performance may have developed simultaneously from the earliest times.

Whatever the truth of that process, Greek tragedy by the time we

INTRODUCTION

first have an opportunity to experience it, in the earliest surviving
play of Aeschylus, *The Persians*, dating from 472 BC, had acquired
largely the form it was to have over the whole of the classical period.
Each of the three tragic poets whose work survives from the fifth
century BC modified that form to suit his own work, but the form
itself, socially and aesthetically, changed hardly at all.

The principal performance of plays took place during the festival
of Dionysus, the god of wine and ecstasy, in the month of March,
in the theatre of Dionysus on the Acropolis in Athens. A second
festival, the Lenaia, was held in January, and there were minor local
festivals held all over the Greek world at which the performance of
plays was of principal importance. In the fourth century BC these
were numerous enough to support what we can only call touring
companies of professional actors, though whether such companies
existed in the years when the playwrights were at work is less
certain. The lesser festivals certainly did, and the four great
playwrights seem likely to have written new plays for them
occasionally.

The Dionysia was a religious event, and began with a day of
religious rituals and ceremonies, which may well have been fairly
lively occasions where a great deal of wine was consumed. A
January festival, and indeed a March one too, indicates an origin
to do with the first tasting of the previous year's wine. The dramatic
part of the festival though, certainly by the early fifth century, when
our interest begins, clearly had a life of its own, and took the form
of a competiton between playwrights, a competition which must
have been as intense and demanding as anything playwrights have
experienced in any succeeding culture. Five days were set apart for
the festival, and one playwright was required to occupy a whole day
of performances, the order of days being decided by drawing lots.
Obviously, it was more advantageous to be the last playwright, least
lucky to be the first. During that day, the playwright had to offer
three tragedies, and a satyr play, on subjects which may have been
in some way linked, though not necessarily as part of a formal
trilogy, and the satyr play would end the sequence in what was
probably a very satisfying manner, by making a comic comment,
perhaps on some of the issues and characters which had been
presented during the day. Finally, a comedy would be presented,

written by a different playwright, and part of a separate comedian's competition. Aeschylus seems to have written naturally in trilogies: his *Oresteia* is the only actual trilogy to have survived, and the other four plays of his we have seem to be amputated thirds of lost three-part works. With the two later playwrights we are on less certain ground. Euripides certainly wrote at least one Trojan War trilogy: we have the titles of the two lost plays which preceeded the *Trojan Women*, though we cannot be sure whether the three plays were tightly linked in subject and theme, as the *Oresteia* is, or merely three plays telling separate stories with the common background of the Trojan War. In Sophocles' case, one thing is clear. The three plays in this volume, although they are often referred to as the *Theban Trilogy*, and although they make a very satisfying dramatic unit, were certainly not written as a trilogy, but on three separate occasions, probably over a period of thirty years. *Antigone* is generally considered to be the earliest, *Oedipus the King*, dating from the early years of the Peloponnesian War, the second, and *Oedipus at Colonus*, dating from the final shattering years of the war, as Athens approached its final defeat, the last, 407–406 being the usual date suggested. *Antigone* probably won first prize, *Oedipus the King* came second, and in the case of *Oedipus at Colonus*, nothing certain is known about performance at all, beyond the possibility that it may have been performed posthumously, directed by the poet's grandson. These plays must have been presented with two other plays and a satyr play, but it seems likely that Sophocles' trilogies were not connected ones as Aeschylus' were. There has never been any serious suggestion that there were three *Oedipus* plays, three *Antigone* plays, three *Colonus* plays, and the plays themselves do not read like bleeding chunks of a three-part work, as Aeschylus' *Seven Against Thebes*, *Prometheus* and *The Suppliants* certainly do. It seems likely that Aristotle, mentioning *Oedipus the King* by name, would have mentioned the other two plays at some point if they had existed, and it seems at least possible that the notorious fact that *Oedipus the King*, certainly one of the world's greatest plays, could only gain second prize, can be explained not simply by the lack of critical sense among the original judges, or even by the more likely political bias or inadequate performance, but by the fact that the other two lost plays were not as good as the one that has survived.

The making of plays started not with the playwright, but with the Chorus. Five rich men were selected by the city authorities, and each was required to select, train and produce a chorus for one of the five days. These choruses were amateurs, young men of the city, and there was intense competition for the honour of being asked to provide a chorus, and for being selected to perform in it. Financing a chorus was an expensive business. The twelve or fifteen young men had to be provided with food, and an intensive training, sometimes conducted by a professional who would need to teach them the music and complicated dance steps that went with it. In addition, the producer – that's what he was, in effect – had to commission the design and manufacture of costumes and masks for the chorus, and all the evidence suggests that the success and novelty of these aspects of the play had a great deal to do with who eventually won the prize.

Only after the choruses had been selected were the five playwrights chosen. They seem to have been chosen by the Archon Basileus of Athens, as part of his responsibility for religious ritual, and then matched up with one of the five producers and his chorus. Nothing at all is known about how the poets were chosen, or by what judgement poet and chorus were matched. The opportunities for graft, political in–fighting and aesthetic bias must have been widespread in both these processes, and if theatrical people in classical Athens were anything like what they seem to have been in all European cultures since, they were doubtless exploited to the full. The texts make it clear that a good or bad chorus must have been quite enough to enhance or ruin a play, so this initial matching must have been crucial. When the poet had been awarded his producer and chorus, the producer was assigned his one, two or three actors, again at the whim of the Archon. The actors were professionals, and to be lucky enough to be granted the services of a well-known or popular actor must have been a great advantage for a playwright, particularly when we consider how the tragic protagonists dominate their particular plays.

Aeschylus is credited with having introduced the second actor, thus enormously enlarging the dramatic possibilities of Thespis' one actor and chorus, and Sophocles himself, by tradition, introduced the third actor, making possible scenes where A conflicts with B but agrees with C – and all the possible permutations of that triad. The way parts were divided between the three speaking actors – non-speaking walk-ons were often used in addition – is a subject worth much study in itself, but it is interesting to note that a character in a play might sometimes be played by more than one of the three actors. Indeed, assuming that the principal actor played the main part throughout, it is often impossible to share out the parts without this happening. At the end of *Oedipus at Colonus*, the actor playing Oedipus must have returned at the end to play Theseus, unless the Messenger crept offstage after his speech to assume the role – which seems an unlikely possibility in that dramatic situation. It is worth noting, too, that on the occasions when four characters appear together, only three of them speak. When Theseus brings the rescued Antigone and Ismene back to their father, Ismene says nothing, and she remains silent for the length of a chorus, two scenes and a choral dialogue, till her exit, clearly because the part was being played by a mute actor wearing the Ismene costume and mask. It is not easy to convince a modern actress playing Ismene of the validity of that argument! ('My God, I've just been rescued, can't I say something?') Aeschylus himself, in his last work, the *Oresteia*, certainly needs three actors. What more natural than that the older playwright should follow the lead of his younger and highly successful colleague?

The Greek theatre was an intensely competitive business. There seems very little evidence that plays were ever performed outside a competitive context. For us, accustomed to the gruesome charades of Oscar awards and BAFTA ceremonies, it seems extraordinary, given the seriousness of the plays, that this should be so, and it is likely that the Dionysia, with their religious basis, were more dignified affairs. But Greek drama declined into decadence quite quickly, becoming in the fourth century and later principally a competition between star actors, who mutilated the old plays and encouraged the production of few good new ones: so perhaps for Alexandrian or early Roman Athens the tawdry show-biz glitter of our own awards ceremonies might be some kind of analogy. In the good years of the middle and late fifth century, when the great plays were being produced, we know fairly well what happened. For five days the playwrights showed their productions (cut down to three days during the Peloponnesian War, doubtless for good economic reasons), and the audiences made their preferences clear, cheering or barracking as the mood took them. The plays were then judged by ten judges, each one selected from one of the ten tribes of Athens. These ten then cast their votes into an urn, and five of the votes were drawn out at random. From these five votes, the result was announced. Simple mathematics indicates that the result may well have been unrepresentative of the ten judges' opinion. What the system does make quite clear though, is that the Athenians were prepared to go to extraordinary lengths to try to avoid bias, corruption or threats having an undue influence on the result. This in its turn suggests that this must have been a problem. Winning the playwright's, or the producer's, or the actor's crown was a matter of great import and significance, about which people were prepared to cheat, or bring all kinds of unwarranted pressure to bear.

The theatres themselves were the familiar open-air structures, based on a half-circle design, with the stage across the diameter. They were very large, seating as many as 15,000 spectators, but were designed by men who were clearly masters of the art of acoustics. In most ancient theatres a whisper delivered by an experienced actor can be clearly heard in all parts of the vast half-circle, and though the presence of an audience would have absorbed a lot of sound, it would also have muffled the echo, so that it seems likely that the words were clearly audible. Indeed, they must have been. Audiences except in modern prestige theatres do not tolerate inaudibility, and the Greek theatre in this form flourished for many hundreds of years.

The area in the middle of the half-circle was flat, and normally occupied by the chorus, though the actors often came down to join them. The actors' natural home was the stage, a well-raised structure, drawn like a straight line across the half-circle at the diameter. The stage seems to have been backed by formal buildings with central doors, a door at either side, and a usable roof. Most surviving theatres are Roman, or were rebuilt by the Romans, and their stage buildings are immovable stone structures. But there are grounds for believing that Pericles' Athenian theatre was backed by wooden buildings, and the pre-Periclean theatre almost certainly was. This could have made it possible for the stage backings to be changed from play to play; so it may be that the permanent stone structures we are accustomed to would have been alien to many Greek theatregoers.

Whether or in what way this stage was decorated is a question for which the evidence is so flimsy that educated guesswork must suffice. The ancient biographers credited Sophocles with the invention of scene painting, and *Oedipus at Colonus* is set in a rustic landscape, in front of a grove of trees sacred to the Furies. But what this meant in practice is unknown. The lines in the early part of *Colonus*, describing the scene in some detail, could either be drawing the audience's attention to some new feature of this particular play – look at all this beautiful scenery our painters have made – or they could, like many similar passages in Shakespeare, be a substitute for scene painting, a creation in the imagination of what was lacking in fact. There is evidence to suggest that painted panels were inserted into the permanent structure, and that these could be varied for different plays. Costumes were certainly spectacular – Aeschylus, on several occasions, draws attention to the fact in his text – and so, probably, were masks, though what evidence there is suggests that they were not grotesques, as Roman masks were, but rather naturalistic, certainly when the three great tragedians were working. Aeschylus' masks for the Furies in the *Eumenides* were reputedly so powerful that they caused women to abort, and drove people screaming from the theatre. Such traditions and myths don't usually arise without good cause; clearly those masks and costumes were particularly impressive, and long remembered: and here we may have the best clue to the nature of the scene painting. The best backing for spectacular costumes, as any modern director knows, is neutral, something that will allow the shapes and colours to read most effectively. Perhaps the backgrounds were kept simple for this reason, or, more likely, perhaps the spectacular costumes and masks emerged because the permanent or semi-permanent backgrounds were difficult to make visually exciting.

It would be a grave mistake to assume that this basic simplicity of staging indicates any degree of theatrical primitiveness. The playwrights were working in a well-established and popular tradition, and far from seeming simple, their dramaturgy indicates a pronounced degree of theatrical sophistication. Many of the tragedies require – and Aristophanes makes it clear that the requirement was satisifed – staging techniques that we usually associate with the emergence of sophisticated indoor theatre during the Renaissance. The Greeks clearly had developed some kind of revolve or reveal mechanism, whereby what was going on in an inner room could be exposed to the audience. Bodies are often revealed in this way at the climax of Greek tragedies – the dead Erydice, for instance, in *Antigone* – and Aristophanes in *Thezmophoriazusae* used it to show us Agathon at work in his study. In Euripides we often have gods and goddesses appearing, and the texts indicate that this was sometimes high above the actors. It is apparent that some kind of crane was in use, and given the size of Greek theatres and the theatrical necessity of making this happen, at least on some occasions, in the middle of the stage, they must have had a quite substantial and sophisticated piece of theatrical machinery. For these two devices we have hard evidence, but we should not assume that the lack of evidence for any other stage machinery or effects means that there were none. By the time the great playwrights were writing, the Greeks had developed their theatre into a very flexible and sophisticated instrument, capable of doing anything they asked of it: nothing, it seems likely, was beyond their theatrical technique, though some things were limited by the geography of their theatres – all Greek tragedies, for instance, are set in the open air.

The very essence of theatre is performance, the act of live communication, and it is the greatest frustration of the classical Greek theatre that about this crucial aspect we know almost nothing. That the formal choruses were sung, to the accompaniment of a solo flute and other instruments, which must have included percussion, is as certain as these things can be. But what was the music like, and how was it interpreted? Was it more like operatic aria, or *Sprechgesang?* Was it performed in unison, or was it harmonised? Did all the actors sing at once, or were they broken up into small groups; or were some lines sung individually, or even spoken? How did music and dance interact? Any director of musicals will affirm that energetic dancing and decent singing are difficult to pull off at once. Did the actors sing, or declaim, or speak with any attempt to imitate natural speech? In the choral dialogues, did the chorus sing, and the actor speak, or both sing, or both speak? Did the actor too join in the choric dances? Fragments of evidence float down to us across the centuries – that Euripides' music was too advanced for traditional tastes for instance – but on all these questions, history contributes little more than a great silence. It's dangerous to extrapolate anything at all simply from the texts, particularly in a foreign language, but any director's instinct will tell him one thing about these plays, namely that the protagonists' parts demand great acting, and great acting in a grand and heaven-storming mould. A Greek tragedian, regardless of whether he actually sang or not, must have used his voice like a musical instrument, to create emotion by the tone colouring of the words, as the older generation of actors, Gielgud, Olivier, Richardson, Quayle and Burton still do, or have done, in our own day. Sophocles' characters are drawn with great emotional subtlety, very satisfying even to today's post-Freudian, post-Chekhovian actors, and Euripides clearly experimented with very direct and natural styles of speech; but modern experience again tells us that it is quite possible to marry this kind of naturalism with the grand style. Our own Renaissance drama pulls this trick off again and again, with the subtlety of Hamlet's characterisation, or Lear's cry of 'pray you, undo this button', at the height of his passion, the most striking examples in our language. Nevertheless, the brutal fact remains that what Greek tragedy was like in performance is utterly unknown.

Trying to see Greek drama whole, as a cultural and historical phenomenon, is difficult over a gap of so many centuries and with so little reliable evidence to hand, but some points may be made with reasonable safety. The first is how effectively and practically the theatres and the dramatic techniques interact. All drama is first of all the solution of a physical problem, how to present an enacted story within a certain set of physical conditions, and all the great periods of drama in the world begin with its triumphant solution. Shakespearean and Jacobean drama finds its unique form initially from the problem of presenting ambitious and wide-ranging stories in an inn yard, and the first custom-built theatres were developments of the spatial relationship of that original inn yard. Looking at Greek drama, we see an ideal matching of physical conditions and dramatic techniques, so that it is difficult to imagine a form of drama more suited to that kind of space than the one the Greeks evolved. The orchestra, or area for the choral dances, like the chorus itself, is the Greeks' unique theatrical contribution, leaving a large circular space free for dancers, which allowed them plenty of freedom of movement, well away from the main actors. In modern productions, unless they are staged in ancient theatres, the chorus is invariably weaved into the action upon a single stage: but then in very few modern productions does the chorus actually dance.

As a social and cultural phenomenon, what is most striking about Greek drama is its seriousness, or rather, seriousness of purpose. Vulgar opinion labels Greek drama as gloomy, a pastime for serious-minded intellectuals, and box-office death, but this is surely a comment upon how we produce Greek drama in translation, not on the original phenomenon. Through all our ignorance, it seems clear that Greek drama was popular art, a tremendous and spectacular event, very much enjoyed by an audience which was a cross-section of the whole city. The opening lines of *Agamemnon* delivered as the sun came up – if that is indeed what happened – must have been a stunning experience, and some of the great choruses of the canon, sung, danced, with instrumental accompaniment and spectacular costumes and masks, in a very dramatic situation, must have been as exciting to the Greeks as the première of *West Side Story* was to us. And yet the seriousness of purpose remains. Aristophanes was and still is very funny, yet his desperate concern for his city as defeat by the unlovely Spartans loomed shines through his plays; and the tragedians, though the content of their sensational mythology invites it, never descend to vulgar melodrama or sensationalism. Tragedy exists for them to present a powerful image of the suffering of man, but also to consider all kinds of ethical and moral dilemmas, which civilized men must learn to resolve if their civilisation is to survive. What moral and ethical necessities surround the idea of revenge? What are the limits of civilised behaviour in the uncivilised business of war? How can we reconcile the conflicting demands of the individual conscience and the State? What does man's life mean, living always under the immanent but indefinable shadow of the gods, whoever or whatever they are? Where is the line to be drawn within the human personality, and in social life, between instinct and reason? The Greeks confronted all these questions in their drama, and what they said is still burningly relevant, because the human race is a long way from finding acceptable answers to them.

This high seriousness must initially spring from the drama's religious origins, and we cannot be sure just what was the relationship between the religious and dramatic aspects of the festival in the great playwrights' time. What is apparent is that the poets were speaking to their city on political and moral matters, and expected to be heard. The tragedies never explicitly indulge in party politics – though Aristophanes clearly does – but they do concern themselves with the underlying moral issues that are at the heart of political action in civilised societies. There seems no reasonable doubt that when Aeschylus, Sophocles or Euripides spoke, what they said mattered, and their voices were listened to with great attention. In Aristophanes' *The Frogs*, the debate between Aeschylus and Euripides is not about who is the better playwright in aesthetic terms, but whose message would be most useful to the Athenians as they plunge towards defeat and disaster. The decision to bring Aeschylus back from the dead reflects not so much the awarding of a literary prize, as a realisation that the old-fashioned virtues embodied in his plays are exactly what Athens so desperately needs in her moment of crisis. The poets and playwrights of Eastern Europe have always lived similarly, within the sound of gunfire, and many of them have paid with their lives for the influence of their words. What political pressures were brought to bear on the Greek playwrights we don't know. We do know, however, that both Aeschylus and Euripides chose to end their lives in exile, and that the Athenians were prepared to execute Socrates for saying unacceptable things. Plato's famous attack on the drama indicates how seriously playwrights' verses were taken by society at large, and how widespread their influence was. In an age which produces as many frivolously empty plays and films as ours does, and where a moral or ethical idea in a popular play is about as common as a diamond in a dustbin, this is only one of many lessons the Greeks still have to teach us.

In trying to trace a more direct relationship between the tragedies and historical events we are on uncertain ground, because the tragedians hardly ever spoke directly to their audiences on these matters, as the comedians certainly did. In the plays we have, with the single exception of Aeschylus' *The Persians*, the poets always speak through the dramatisation of their rich legacy of myth, knowing what many modern playwrights have forgotten, that the distancing of drama from actual daily event and daily politics, quite apart from being a safer tactic in disturbed times, enables the writer to speak far more seriously and wide-rangingly about the deeper issues underlying those events. *The Persians* is a fairly straightforward celebration of national political and cultural triumph, written at a time of great confidence and national expansion. But *The Trojan Women* seems likely to be Euripides' impassioned comment on the punitive expedition the Athenians sent against the Island of Melos. Melos had always managed to avoid becoming part of the Athenian Empire, but in 416 BC Athens demanded it pay tribute as an ally, which the Melians refused to do. The Athenians sent a punitive force, and when, after a long siege, the Melians surrendered, the Athenians executed all the men on the island, down to boys of military age, and enslaved all the women and children. Euripides' play says nothing about this. He tells the story of how the women of Troy are taken into captivity by the victorious Greeks, who commit the atrocity of murdering Hector's small son Astyanax, because they are afraid to let the son of so great a hero live. Thunder rumbles and Troy burns as the Greeks prepare to leave; and though Euripides' view is not hammered home, it does not need to be. All the audience knew that in the story, the return of the Greeks to their homes was utterly disastrous, and the root of their disaster was their dishonouring the altars of the gods when they sacked Troy. Euripides' point must have hit home with even greater force, enacted by the heroes of Homeric epic, on the eve of the departure of the huge and ultimately disastrous Athenian expedition against Sicily. It is perhaps not surprising that *The Trojan Women* did not win the crown that year.

Of the plays in this volume, *Oedipus at Colonus*, the only one that can be dated with reasonable accuracy, is full of the poet's comment on the atmosphere of its time. Athens was in a desperate state when the ninety-year-old playwright wrote his last play. The Spartan Army was camped only twelve miles away at Deceleia, and the city and its regime were close to military defeat and collapse. Politics had reached a low ebb, and the leadership of the city had deteriorated into a series of squabbles between the second-rate. Sophocles' play resonates with a rallying patriotism, of the kind that we are well accustomed to in our films of the Second World War, and in Olivier's film of *Henry V*. The play repeatedly praises the greatness of Athens, and the justice of its institutions, and in the figure of Theseus, Sophocles portrays the ideal military and civil leader, the just and serious-minded man Athens so badly needed. The choral odes in praise of Colonus and of Theseus' victory over Creon – Athens had had a sadly minor victory over Thebes in a cavalry skirmish near Colonus less than a year earlier – must have sounded stirringly relevant to the first Athenian audience, if indeed the play was presented before the city fell. If, as some scholars argue, it was produced by Sophocles' grandson some years after the poet's death, those same odes, and the whole panegyric of Athenian democracy, must have been painfully sad. Most strikingly of all, the whole action of the play seems designed to make Oedipus a kind of defensive icon, whose magical powers would protect the city against all enemies. We suddenly get a sad picture of a very old man, who had flourished in the city's greatest days, when it was undisputed master of the Aegean and Ionia, and who had known and been on intimate terms with the great men who made it so, desperately trying to use his poetic powers to shore up the collapsing wreckage of his much-loved city as it slid towards disaster.

Of the historical context of *Oedipus the King*, which has been dated by some scholars in the year 427–426, just after the beginning of the Peloponnesian War, there is little worth saying. It has been suggested that in Oedipus, Sophocles drew a portrait of Pericles himself, but there is no evidence, beyond the fact that the play begins with a plague, there was a plague in Athens in 429 BC, and

Pericles himself died of it. About *Antigone* however there are some few fragments of historical context, and one provocatively interesting suggestion. The traditional view, based on a note by Aristophanes of Byzantium, states that Sophocles was awarded his generalship on Samos because of the golden opinion he won from the production of *Antigone*. As the Samian expedition was in 441– 440 BC, this would date *Antigone* at around 442 BC at the latest. Geoffrey Lewis, of the Department of Ancient History at Edinburgh University, points out to me that Douris of Samos, a sensationalist and not totally reliable ancient source, states that the Samian prisoners were tied to posts and left for ten days, before being clubbed to death; and that their bodies remained there, unburied. There is clear evidence that Sophocles won first prize at the Dionysia in 438 BC, but unfortunately none for the titles of the winning plays. So why should not 438 BC, when we know he won, be the date, rather than some date in the mid-forties for which the evidence is uncertain? The award of a generalship for writing the play may be quite simply a reversal of what actually happened – that the generalship provoked the writing of the play. Or, as Geoffrey Lewis argues, it might refer to Sophocles' presence on the expedition against the Samian refugees in Anaia in 433 BC, after the play had been presented in 438 BC. Works of art are sometimes directly inspired by historical events – Picasso's *Guernica*, for instance – and the subject matter of *Antigone* can't avoid political relevance. The idea, which Geoffrey Lewis is developing, and will eventually offer in the correct scholarly context, is certainly a piquant one. Maybe here too we see an example of the Greek playwright warning his city that uncivilised behaviour, even enacted with the full force of the State behind it, brings its own punishment.

For whatever sins the playwrights may have committed, the gods have wreaked a terrible vengeance on Greek drama. Only thirty-one tragedies survive, by three writers, some of them in a mutilated condition, and, of the comedians, only works by Aristophanes survive in a reasonably complete state. We have seven plays only by Aeschylus, seven by Sophocles, and nineteen by Euripides – seventeen tragedies and two satyr plays. The manuscripts we have are Byzantine copies of much earlier editions of the plays, probably prepared for study purposes, and the preponderance of Euripidean texts indicates his great popularity in the fourth century BC. Sophocles is stated to have written 123 plays, Aeschylus more than seventy, and Euripides ninety-two. It is likely enough that the plays preserved by each author were considered, at least by one ancient editor, to be those authors' best works. But when we consider the quality of the extra Euripides plays we have, and even more, when we think of the lost plays of the Aeschylus' *Danaids*, *Prometheus* and *Theban* trilogies, as well as the lost *Alexandros* and *Palamedes* that comprised the Euripidean *Trojan Women* trilogy, the mind despairs at what we have lost.

But the loss is even greater than that. The Greek theatre flourished for at least 700 years, from the time of Thespis, till Hadrian visited the theatre in Athens and saw tragedies performed. For a great deal of that time, it has been asserted, the theatre was sunk into decadence, with nothing worthwhile being written. But there is no way we can test that assertion, because no complete play survives beyond those written by the three great tragedians within a span of about seventy years. Of Thespis, Phrynicus, Agathon, Chairemon, Aphareus, Theodektes, Meletos, Philokles, Polyphrasmon, Aristias, Pratinas, we have nothing but their names, and a few odd lines quoted in other texts. English drama has been going for about 700 years. The situation is as though we had only seven plays by Marlowe, seven by Shakespeare, nineteen by Webster (!), a clutch of Jonsonian comedies, and nothing else: no Congreve, no Wycherley, no Sheridan, Shaw, Pinero, Wilde. The whole of Greek theatrical culture, with the exception of a few priceless pinnacles, has been wiped out. What we lose, apart from the plays themselves, is the power of comparison. It is only when you have heard J C Bach, Salieri, Paisiello, working in the same musical language, but without the insight of genius, that you realise the full stature of Mozart, and that comparison is denied us with the great Athenians. More crucially, we get only a glimpse of what must have been one of the most vital points of Greek tragedy, the originality with which each writer handled the myths. The great majority of the works we have draw their subject matter from Homer's two great epics, or from the lost epic, *The Thebaid*, which we know to have existed, and which told the whole story of the House of Labdacus, presumably from Cadmus' original founding of Thebes down to the final *Götterdämmerung* of the slaughter of the children of Oedipus. Some comparisons we can make, between all three dramatists' treatment of the story of Electra, and between Aechylus' *Seven Against Thebes*, Euripides' *The Phoenician Women*, and Sophocles' *Oedipus at Colonus*, and *Antigone*, all of which portray the final chapters of the Theban saga. These plays are so utterly different from each other, and the comparisons between them so revealing, as to sharpen our regret for what we have lost.

No one knows how much survived, or for how long, but in my own mind I always see two images of mankind at its most stupidly brutal destroying these evidences of mankind at its most supreme. The first is the burning of the library at Alexandria during Caesar's Egyptian expedition. Alexandria was the great university of the ancient world, the centre of Hellenistic culture, and there can be little doubt that it contained a great many more than thirty-one tragedies. The other disaster was the sacking of Constantinople in 1204 by the Crusaders, who, deciding that the pickings in the Islamic Middle East were likely to be too slim, turned left up the Aegean, and sacked the greatest city of Christendom instead. For four days the Frankish yobs and layabouts ran riot in the city, destroying and burning everything. The Venetians had their share too, but at least they simply stole the horses of St Marks, instead of melting them down for ready cash. Constantinople had existed in an unbroken line from its foundation, and was widely regarded as the treasure house of the Ancient world. It is likely that the drunken French and Italian soldiers, warming their hands round fires of manuscripts, and burning down libraries for the sheer pleasure of it, destroyed our last chance of knowing what Greek theatrical culture was really like.

We must be content with what we have, and indeed, the three plays in this volume alone have produced many thousands of pages of scholarly exegesis and analysis. In directing them, even in translations which make them several hundred lines longer than their Greek originals, what comes across most strikingly is proof of the long-praised Sophoclean mastery of structure. Formally, they have the perfection of a Greek vase, of the Parthenon itself, of a

Mozart symphony. But what does this grandly abstract statement mean in fact? At the simplest level, it is a scarcely definable feeling of rightness, an emotional and intellectual conviction that the poet has said not one word more nor less than his subject requires. His principal weapon is a directness and economy in story-telling which many generations of playwrights have admired but none have matched. Each scene is emotionally and intellectually satisfying, telling us what we want to know, and no more, moving to the next scene just when we are ready for it, at the same time satisfying and surprising our expectations. A good play in any period has backbone, that which moves it lineally from one scene to the next. However well-written it may be, if it lacks backbone it will fail. But if the structure is right, it will always work, carrying its actors along with its own dramatic energy, as a wave carries surf-riders. This is the action, which Aristotle puts first in his list of the constituents of tragedy, and Sophocles is the supreme master of it. There is a wonderful inevitability about the movement of *Oedipus the King*. Once the first words have been spoken, we feel that absolutely nothing can stop the progress of events till the chorus' last sad moralisings, which may or may not be spurious, but end the play in an utterly satisfying manner. It is so marvellously done that it has acquired the force of myth. We have to keep reminding ourselves that it is just Sophocles' own story, a play he made to suit his own preconceptions. A glance at Euripides' *The Phoenician Women* reveals that there was nothing given about the story beyond very broad outlines. Sophocles' skill has enabled him to tell it in a way that has become definitive.

What keeps our eyes glued to the play is the most celebrated use of dramatic irony in theatrical history. We, the audience, know the story. The Greeks all knew it of course, as part of their cultural heritage, and those members of the modern audience who don't know are likely to suspect the truth within the first few minutes. Only the characters on stage are completely unaware, with the single exception of Teiresias, whose testimony is not believed. We watch with a kind of mesmerised attention as the determined King unravels the skein of crime which we know is to lead to himself. It is in the juxtaposition of situation and character that Sophocles pulls off this masterly trick. The Greeks were not grey-faced determinists, however much they may seem to be at first glance. The gods have not decided in meticulous detail what is to happen. As Kitto succinctly puts it, Apollo prophesies, but he does not compel. Within all the great tragic sagas there are several hinge points where the human protagonists could have behaved differently. Indeed, if Laius had obeyed Apollo's initial command not to have children there would have been no tragic cycle. What the gods know is what will happen, and the fascination lies in seeing how the human beings bring it about, in spite of all their efforts to the contrary. Oedipus is certainly put into a wickedly neat trap by what looks like Olympian malignity, but it is a trap a lesser man, or a more moderate man, might have found a way out of. Oedipus is neither of these things. He is a great man, full of profound talents, and with a very high, almost sacramental concept of the duties of a king. It is out of the question that he should not hunt down the criminal who is causing such suffering to his people, and the closer he gets, the more determined his hunt becomes. Teiresias knows his character, as well as the dilemma he is placed in. He knows that if he begins the investigation, he will see it through, and horror must result: which is why he tells Oedipus not to begin. He knows, too, that the briefest possibilities of escape for Oedipus from the closing trap of his destiny will present themselves. But we have already seen enough of the man, and Teiresias surely knows enough of him too, to understand that he will not take those opportunities, and that his very virtues will bring him down. Jocasta sees a final possibility of escape. At the very last moment, when everything has become clear to her, she is even prepared to live with the horror of that knowledge, as long as it is not brought out into the light, so as to save her husband, and herself. But Oedipus is incapable of that sort of greasy compromise, indeed, it is his inability to do such things that makes him the great king he is. And yet he is not an idealised figure. He has one great failing, which we see demonstrated again and again, and which makes his doom inevitable: his propensity to violent anger. Irrational outbursts make enemies of Creon and Teiresias, and indeed, in the past, it was the same irrational anger, expressed by both father and son, that caused the act of parricide at the place where three roads meet. We recognise the inescapable necessity of human character at work when his reaction to the two brief chances of escape offered him by Teiresias and Jocasta is the same angry refusal even to contemplate what they are saying. It is this remarkable man, with his brilliant intellect and relentless integrity, prone to violent anger, who is placed at the nexus of the gods' malign plot, and the combination is fatal. That man, in that situation, is doomed. When the doom is realised by the man himself, we watch with appalled horror the way in which he continues to behave like himself. Who but Oedipus would act with such furious logic as to blind himself in the height of his passion? Who but Oedipus could go through the anguish of that passion with such relentless honesty, such untrammelled grief? At every level, what Sophocles has created convinces us, so that the man and his destiny are hopelessly ensnared. He has been destroyed by circumstances and his own best and worst qualities, all working together. Nothing else in world literature produces quite the shiver we experience as we watch his heroic determination to do all that human ingenuity can achieve to avoid killing his father and marrying his mother, when we know that those very crimes have already been committed, long before the play begins; and that feeling is only intensified as we see his last chances of salvation disappear, knowing that there is not the slightest chance that he will take them. By the time the great passion of his blinding and despair arrives, the qualities of his character, his virtues, and his failings, have been so completely demonstrated that we are ready to experience with him the tragic grief and anguish that is his, and ours.

The gods in Sophocles are remote, and implacable. With the single exception of *Ajax*, his first extant play, they do not participate in the action as they do in Aeschylus and Euripides; and in *Ajax*, Athena's role is conventional, taken unmodified from Homer. But the laws they stand for are monolithic and immovable; and in the third chorus of *Oedipus the King*, the Theban Elders express their fear of the moral anarchy that will ensue if they are not applied to everyone. The gods' one contact with the human race is through oracles, which tell the protagonists not how they should behave, but what will happen. But the oracles are enigmatic, and fatally easy to misinterpret, as Oedipus misinterprets them by wrongly identifying his father and mother. Teiresias is the gods' representative among men, and his spiritual insight is theirs, the ability to know what will unavoidably occur, but it is his fate not to be believed. The gods themselves stand monumentally aloof, as the human actors hurl themselves against their immutable laws and unalterable predictions, and smash themselves to pieces. They neither help nor hinder. Simply, they know how the story will end, and they stand back and contemplate the tragic protagonists as they find their way, by however indirect a route, to that prophesied ending.

Sophocles has traditionally been considered the most conventionally religious of the three tragedians, but a modern consciousness, contemplating him, hardly sees that. What strikes us with great force is the essential ambiguity of his viewpoint. The gods are all-powerful. When they decide upon a course of action with regard to a human being or a family, that action will take place, even if it takes generations to come to full fruition. The ambiguity arises in the justice of their actions. Are the gods, by any definition of the word, just, in Sophocles? Are their decrees related to the actions and deservings of men, or are they merely arbitrary? Sophocles repeatedly asserts the power of the gods, and that their ordinances must be obeyed, but his story-telling leads the mind in other directions, so that the plays ask as many questions as they answer. Oedipus' human failing, his anger, prevents him from extricating himself from the trap the gods have devised for him, and to that degree he is culpable. But what has he done to deserve the destiny inflicted upon him in the first place, the crimes of parricide and incest for which he is punished? He is not exiled from Thebes because he acted unwisely in his anger, but for murdering his father and marrying his mother, and for those two actions he has no more responsibility than that of being his father's son: indeed, he has done just about everything a reasonable human being can to avoid his fate. *Oedipus the King* does not stress this point, beyond Oedipus' statement that Apollo has been the author of his pain, uttered at the height of his agony, but the whole structure of the play raises the question in an unavoidable form. This is the first matter that must be discussed, and discussed at great length, between the director and the actor playing Oedipus, because the first question is always 'what has the poor fellow done wrong, he has fallen over backwards to avoid committing the prophesied crimes, and has only committed them in ignorance.' Our modern consciousness might argue that at the crucial point in the saga Oedipus' uncontrollable anger has provoked him to murder an innocent old man at a crossroads, thus fulfilling the essence of the gods' prediction with an action for which he alone is entirely responsible; but the fact remains that in the story as Oedipus tells it, he was clearly provoked by Laius' servants, one of whom barged into him. Oedipus retaliated by hitting the man, but Laius himself intensified the conflict, by hitting Oedipus hard on the head as he stepped aside to allow the carriage to pass. What followed was an act of self-defence, made murderous by the fury at the heart of Oedipus' character, and though his actions are certainly morally questionable by our terms, if not by the Greeks' own, they hardly seem to justify the massive retribution they bring down on Oedipus' head. 'Yes,' we say, 'he was in the wrong, his own actions have contributed to his downfall, and the self-blinding is entirely his own responsibility.' But in the same breath we have to affirm that the gods have victimised him in a particularly determined way, and that the punishment seems out of all proportion to the offence. It is this Sophoclean ambiguity, his refusal to discuss the philosophical question at the heart of the play, while being willing to demonstrate it, that gives the play its unique quality. We feel for the man partly because we feel he does not merit such shattering punishments. In *Oedipus at Colonus* the criticism has become overt. Oedipus again and again asserts his own innocence of any crime, and accuses the gods of pure malignity against him: indeed, the idea of the gods' justice, or lack of it, and the very relevance of such an idea on the brink of eternity, is the whole subject matter of the tragedy. Perhaps if we had some more of the 116 lost Sophocles plays, the answer to these questions would become clearer. It seems very likely that on this crucial issue, central to the thinking of all three tragedians, Sophocles' own thinking developed and changed over such a long writing life, which must have spanned something like sixty years at the very least. We can certainly see a development in the three plays in this volume. *Antigone*, the earliest, accepts the gods' laws as immutable, and sets up a story which does not question their justice, but shows two equally powerful imperatives in direct conflict. *Oedipus the King* unavoidably raises the question of justice and deserving, but retains an ambiguous position. *Oedipus at Colonus*, written at the age of ninety, in the disillusion and collapse of the Athens that Sophocles stood for, openly questions the whole ethical basis of the gods' decrees, and in so doing, allies itself with the contemporary Euripides, who at this disastrous stage in Athenian history was writing plays which showed the gods as near contemptible figures, persecuting mankind for the most petty motives, even, as Apollo says at the end of Euripides' *Orestes*, to rid the earth of the burden of superfluous people: an idea quite certain to strike a chill into the twentieth-century mind.

It is the essential ambiguity of Sophocles' position that keeps his plays so thrillingly alive. Of course, his Olympian deities are no more than marvellous fictions for us, but the necessities they embody are real, and manipulate our lives as completely as Apollo manipulated Oedipus. Indeed, it is the very reasonless injustice of the gods' actions that speaks so directly to our consciousness. We have good reason to know that certain individuals are sometimes born at the focus of the gods' malignity, and are brought to undeserved disaster, in spite of the most remarkable qualities or most determined efforts. A Jew born in Krakow in 1930 was trapped as desperately as Oedipus, and almost certainly endured an even more terrifying tragedy, one enacted on a continental scale. We know about chance, and the deeper necessities moving under the surface of society which bring dreadful events to a focus, so that at a certain time and place disasters are likely to occur; and we know, too, that such disasters are never utterly determined, that somewhere the hand of man participates, making the disasters avoidable or inevitable. Sophocles would have recognised in Salvador Allende and Leon Trotsky the materials for his kind of tragedy, and looking at our world, would have been quite sure that his Olympians are not dead. They have changed their names, and their instruments of action have changed with the times; but chance, arrogance, greed and the lust for power are still with us, and economic and political necessities construct traps for men and women as intricate as anything Apollo devised for Oedipus.

Historical events, and the desperate patriotism of a ninety-year-old man near to despair, are powerful elements in *Oedipus at*

Colonus, but there is a great deal more to the play than that. Sophocles' last work is one of the great summits of the poetic drama, of a richness, range and wisdom to rival *King Lear*, with which it has much in common. To direct it was one of the most extraordinary experiences of my thirty-year directing life, and to confront it day by day was to be reminded of Keats' lines about Lear, 'once again . . . Must I burn through . . . the bitter-sweet of this Shakespearean fruit.' The power and intensity of the anguish it contains flows like a wave from the text as soon as the actors begin to speak it, and carries everyone from the leading actor to the ASM and props boy unavoidably through to its quiet conclusion. *Lear* ends on a summit of pain, but *Colonus*, like *The Tempest*, has a sunset quality about its conclusion, a sense of everything being correctly and rightly finished, which conjures up Milton's conclusion to his Greek-inspired *Samson Agonistes*:

> His servants he, with new acquist
> Of true experience from this great event
> With peace and consolation hath dismissed
> And calm of mind, all passion spent.

In telling the story of Oedipus' arrival at Colonus in search of his prophesied death, Sophocles creates a profoundly religious play, but its religion is not of the kind that attaches itself closely to any particular creed, rather the spirituality of everyman confronting the paradox of human life and eternity, the necessity to die which is laid upon all of us. How to die is the play's subject, or more specifically, how to die if you have been branded as the supreme criminal and outcast of the world. When the old man arrives at the grove sacred to the Furies, convinced that this is the place of his long-prophesied mysterious death, the Chorus of local men of Colonus is horrified to discover who it is who is seeking sanctuary with them, and their first instinct is to throw him out, as he has been thrown out in so many places before. The progress of the play shows how this criminal outcast and much-punished man becomes acceptable to the gods. They grant to him an extraordinary death, unlike any death ever experienced by a mortal man, so that the memory of his pain will become one of the icons of Athens, a local deity to guarantee protection for all time. The nature of his death is prophesied, because as always in Sophocles the gods know what will happen: the drama lies in seeing how it will come about; in particular, how this ragged and despised outcast can possibly attain the magical ending reserved for him, when all the pressures of the world seem combined to deny it. Once again, as in the earlier play, Sophocles conceives his protagonist in an essentially sacramental role, the one who suffers for the sake of his people, and the parallels with Christian mythology are obvious. Nineteenth-century critics and twentieth-century Christian apologists have seized upon *Colonus* with delight, even with relief, as a pre-figuring of Christian values, as though they were marking Sophocles out as one of the virtuous pagans, consigned to the most comfortable circle of Hell, one of us really, just unlucky enough to have missed out on baptism. In fact, though the sacramental role of Oedipus is obvious, the play is profoundly unchristian in its thinking. There is no nonsense about forgiving one's enemies in Oedipus. On the contrary, one's enemies are to be lacerated, and cursed, with an intensity of hatred that is frightening in any language. More interestingly, there is no spiritual development in Oedipus in the course of the play. With any Christian dramatist, or even any dramatist influenced by centuries of Christian thinking, the pattern would have been clear. The much-persecuted Oedipus would have entered enraged, full of hatred for his sons and Creon and all who have been the authors of his sufferings, and through the progress of the play we would have seen his spiritual rehabilitation, till at the time of his death he would have been reconciled with the world, and those who persecuted him, and ready to die in humility and love. Milton's Samson endures that sort of journey, from savage despair at how his God and his people have betrayed him, to an acceptance that all is for the best, and that God is working through him still, even if the work in hand is the mass murder of the Philistine/Royalists; and Hamlet and Lear progress from the depths of despair at the horror and meaninglessness of the world, to an acceptance of some sort of necessity. Oedipus travels no such journey. He goes into the grove the same man who arrived before it, having stubbornly asserted his innocence, and his unrelenting hatred for his two sons, from his arrival to his exit. He is still the same arrogant, angry, giant of a man we remember from the first play, and none of his anger or bitterness has cooled. He has merely put it aside to confront the greater reality of his own imminent death, and the necessity to help Athens, the city which has helped him. If the gods are prepared to accept him, as they do with signs of exceptional honour, they accept him 'with all his imperfections on his head', not as the penitent sinner coming through humility to salvation. Nothing could be further from Sophoclean tragedy than that concept. To the last Oedipus is a rock, standing alone in a waste of northern ocean unmoved under whatever battering the gods feel tempted to inflict upon him. Nothing can stop him from being marvellously and heroically himself, and it is in that courage that the essence of Sophoclean tragedy lies. Genuine tragedy is in this sense an essentially pagan idea. Christians must eventually submit, but Greek tragic heroes never do: which is perhaps why Milton, who belonged to a personal religious party of one, and who never really submitted to anyone, even God, succeeded in creating the nearest to a Greek tragedy in English letters.

Religion, mankind under the eye of eternity, is not Sophocles' only concern in this inexhaustible play. Political matters, how men organise themselves into societies, are never far distant in Greek tragedies, and this most spiritual of plays still has a lively concern for hard material realities. The portrait of Theseus as the ideal political leader Athens so desperately needs, is balanced by the brutal realism of the portrait of the power-politician Creon, a man without morality, concerned only with political advantage for his city and himself. Violating the sanctuary of the sacred grove means nothing to Creon. He is quite prepared to seize Ismene in the very act of prayer, and intends to drag both girls off to Thebes to serve as hostages for Oedipus' return. Creon's actions are horribly familiar to us, as they doubtless were to the war-torn Athenians. We, too, live in an age where innocent hostages can be captured and murdered simply as pawns in an international game, and Creon's diplomatic hypocrisy and immediate resort to force when diplomacy fails make it quite clear that whatever else may have changed over two and a half millennia, mankind's political cloven hoof has not. Creon is in fact one of the most remarkable of Sophocles' creations. His hypocrisy and amorality are required by the structure of this particular play to balance Theseus' integrity and concern for ethical behaviour, but even so, and over the period of something like forty years of his creation, Creon is recognisably the same human being in all three plays. In the first play he demonstrates that he has already learned the politics of living as third in command, and when he becomes regent, after Oedipus' fall, there is no doubt that he relishes the taste of power in his mouth and the spectacle of the great Oedipus on his knees before him. In the second play, years of anarchy and disorder have made him a cynical authoritarian materialist, prepared to do anything to achieve his own political ends, and in the third play, the trap that has been so carefully set for him over his long life is finally sprung, when the unimaginative authoritarian realist is confronted with the one person all his experience has left him unfitted to deal with, the intense and idealistic Antigone. It is a masterly portrait, and a source of great delight to any actor lucky enough to play the part in all three plays.

Polynices too is an unforgettable character, and the whole intense and destructive relationship between father and children is drawn with total conviction. Sophocles presents Polynices as a slob, a born loser, a man who in the first part of the scene seems completely unaware that Oedipus has any reasonable grounds for complaint against him. Of course, he has treated his father badly, he admits, but that's all over now, and ought to be forgotten. His selfishness shines through every word. He needs Oedipus, very badly; otherwise, we are sure, he would not have been seen dead anywhere near the old devil. It is this unlovely character that Sophocles brings before us in the first half of the scene, shifty, boastful and, in his desperation, almost embarrassing as he crawls before his unyielding father. The final bait which he holds out to tempt him is the opportunity to participate in the total destruction of his younger son, Eteocles. Nothing could be more carefully calculated to convince us that everything Oedipus has said about Polynices is true, that he is indeed a totally worthless character. Then Oedipus launches upon his terrible curse on both his sons, and its power is frightening. Polynices himself is visibly shaken, as if he had never fully realised the depth of his father's hatred. He calls upon his two sisters to help him, and it is here that Sophocles pulls his master stroke. The girls' love for their unpleasant brother is patent, and immediately the family group is completely convincing. What more likely than this adoration of their prodigal elder brother by the two sisters whose own actions have been so different, and particularly by Antigone, whose intensity makes her do everything by extremes? Polynices' beaten stoicism, the grim realisation of a man who knows he is already defeated, and must now endure the enacting of his defeat, is powerful and unexpected, and the anguish of the final farewell between Antigone and her bad-hat of a brother is one of the most moving scenes in the whole of Greek drama. Sophocles performs the feat of completely reversing our sympathies within a single scene. The character whose self-centred unpleasantness has dominated the first half leaves with something like our sympathy. It is a masterly stroke of playwriting, which in its complete sureness in the manipulation of dramatic material and technique, puts Sophocles with his natural colleagues Shakespeare and Chekhov.

A great deal of nonsense has been talked about the structure of *Oedipus at Colonus*, as it has about many of Euripides plays', by critics who have never set foot in a rehearsal room. It has been remarked that the play is broken-backed, that Polynices is dragged in without any good reason, that the play wanders from event to event, and lacks the dramatic logic of *Oedipus the King* and *Antigone*. Certainly Sophocles does not employ the causal dramatic logic that he had employed in the two earlier plays, but there is no reason why he should. There is no set pattern for the employment of Greek dramatic form, and each play that we have modifies the basic structure to suit its own ends. Kitto has very helpfully compared *Colonus* to the late Beethoven Quartets. They too lack the tight structure of the middle-period works, just as the late Mozart piano concertos treat sonata form as a starting point rather than a strait jacket. When artists become complete masters of their craft, they no longer need tight forms to unify their work, and *Colonus* too suggests a total master, who can do anything with the material under his hands. The formal artistry of the play is carried to very great heights in the repetitive patterns of the choruses and choral dialogues, and in performance and rehearsal the play is as tightly unified, and moves with as convincing a sweep of action, as either of the two earlier plays. Sophocles throws connective logic to the winds, and relies on pure dramatic instinct, just as he does in the huge entry song of the chorus, which he casts in the form of a choral dialogue, rather than an ode, and which contains long passages, between the formal strophe and antistrophe, of what we can only call free verse. In every aspect of the play's structure, the supreme master of form is prepared to improvise. His choruses are used with masterly variety, to create contrast – as between the lyrical ode in praise of Colonus, and the terrifying arrival of Creon, and between the Thunder chorus, and the sense of mystery which follows it – and even as crucial participants in the plot, when they prevent Creon from taking Oedipus back to Thebes by force; and the Polynices scene, far from being in any way structurally inadequate, is in fact the structural climax of the play. His arrival may not have the logical necessity of events in the earlier two plays; but Oedipus has been talking about his two sons, and cursing them, almost since the play began, and it is a compelling emotional necessity that the confrontation between father and son should occur. Without it, the play would lack its essential ingredient, and Sophocles, knowing that, has placed the scene at the climactic point of the drama, the final confrontation before the old man enacts the ritual of his death. The scene, when it comes, in all its anguish and pity, fully lives up to all the emotional expectations Sophocles has raised throughout the play, and crowns the structure like the capstone that holds the whole building together. From this point on, Sophocles keeps the play at the very heights of drama, sustaining the action at an unrelenting level of pathos, tragedy and grief through to the end. Polynices' exit is followed by the spectacularly dramatic Thunder chorus, a marvellous scene of sustained poetry between Theseus and Oedipus, a choral ode of grave beauty, praying for a quiet death for the long-suffering man, a Messenger speech which has always been considered one of the greatest in the canon, and, as a final demonstration of genius, a choral dialogue of such sustained pain and grief that it rounds off the whole work, as a great chorale rounds off an oratorio, giving us full opportunity to weep with Oedipus and his two girls, but like the end of the St Matthew Passion, bringing us, after our tears of grief, to a quiet close. Such is his sureness of touch, he can even introduce his last fragmentary irony, Antigone's desperate hope to save her brothers, which we know is doomed to fail, without spoiling the grand and solemn music of his finale. Sophocles lays down his pen at the very height of his powers, having written nothing, at least in the seven plays we have, of greater range or more supreme artistry.

In considering *Antigone*, we leap back to Sophocles' first great play, but it is worthwhile remembering that if the conventional dating is anywhere near correct, he was at least fifty when he wrote it, and must have had very many of his 123 plays behind him. It is not the work of a brilliant beginner – all that is lost – but of a well-practised artist well into middle age.

Perhaps the most extraordinary thing about the play is the unique place it has occupied in the European consciousness. In Sophocles' own day it was the play most often mentioned in anecdotes about the poet, and at least since the end of the eighteenth century, the figure of Antigone has become a cultural archetype, the symbol of personal integrity, even at the expense of martyrdom, and an icon of political freedom. The figure of the frail girl confronting the power of the State, refusing to be broken, and choosing to die for what she knows are the greater truths, flew like a banner over the Romantic movement – she was the girl they were all looking for – and she finds herself today inspiring all kinds of political positions and ideals of revolutionary purity far removed from anything Sophocles conceived. Creon in all these schemes hardly gets a look in. He is cast as the baddie, the power of the repressive State, the grim force of reaction we are all in arms against. This symbolism is particularly widespread in our own age, and yet nothing could be more calculated to destroy Sophocles' tragedy than this kind of thinking. The nineteenth century made the same mistake, even to the extent of criticising the play's structure, because the leading character or tragic protagonist leaves two-thirds of the way through. In fact, the structure of the play has all the flawless logical perfection of *Oedipus the King*, and the tragic protagonist is Creon, not Antigone. The presentation of the two leading characters is much more subtle than the popular symbolism assigned to them gives credit for, and, as we come to expect in Sophocles, it is their own action in a situation that their characters make unavoidable that leads them both to destruction. The play is not a confrontation of the forces of darkness and the forces of light, but a clash of the two great imperatives that underlie all political action, the needs of the individual and the needs of the State. History has turned this question into the principal political subject matter of our century, and consequently made this the most popular of Sophocles' plays at the present time; but perhaps the most extraordinary thing is the continuing validity of what Sophocles presents to us, even in our unimaginably changed circumstances. No one has written better on this subject since Sophocles. No one has put the nature of the conflict more succinctly, or demonstrated the price that must be paid on both sides with more unrelenting honesty.

The key to the play is that Sophocles doesn't present us with a picture of a frail idealist destroyed by Auden's ogre, but with the tragedy of a king trying to rescue a State from civil war and anarchy, so that it can be brought back to the order and reasoned justice that was the Greek ideal of political life. On his first day in power, Creon confronts the biggest of all political questions, and his inability to solve it destroys him. At the beginning of the play, both ideals are presented as equally valid. Conscience is above the law. Spiritual realities, long-held human values, the laws of the gods, call them what you will, have a lasting validity which is ultimately superior to man-made laws, which change from day to day, reflecting the needs of the men who make them. There comes a time for everyone when, if the deepest-held beliefs are pronounced to be against the law, then the law must be broken; indeed, it is the duty of the honest man or woman to break it. On the other side of the question, a State must have laws, and they must be obeyed if human society is not to decline into anarchy. Individuals cannot be allowed to obey the laws or not to obey them, as they please, obeying the ones they approve of, disobeying the ones they disapprove of: disaster and bloodshed, never very far from the walls of Greek City States, will inevitably follow. These are the two general principles Sophocles embodies in his two leading characters, and as absolutes they are irreconcilable. But Sophocles does not present them as absolutes. They are embodied in two recognisably human beings, so that instead of an arid debate about abstract issues, we see the clash and interweaving of human passions and human failings.

Antigone is no saint, though she has often been presented and written about as though she were. She is an infuriatingly stubborn and indeed half-mad girl, whose intensity of experience is so great as to leave her on the borders of sanity. Sophocles describes the fear Ismene feels as the power of the fire burning inside Antigone scorches her and seems likely to reduce both of them to ashes, and Antigone herself admits that her actions are of a kind very few would be prepared to undertake. It is nowhere suggested that Antigone's intensity unbalances her judgement, or makes her position in any way less valid, but the action of the play makes it clear that this kind of individual is a particular thorn in the flesh of any State trying to organise itself into some kind of rational pattern. History is littered with Antigones of both sexes, the non-conformists who are the makers of political liberty and the despair of rational statesmen, even if they are a great deal more successful at the job than Creon is. What is a statesman to do when confronted with such a figure: merely capitulate? Antigone's absolutist answer would be plain enough: don't enact unjust laws, and you won't be confronted with an Antigone. But all politicians know, as Sophocles knew, having been one himself, that daily politics doesn't work like that, and sometimes genuine individual truths have to submit to greater political necessities.

Of the validity and justice of Creon's opening statement there can be no doubt. His initial speech is a definition of the Greek ideal of a just king. If he acts up to his words, then Thebes, shattered by disasters for a generation, and reeling from the effects of a massive war against Argos, which was in effect a civil war because Oedipus' two sons led the opposing armies, is in for happy days indeed. When at the end of his speech Creon announces that Polynices is to remain unburied, as a warning to any future disturbers of the peace of Thebes, the Chorus articulates our own uneasy feelings. This is not the correct behaviour, it violates religious imperatives and common human decencies. But we can see the point. Creon's propaganda is well calculated. His regime is to be a firm and authoritarian one, determined that the days of anarchy will not return, and in choosing to make a hero of the brother who defended the city and a villain of the one who attacked it, he is showing a mature sense of political tactics, what one would expect from a man who has been in or near power for so long. Of course, to Polynices it is an injustice, but in the real world losers expect to be treated unjustly, the demonstration will make Creon's point forcibly for him, and no one is likely to complain. Unfortunately for Creon, there is one person who is quite certain to complain, and even more unfortunately, that person is Antigone, the one individual in Thebes Creon's authority is not likely to frighten, nor his political experience buy off. Like John Lilburne, one of England's Antigones, she knows that 'what is done to anyone, may be done to everyone', that one man persecuted in a remote dungeon matters as much as a whole nation in chains. She confronts Creon with the implications of what he is doing: she will not allow him to use her dead brother to make a political point, and by her action she places him in a wicked dilemma. His long experience tells him that on this issue he must win. To be defeated by Antigone, to have his first decree on his first day of power overturned by the refusal of a young girl to obey him, will be fatal to his authority. She must be punished, and, family or not, he will carry out the letter of the law. Creon, as we have already seen, is not a man who is deeply involved in the morality of politics. What practical politician is? As he gets deeper and deeper into the crisis of his authority, he forgets what the Chorus has told him at the beginning, that the decree is fundamentally unjust, and offensive to religious feeling. Once Antigone is captured, and he is confronted with the necessity of carrying out the punishment he has announced for anyone who dares to bury Polynices, Creon shows that though he may make good speeches about the duties and responsibilities of a king, he has none of the qualities necessary to a good ruler. He is the perpetual second-in-command, the Anthony Eden, who when the tiller is in his hands, steers unerringly for the rocks. He makes decisions rashly, in anger, on the spur of the moment, and is quite incapable of taking advice, from his wise son, from the Chorus, even, most rashly of all, from Teiresias. Teiresias reveals the nakedness and emptiness of Creon's position. For all his stately pronouncements about kingship, all Creon is actually concerned about is losing face. He has the insecure man's determination not to be seen changing his mind, even when he is patently in the wrong, and it is this arrogant stupidity that leads him to his downfall, and the relentless unrolling of events following Antigone's burial alive. In the final moments of his kingship, before the mad dash to Antigone's tomb, we see him in a state of panic, all authority gone, his mind whirling out of control, like a weathervane in a hurricane. Once again, Sophocles demonstrates to us his conception of tragedy, just as he is to show it later in *Oedipus the King*. Over many years, patterns of events emerge which, at a crisis point, bring two individuals into conflict, and by the rich irony of the Sophoclean tragic process, they are the two individuals most likely to be unable to make an accommodation with each other, and most likely to inflict destruction upon the other. Character and destiny become hopelessly ensnared. Creon, the arch political manipulator, tries to manipulate the one person who will not accommodate his deviousness; and Antigone, the daughter of Oedipus, whose sense of what is right and what is wrong has kept her on the road with her father for years, regardless of the cost to herself, finds herself placed in the one situation in which her unrelenting strength of character will bring about her own destruction. Justice is on Antigone's side of course, and she dies a martyr, but Sophocles is not really interested in that. He is interested in the confrontation between an experienced but unimaginative politician and an intense, unbending idealist, and the destruction that results from their collision. Perhaps he was speaking directly to Pericles in the aftermath of a military atrocity on Samos, taking the playwright's privilege of warning the great of the dangers of sacrificing morality to political expediency. The truth of that we will never know. If he was, his artist's sense of form overrode his politician's need to persuade, and left us with a cunningly balanced clash of principles and entanglement of personalities that lives on the stage and in our consciousness many hundreds of years after the particular political argument between the two men is forgotten.

One final point seems worth making, to do with Sophocles' use of the Antigone story, because it is the perfect illustration of the Greek tragic method. As with *Oedipus the King*, Sophocles' version of the story is so perfectly put together that it has achieved the force of myth. We must continually remind ourselves that it is simply one playwright's version of a much-told tale, and that the characterisation and story-telling are very much his own. Other playwrights, we know, treated the story differently, and it is in what Sophocles decided to leave out that others included that we see his playwriting hand most clearly. In Euripides' *The Phoenician Women*, Creon refuses burial to Polynices under strict instructions from the dead Eteocles, the former king, and Polynices' brother. This would have weakened Creon's position in Sophocles' play, and he leaves it out. If he had included it, Creon could have argued from an equal religious imperative, the vow sworn to the dead king, and the play's clear conflict of values would have been muddied. What Creon does, he does on his own initiative, for reasons which are clear, and quite opposed to Antigone's, and the drama is the better focused for it.

The question of Creon's sons is even more fascinating. According to Aeschylus, Creon's son Megareus was one of the defenders of the seven gates of Thebes, and presumably died in the battle as Eurydice, just before her own suicide, weeps over his empty bed. In Euripides' play, Creon's son, Menoeceus, commits ritual suicide on the walls of Thebes, because Teiresias has prophesied that only this way will the city win the battle. We don't really know to what extent Attic playwrights were following different variants of the old stories, or how much they were prepared to invent new incidents to suit their own purposes, but we do know that Aeschylus' play was written before *Antigone*, and therefore that the Megareus story at least was available to Sophocles. So, let us get the situation quite clear. On the day before *Antigone* begins, Creon has lost one, perhaps two sons in the battle against the Argive forces. I can think of no modern playwright, nor any playwright perhaps since the Renaissance, who would not have been tempted to incorporate this material somewhere in the play. The grieving father of heroic sons is surely too tempting a dramatic morsel to be ignored by even the most classically chaste of playwrights. Sophocles ignores it, because it is not relevant to the play he is writing, and because another body or two on the battlefield would have fatally obscured the clear outlines of the conflict he has created. Eteocles is the hero to be honoured, and another is not required. Any personal grief Creon might feel is not relevant to what confronts him on his first day in power, and would have confused the direct line of drama when he finally confronts his surviving son Haemon. Nothing could be a purer indication of the dramatic methods of Greek classicism, nor could indicate more clearly why the dramatic structures of

INTRODUCTION

Sophocles' Theban plays have been a byword of excellence since they were written.

In calling this introduction *Sophocles, Our Contemporary*, I tip my hat to Jan Kott's influential sixties book on Shakespeare, and encapsulate my own view of the Athenian master, both as reader, director and playwright. To me, his works feel less out of date than some plays I could name by living authors. Nothing could have illustrated that more clearly than the fact that we were rehearsing *Antigone* during the summer of 1984, in the first months of the miners' strike, and throughout the drama of the Sarah Tisdall trial. In both cases, the words being spoken in our rehearsal-room exactly paralleled the arguments being rehearsed in the papers and on the TV political discussion programmes, but for the fact that Sophocles, even in the Don Taylor version, treated these matters with far greater insight and subtlety than any journalist or politician. Indeed, some of the latter, in their absolute assertion of the rights of the State and denial of conscience, seemed to be quite unaware that *Antigone* had ever been written, or that these ideas had ever been considered by finer minds than their own. Somewhere in the world, every day, on a larger or smaller stage, the real-life drama of Antigone is being enacted, just as, to our shame, year after year and in country after country, our modern Trojan Women raise their cry of despair; and the tragic metaphor of the life and death of Oedipus, including political considerations, but going far beyond them, continues to enact for all of us the daily tragedy in which we are all involved as we move towards our own mysterious ending. It is my sense of the relevance and immediacy of these great plays that has moved me to transform them into my own language as it is used at the present time in the theatre and on television. Plays in which subject matter and dramatic form are wedded with such perfection as they are in Sophocles are never likely to be dead, but each age has to make them live in its own characteristic way. This way, I hope, is ours.

Don Taylor
February 1986

OEDIPUS THE KING

Characters

OEDIPUS, King of Thebes
A PRIEST of Zeus
CREON, brother of Jocasta
TEIRESIAS, a prophet, blind
JOCASTA, wife of Oedipus
CORINTHIAN MESSENGER
OLD SHEPHERD
MESSENGER
CHORUS of Counsellors of Thebes
TEIRESIAS' BOY
ANTIGONE
ISMENE } daughters of Oedipus and Jocasta
PEOPLE OF THEBES
JOCASTA'S WOMEN
SHEPHERD'S ATTENDANTS

This translation was commissioned by BBC Television and first produced in the autumn of 1986, with the following cast:

OEDIPUS	Michael Pennington
CREON	John Shrapnel
TEIRESIAS	John Gielgud
JOCASTA	Claire Bloom
SHEPHERD	David Waller
MESSENGER	Gerard Murphy
PRIEST	Cyril Cusack
CORINTHIAN MESSENGER	Norman Rodway
CHORUS	Nigel Stock, Edward Hardwicke, Donald Eccles, Robert Eddison, Alan Rowe, Denys Hawthorne, David Collings, Michael Byrne, Noel Johnson, Ernest Clark, Clifford Rose, John Woodnutt
ANTIGONE	Cassie Shilling
ISMENE	Kelly Huntley
TEIRESIAS' BOY	Lincoln Saunders
PEOPLE OF THEBES	Gabrielle Blunt, Imogen Claire, Edwina Day, Mary Lincoln, Heather Ramsay, Judy Liebert, Catherine Shipton, Mary Llewellen, Czeslaw Grocholski, Stuart Saunders, Bill Gavin, Gordon Faith, Philip Wright, Alan Collins, Richard Tate, Timothy Block, Stanley Dawson, Michael Eaves, Hugh Hayes, Eric Longworth, Judith Cox, Anne Higgins, Hazel Stock, Susie Sapsford, Elizabeth Page, Gioia Izquierdo, Jacqui Cryer, Mike Vinden, Colin Thomas, Kenneth Lawrie, John Coleman, Andrew Thompson, Bernard Losh

CHILDREN OF THEBES   Tamsin Alker, Erica Rossi,
Nicola Whitehead, Dean Gunter,
Nicola Sideris, Emma Cook,
Tom Hammond, Lincoln Saunders,
Jonathan Taylor, Lucy Hammond

Directed by   Don Taylor
Produced by   Louis Marks
Designed by   David Myerscough-Jones
Music by   Derek Bourgeois
Costumes by   June Hudson

The scene is set before the palace of King Oedipus in the city of Thebes.

Citizens of Thebes, of all ages, enter, or are discovered. They carry with them garlanded laurel branches and incense burners, and they show all the signs of the sickness which is ravaging the city.

Led by a Priest of Zeus, they gather in groups in front of the king's palace, adopting attitudes of desperation and prayer.

The palace doors open.

Enter Oedipus.

OEDIPUS. My children. You are the modern descendants
    Of King Cadmus, who founded our city.
    Why do you come here with these laurel branches,
    Ritually dressed, and all the signs
    Of desperate people begging for help?
    In the city I hear prayers for the sick,
    And the sound of weeping. The air is heavy
    With incense and tears. What more do you want?
    I can't rely on second-hand reports,
    I have come to find out for myself.
    I am Oedipus the king. Everyone knows my name.
    You, sir, you are a priest,
    A man old enough to be wise
    And entitled to speak first. A sudden panic
    Is it, or a demand for action?
    Anything I can do, I will do, of course.
    I would have to be a man without feeling
    To close my eyes and stop my ears
    To a petition from everyone, such as this.
PRIEST. King Oedipus, Lord of Thebes,
    You see us, many hundreds crowding to your palace:
    Youngsters, like birds still in the nest,
    Old men, whose eyes have seen everything,
    Priests – of Zeus, like me – and of other gods,
    And the very best of our young men.
    We have all come here: there are thousands more

Sitting in the market place, carrying emblems like these,
Others at the two altars of Pallas Athene,
And at Ismenus' shrine by the river bank
Where the future can be read in the ashes,
And we are all offering desperate prayers.
You've seen yourself what's happening here.
This city is like a warship, defeated in battle
Wallowing aimlessly in a sea of blood.
The crops are rotting in the fields,
Disease is killing all the cattle,
Babies are born dead, or decay in the womb,
And as if that weren't enough, some god has sent plague
Like a fire-demon to scorch our people.
The courtyards Cadmus built will soon be empty,
And the underworld is already crowded with Thebans
Weeping in the darkness for themselves and their kin.
If we choose to come here to beg for help,
It's not because we think of you as a god,
But because we know you to be the best of men,
Not only in the daily business of the state,
But in those deeper mysteries of life
Where the mind of man touches eternity.
We haven't forgotten that it was you,
A young man, newly arrived here,
Who solved the riddle of the Sphinx,
That monstrous perversion of woman, lion and bird,
And freed us from her magical tyranny.
We could do nothing to help you then,
And I think – we all think – some god helped you.
That's why, world-famous Oedipus,
We're asking for your help again. Find us
Some remedy, either from your own experience,
Or by calling on supernatural powers.
You've solved terrible problems in the past,
And that gives us confidence in your abilities now.
Indeed, you have a reputation to live up to.
Your genius has saved us once. It would be
Ridiculous to have preserved us then,

Only to see us wasted now.
Save us again, as you did before.
Sail under that same lucky star,
And guide us, as a real prince should,
Into the harbour of good fortune and peace.
An unmanned ship needs no captain:
A city that is empty because its people are dead
Has no further use for a king.

OEDIPUS. My children, believe me when I say
I know everything that you are suffering,
Why you come here, and what you ask of me.
I suffer as much, perhaps more than you do.
You carry your personal burdens of sorrow:
I carry them too, and my own, and the city's.
I have not been sleeping. My eyes, like yours,
Are bloodshot with too frequent tears.
I have walked every corridor in the palace,
And all the secret galleries of my mind,
Searching and searching what best to do.
And this much I have done – because I haven't been idle –
The one thing that seemed sensible.
My brother-in-law, Creon, the son of Menoeceus,
I have sent to the oracle of Apollo, at Delphi,
To ask the Pythia, the sacred priestess,
What action or word of mine might help.
He ought to be here, his mission has taken
Far longer that it should, and I begin to wonder
What keeps him so long. When he arrives,
Whatever the oracle demands, you have my word
Will be meticulously performed.

PRIEST. No man could say better than that;
Nor upon a better cue. Look, there's the signal!
Creon himself is approaching.

OEDIPUS. Whatever the message, he's certainly smiling!
Apollo, god of healing, let the news be good.

PRIEST. It must be good. He moves like a man.
Confident of his success.

OEDIPUS.   He can hear us now.

9

Dear brother in law! Son of Menoeceus!
Enter Creon.
What's the god's message? What does the oracle say?

CREON. It's good news. Or perhaps I should say
It will be good news, if all turns out well:
Though perhaps painful to begin with.

OEDIPUS. And what does that mean! At such an answer
I don't know if I should laugh or cry!

CREON. Do you want me to say it all here, in public,
Or shall we go in?

OEDIPUS.   In public, of course!
While these people suffer, I suffer too.
Their life concerns me, more than my own!

CREON. The answer is straightforward, and the command simple.
There is something unclean in our city.
Born here. Living here. It pollutes everything.
We harbour it. We must drive it out.

OEDIPUS. How can it be purified, the pollution of
This unclean thing? What is it?

CREON. By banishment. Or by blood for blood.
It was bloodshed, the oracle says,
That whipped up this storm that's destroying us.

OEDIPUS. Whose blood was shed? What sort of man?

CREON. There was a king here sir, before you came.
His name was Laius.

OEDIPUS.   I know the name.
I never saw the man.

CREON.   The man was killed:
And the oracle's meaning is clear enough.
The murderers of Laius must be found,
And the unknown killers brought to justice.

OEDIPUS. But where are they? The trail's gone cold.
It's an old story now. Where shall be begin?

CREON. Here. The god said here. Search,
And you won't be disappointed. No evidence
Is ever found if you don't look for it.

OEDIPUS. Where did it happen – this unexplained murder?
Was it here in the palace? Or in the country?

Or while he was travelling abroad?

CREON. He left the city to make a pilgrimage.
And he never came back, except in a coffin.

OEDIPUS. Who was with him? Didn't anyone see it?
There must be evidence, some scrap, some rumour?

CREON. One of the servants escaped. He ran
So fast, he could only remember one thing.

OEDIPUS. What thing? Tell me. The smallest clue
Might lead to others.

CREON.   He said that robbers,
Not one man, a whole band of them,
Met them on the road and they murdered the king.

OEDIPUS. Robbers? Would they dare attack a king?
Perhaps they were bought. Theban money,
And political ambition the motive.

CREON. We thought that too, at first. But the crisis
Blew up almost at once. We had other troubles,
And Laius was dead. No one pursued it.

OEDIPUS. What crisis could be greater than a murdered king?
So there never was a full investigation?

CREON. The voice of the Sphinx seemed to mesmerise us.
She drained all our energies with her riddling.
It was a question of survival: no time
For unsolved mysteries, even regicide.

OEDIPUS. Then I shall begin it. There's time enough now.
We'll shine a fresh light into every corner
Of the whole dark and musty business.
Thanks to the Lord Apollo! And our gratitude to you,
Creon, for reminding us what we had forgotten,
Our duty to the dead. I am determined
To do everything I can to help our city
And show the god's justice. It's in my interest too
To avenge this crime, not only for Laius' sake,
But for my own protection. This unknown killer
Might strike at me. Justice for Laius
And my own safety go hand in hand.
So go to your homes, dear people, my children,
Pick up your sad sprays of laurel

11

Call the Theban counsellors here, and tell them
That I will do everything a man can do.
With the god's help, we will find out the truth
And save the city. We must, or be destroyed.
Exit Oedipus, into the palace.

PRIEST. Go home, now, good people. The king has promised
Everything we came to ask for. Apollo
The healer, whose priestess gave us good answers
May come himself to cure this sickness
Of man and beast. Let us pray for that.
Exit Creon.
The people disperse and leave the stage.
Enter the Chorus of Counsellors of Thebes.

CHORUS. With a voice sweet as music from the house of gold
The priestess speaks to sunlit Thebes,
And the god speaks through her. But his meaning's obscure.
My hands are shaking, my heart is cold,
On the rack with fear.
From your island of Delos, supreme physician,
Send us your antidote to ease these plagues.
Is this torture unique, or the old condition
Of suffering man through the centuries?
The golden child of hope never dies
And we live by her prophecies.

Ever living Athene, wise daughter of Zeus,
We sing first to you, and your chaste sister
Artemis, the deer-slayer queen,
Whose stony eyes watch in the market-place
From her marble throne:
And bowman Apollo, infallible marksman,
Trinity of deities, show us your power,
Purge our diseases, and save our nation,
If ever you saved us in the days of disaster,
When the plague enforced its reign of terror
And a fire consumed us that no man could master.

Our agonies are beyond telling,
A whole city slowly dying
From an enemy no man can fight.
Slime and fungus on orchard and meadow,
Death in the womb, and birth in the shadow
Of death, and in the mother's sight.
Men die without number, like birds flying,
Like fire consuming, despairing, crying,
As they pass to the shadows of night.

The smell of the dead, the street stinking,
Breeds death and more death, beyond all counting.
No tears as her children die
From the girl wife and the grey-haired mother,
Tearing their nails at the crowded altar,
Accusing the implacable sky.
Healer Apollo, Athene all-knowing,
Can you not hear a whole city screaming,
Will you not answer our cry?

Now let the bloodstained god of war
Whose savage music I hear
Though no swords clash or shields ring,
Be driven from our city, where the only song
Is the groan of the dying, the whimper of fear.
Rout him, the man-slayer, let him fly
In disorder, let him hide his head
In some bleak Thracian bay,
Or ease himself in Amphitrite's bed.
Now, whoever survives the night
Dies at first light.
Great Father Zeus, you who punish with fire,
Incinerate the god of war
Before we all lie dead.

Stand by us now, wolfish god-king,
Pull taut your golden bowstring
And let fly your shaft that never misses:
And hard-riding Artemis, whose torches

Flare on the Lycian slopes, trailing
Sparks as you pass – and god of ecstasy,
Bacchus above all, whose drowsy peace
Inspires and protects our city,
God of the golden turban and flushed face
By your resinous torchlight we stamp and cry
As your Maenads sweep by
From the frenzied east: fly to us, wielding
Ecstatic fire to burn this killing
God, whom the gods themselves despise!
Enter Oedipus, from the palace.
OEDIPUS. You have prayed to the gods. Now listen to me.
If you act as I tell you to act,
Follow my instructions in every detail
Those prayers will soon be answered.
I speak as an outsider. I know nothing of this story,
The murder or the murderer. So, without your help
And hardly a clue to go on, alone,
What trail can I follow? When the crime was committed
I wasn't even a citizen of Thebes.
So, first, I'll make a public proclamation.
If any man here knows the killer's name,
He must speak out now, in public, to me!
Silence.
Or perhaps one of you is the guilty man?
If that man is here, and gives himself up,
Now, it will be easier for him.
There will be no capital charge.
The severest sentence I shall pronounce
Will be exile. No greater punishment than that.
Silence.
Or maybe one of you has inside knowledge
That some foreigner was the killer?
If you turn informer, you will be well paid,
I shall see to that. But my gratitude
Will be the truest, most satisfying reward.
Silence.
If, however, that man *is* here,

14

And refuses to speak, or if anyone,
Out of fear for himself, his friends or his family
Ignores these offers, and then is discovered
To be sheltering someone, or himself,
On that man I pass sentence already.
It doesn't matter who he is, I Oedipus, forbid
Anyone to speak with, or give shelter to that man
In this city, or in the country under my rule.
No man may pray with him, make sacrifices with him,
Nor even allow him to wash in his house!
Every man will kick him out of doors
As the perpetrator of the horrible crime
That brings this suffering on our city! —
According to the prophetic word of Apollo,
As revealed to me, by the Delphic oracle.
I stand here as the champion of the god,
And of the dead king too! For the man himself,
The murderer: with all solemnity, I curse him,
Whether he acted alone, or with others,
To bear the mark of this crime for the rest of his life,
Without friends, homeless and in misery!
I'll go further. I don't even exclude myself.
If, knowingly, I should shelter
This criminal in any house or hearth,
Or any place of mine, let the curse I have uttered
Fall on me too, as fiercely as on anyone!
That is my sentence, and it's up to you
To see it fully carried out,
For the god's sake, for my sake,
And the sake of our plague-ridden god-deserted city.
To be honest with you, I am surprised
That no purification ceremonies or investigations
Were undertaken, when so excellent a king
As Laius was inexplicably murdered.
Even without the gods' command
That should have been looked into, I would have thought.
Now, however, I am king.
I enjoy Laius' title, his bed, and his wife:

She is a kind of common ground
Between us, and his children, indeed
If he had had any, would be another bond,
Sharing a mother with mine.
And he was a sad victim of this tragedy.
These links between us, and my feeling for the man,
Make me determined to fight for him now
As if he were my own father. Nothing
Will be too much trouble to ferret him out,
This destroyer of Laius, heir to Labdacus
And all the ancient kings of Thebes,
Back to Cadmus himself, and Agenor, his father.
And if any man dares to disobey these orders,
May all the god's curses fall on him too,
Barren earth, barren cattle,
A barren wife, and all the horrors
This suffering city daily endures,
Without mercy, till the end of his life.
For the honest people of Thebes, who follow me
In intention and action, justice be ours,
And the god's help, today and every day!

CHORUS. That curse would frighten any man,
Great king of Thebes, and it terrifies me!
I'm not the killer. Let me say that at once,
And I can't point him out or tell you his name.
The god Apollo asked this question.
He, if anyone, should tell us the answer.

OEDIPUS. I don't doubt that. But if you can tell me
How a man persuades a god to speak
When the god doesn't want to, I shall thank you for it!

CHORUS. One other thing might be worth saying,
Second best, admittedly.

OEDIPUS.   Second best, third best,
Say what you think. Any man's opinion
Is worth hearing at a time like this.

CHORUS. The prophet and astrologer Teiresias
Has studied the mysteries of men and gods:
He has knowledge and experience and insight.

16

He, more than anyone, could help us now.

OEDIPUS. Which is why I have sent for him already!
Nothing, my friends, has been overlooked.
Creon suggested it. I've sent for him twice
And expected him here some time ago.

CHORUS. There were rumours, of course. Gossip in the market
place.

OEDIPUS. Rumours? What rumours? You must tell me
everything.

CHORUS. That travellers killed him, somewhere on the road.

OEDIPUS. I've heard that already. There are no witnesses.

CHORUS. But when your curse has been made public
Someone may come forward. Hearing that,
It would take a brave man to keep silent.

OEDIPUS. No murderer fears words, if he can stomach murder.

CHORUS. Here comes the man to tease out the truth:
The blind man, the shaman Teiresias.
He sees into the heart of things,
And has solved more mysteries than any man living.
Enter Teiresias, blind, led by a boy.

OEDIPUS. Teiresias! You have made yourself master
Of all the arts of understanding,
Both mystic symbolism and practical wisdom.
The highest spiritual truths, and the most down to earth
Material realities are equally your province.
You see the state of our city. Not with your eyes,
I know, but with your intellect.
We rely on you, as our spiritual champion.
We sent to the oracle: you'll have heard that already,
And the answer we were given: find out the killers
Of the old king: execute them, or banish them
And only then will your city be clean.
So, maestro, we need your talents now.
We know that in the formations of birds
In flight, and many other omens,
You can read the future. For your own sake,
For the sake of the city, and for me,
Help us to end this pestilence.

A dead man walks in our streets,
Blinds us with his shadow. We are in your hands.
A gifted man puts his gifts to best use
In the service of his fellow men.

TEIRESIAS. Mine is a terrifying gift. What use
Is wisdom, if it only leads to suffering?
I knew this before I came: and foolishly
Forgot it. I should have stayed at home.

OEDIPUS. That's a gloomy answer! What is it supposed
To mean?

TEIRESIAS. Please let me go home.
Things will be best that way.
You will bear your burden, I will bear mine.

OEDIPUS. Do you refuse to answer my question?
This is Thebes, your country. You were born here!

TEIRESIAS. I've heard your proclamation. It's misconceived:
So it's best for me to keep silent.

OEDIPUS.   Dear gods!
Do you mean that you know, and won't say?
Look, look around at us, the whole city!
We are all imploring you to speak.

TEIRESIAS. That is because you are all blind
To what I can see. I can't tell you.
The truth is painful. My secret. And yours.

OEDIPUS. You do know it, don't you! And you're holding back!
Are you prepared to watch the whole country die?

TEIRESIAS. I'm saving you from agony. And myself.
Don't ask me again, don't waste your time.
I shall tell you nothing.

OEDIPUS.   Nothing?
What sort of a monster are you? A stone statue
Would be moved to fury, much less a man!
Do you mean this? Are you determined to say nothing?

TEIRESIAS. You lose your temper, make me your scapegoat,
When it's your own anger you should blame.

OEDIPUS. Can you hear him? What this man is saying?
This is an insult to the state,
Every decent citizen will be outraged!

18

TEIRESIAS. I can't change the future: only describe it.
  What will happen, will happen,
  Whatever I say.

OEDIPUS.   It's your duty.
  To say what you know. If *it* must come,
  You must tell me!

TEIRESIAS. Lose your temper, shout, stamp, if that pleases you.
  I shall say nothing more.

OEDIPUS. Oh yes, I shall be angry,
  And more than angry! I understand this much.
  I understand that *you* were implicated,
  Maybe planned this murder, did everything
  But act it: and would have done that too
  In my opinion, if you'd had eyes
  To see your victim!

TEIRESIAS.   Would I indeed?
  You compel me to speak. The curse you proclaimed
  Is now upon your head: from today
  Never to speak to me, or anyone.
  You are the man: the unclean thing:
  The dirt that breeds disease.

OEDIPUS.   Do you dare
  To accuse me? Do you slander me
  In public, and think your fortune-telling
  Gives you some kind of immunity?

TEIRESIAS. I don't need it. The truth is its own protector.

OEDIPUS. Someone's behind this. Who told you to say that?
  There's more to this than fortune-telling.

TEIRESIAS. You did. You made me say it. Against my will.

OEDIPUS. Say it again. So there will be no doubt.

TEIRESIAS. Didn't you hear? Or do you want me to elaborate?

OEDIPUS. I heard. But I didn't believe my ears.
  Say it again. Aloud. To everybody.

TEIRESIAS. You are the murderer of the murdered king.

OEDIPUS. Twice! To my face! You will regret this, old man.

TEIRESIAS. Indulge your anger if it pleases you.
  I could say more, to make you angrier still.

OEDIPUS. Why not! More lunacy! Let's have it all!

19

TEIRESIAS. I know, but you do not,
  That the woman you love is not the woman you love,
  That the relationship is disgusting, taboo,
  And, in your ignorance, will destroy you.
OEDIPUS. Do you expect to say such things and not be

punished?

TEIRESIAS. The truth protects me, if I tell it honestly.
OEDIPUS. The truth? What's the truth to you?
  You're blind all over, ears, mind, as well as eyes.
TEIRESIAS. I pity you. People will scream the same insults
  At you, before long. Everyone will despise you.
OEDIPUS. You live in darkness, permanently,
  You see nothing of the real world!
  My eyes are open. You can't hurt me.
TEIRESIAS. How could I? An old man. It's not my business.
  Apollo will do it. It's in his hands.
OEDIPUS. Creon! Of course! *He* went to the oracle!
  This plot is his doing, not yours.
TEIRESIAS. Creon isn't your enemy. You are.
OEDIPUS. Political rank, wealth and power,
  And men's ambitions clawing at each other,
  Till life becomes a battleground,
  And envy everyone's motive!
  Creon is, and has been my friend.
  I've trusted him completely. This crown
  Was given to me, freely, by the people,
  I didn't ask for it. And this man,
  My friend, is secretly plotting to overthrow me
  With a spiritual quack, a charlatan,
  A paranormal stuntman, whose eyes
  Are stone blind when it comes to prophesy,
  But where money's concerned, very sharp,
  Wide open then! Astrology,
  Fortune-telling, forecasting the future,
  Where was all that when we needed it?
  There was a monster here – do you remember?
  I'm sure you do – with the face of a woman
  And the body of a dog, who terrorised this city.

20

Where were you then? What was your advice
To save this country? She set a riddle
Which no ordinary man could answer. Someone special
Was required. What else are prophets for?
But you hadn't a clue, had you!
Not a word, not the slightest suggestion!
And then I came along, a young man,
Quite ignorant, knowing nothing, with only the wit
My mother gave me. But I stopped her mouth.
I did it, Oedipus! I guessed her riddle,
Without any gobbledygook about birds!
And I, Oedipus, I am the man
You hope to depose, you and Creon,
So that he will be king, and you his guru.
Well. You will regret it. You will both regret
This attempt to turn me into a scapegoat.
If you weren't an old man, punishment would teach you
The difference between prophecy and sedition.

CHORUS. Great king,
To speak in anger, as both of you have done,
Helps none of us, as far as I can judge,
When our city is dying. We must consider
The god's command, and how to obey it.

TEIRESIAS. You may be king, but I am a free man,
And I have the right to answer. I serve
Apollo, the god, not you, nor Creon.
You sneer at my blindness. You have eyes,
But cannot see your own corruption.
Nor who she is you love the most,
Not even whose son you are. In your ignorance
You have committed terrible crimes
Against those closest to you, the living,
And the dead. A double curse,
Like a two-edged sword, father and mother,
Will drive you from this city, into exile,
Forever, and what a cripple you'll be then.
Those bright eyes, that perfect vision
You are so proud of, will become dark,

Like mine. There will be no place on earth
That hasn't heard the sound of your pain.
The wildest heathland of Cithaeron,
Even its cliffs and ravines, will echo
To your bellowing, when you understand
How those melodious marriage songs
Deceived you, when they led you
To that safe harbour you imagined here.
Then unimaginable sufferings, miseries
You cannot guess at, will become familiar
Both to you, and to your children
As you pile your agonies upon their heads.
Accuse Creon of every crime.
Slander him, despise what I say.
Every man in the world will despise you,
And no man has committed crimes like yours.

OEDIPUS. I don't have to listen to you! Why should I?
  Get him out of my sight, now, at once,
  Take him back where he came from.

TEIRESIAS.   Yes.
  I shall go now. You brought me here,
  Remember that. I didn't want to come.

OEDIPUS. If I'd known what I'd have to listen to,
  The ravings of a lunatic,
  Believe me, I'd have left you in peace.

TEIRESIAS. You think I was born a fool. Your parents
  Wouldn't think so.

OEDIPUS.   Why this continual harping
  Upon my parents? Who . . . fathered me?

TEIRESIAS. Today you will father your own destruction
  And conceive the truth of your birth and death.

OEDIPUS. Speak plainly, don't talk in riddles.

TEIRESIAS. Why not! You have a genius for solving them.

OEDIPUS. Yes, I'm famous for it. And your sneers and insults
  Won't make me any the less incisive.

TEIRESIAS.
  That fame is your misfortune.

OEDIPUS.   I saved the state

With my genius. What does it matter to me
What you choose to call it?

TEIRESIAS. Now I shall go.
Give me your hand, boy. Take me home.

OEDIPUS. Yes, take him and good riddance. We can do without
you.
Rave in your own house and spare mine.

TEIRESIAS. I'll go. I've said what I came to say,
And I've said it to your face. Why should I be frightened?
You no longer have the power to hurt me.
But I will say one thing more. The man
You're looking for, the man you cursed
And threatened, the murderer of Laius,
Is here. He passes for a foreigner,
Who lives in Thebes. But he was born here,
And will learn that, to his cost.
He could see when he came here. He'll leave blind.
He's a rich man now. He will go as a beggar.
Groping, with a stick in his hand,
Tapping his way, he will leave this city,
Into endless exile. To his children,
Whom he loves, he is brother and father:
To the woman who bore him, lover and son.
To his father, a killer and the man who supplants him.
Go in. Set your genius to solve those riddles.
Call me a blind man, when you've proved them untrue.
Teiresias signs to the Boy, who leads him away. Oedipus watches
him, then turns and moves, angrily, back into the palace.

CHORUS. Who is this man whose terrible crime
The unearthly voice of Apollo's vessel
Intones from the rock of Delphi?
Far let that man fly,
For his hands trail blood, from a sin the oracle
Blushes to whisper. Faster than the storm
His horse must run, outstrip the wind;
Thundering Zeus's son gallops behind,
Grasped in his fist the lethal lightning,
And the hounds of the gods,

23

The unsleeping Fates,
Close in, like a circle tightening.

From the snowbound crest of Parnassus the word
Was transmitted to Thebes: you must find this killer
Lurking like a thief in the night;
Drag him into the light!
Like a mountain bull where the forests are thicker,
The caves bleaker, he creeps, barred
From the company of men, hopelessly flies
The voice of those bleak prophecies
That buzz and sting at his face. No distance
From earth's centrepoint,
Delphi's sacred summit,
Is too far for Apollo's vengeance.

Teiresias has spread fear and confusion.
Should we believe him or not? For us,
Best to keep quiet. I'm like jelly, uncertain
What's happening, or will happen. Was there ever a row
In the past, or is there now,
Between Polybus' son and the ruling line
Of Thebes, the house of Labdacus?
Not that I ever heard.
What could be more absurd
Than to blacken – with no proof – Oedipus' name
By pinning this unsolved murder on him?

The secrets of man, all the mysteries of his nature,
Are known to Zeus and Apollo. No one
Can claim a monopoly of wisdom. One teacher
Is as good as another, and perhaps no better
Than any of us. Some may see deeper,
And some may not, because widsom is a jointure
Unequally shared among men. But what was done
Must be known, beyond doubt.
Oedipus saved our state;
He publicly outwitted the Sphinx. Like gold,

He was tested and found true. We must see his guilt proved!
Enter Creon, from the direction of the city.

CREON. Citizens! Members of the council. They tell me
That the king has charged me with subversion!
I am innocent of any such charge. The city
Is on its knees. Does he imagine
At a time like this I would injure him
By any word or action? I'd rather die
Than be smeared like that! It is a smear,
To be accused of treason, before you
And my friends and my countrymen.

CHORUS. He lost his temper and made wild accusations.
I think he spoke without thought.

CREON.   Did he say
That the old prophet lied, under my instructions?
Who gave him that idea?

CHORUS.   He did say it:
But why he said it, or whether he meant it
Is a matter of opinion.

CREON.   Is he right in the head?
Did he speak rationally and look you in the eye,
Or has he gone mad?

CHORUS.   I've got more commonsense
Than to make judgements like that on a king's actions.
Here he comes from the palace, he'll speak for himself.
Enter Oedipus, from the palace.

OEDIPUS. So you're here, Creon! What have you come for?
I hardly thought you would be thick-skinned enough
To come knocking at my doors again,
While you're planning to murder me and steal my power.
Do you imagine I'm afraid of you? Or stupid?
Or am I just too blind to notice
A conspiracy to overthrow me? Or not bright enough
To do anything about it? And what a conspiracy!
You need plenty of friends and financial backing
To capture a throne. Revolutions are made
With men, and the money to pay them, or buy them.

CREON. Can I speak in my own defence? Judge me

After you've heard my answer, not before!

OEDIPUS. Creon, you've always been a brilliant talker.
But talk cuts no ice with me. I've seen
The evidence of your actions, betrayal,
Sedition . . .

CREON.   Will you let me speak?

OEDIPUS. Say what you like. But don't protest
Your innocence, that would be too much!

CREON. Do you really believe that closing your mind –
A boneheaded refusal to listen –
Is a sensible way of proceeding?

OEDIPUS. Do you really believe that I can allow you
To plot a palace revolution, and do nothing about it,
Because you are my brother-in-law?

CREON. Only a fool would allow that, I agree,
If it were happening! There is no revolution,
In the palace, or anywhere. No conspiracy!
What am I supposed to have done?

OEDIPUS.   It was you
Advised me to send for that canting prophet.

CREON. Yes it was. Good advice. I'd give it again.

OEDIPUS. Tell me. How long ago did Laius . . . ?

CREON. Did Laius what? I don't follow you.

OEDIPUS. He died mysteriously. How long ago was that?

CREON. Years and years. I can hardly remember.

OEDIPUS. And this fortune-teller. He was here then,
Already in the prophecy business?

CREON. Respected then as now, for his skill and integrity.

OEDIPUS. And did he mention me when the murder happened?

CREON. Not in my hearing.

OEDIPUS.   And there was no inquest,
Nor any kind of investigation?

CREON. There was an inquiry. But it revealed nothing.

OEDIPUS. This respected prophet. Why did he say nothing
Then, of what he has said today?

CREON. I've no idea. I never say anything
Unless I'm in full possession of the facts.

OEDIPUS. But one thing you do know and you'd be wise to tell me.

CREON. What can I say? Everything I know
  I will tell you. I'll keep nothing back.

OEDIPUS. You know this much. Without your prompting
  The fortune-teller would never have dared
  To accuse *me* of the murder of Laius!

CREON. Did he say that? . . . Then you must know
  If he's lying or telling the truth; not I.
  Am I permitted to interrogate you?

OEDIPUS. Why not? I've got nothing to hide.
  You will never pin this murder on me.

CREON. Are you married to my sister?

OEDIPUS.   What sort
  Of question's that? I can hardly
  Deny it, can I. I do have that honour.

CREON. She shares the throne, both title and revenue?

OEDIPUS. Of course she does. What's mine is hers.

CREON. And I'm the third partner? I have my share
  Of power and responsibility?

OEDIPUS. You've always had it. All the more disgusting
  To conspire against me behind my back!

CREON. But I haven't conspired against you! Ask yourself,
  As I ask myself, whether any sane man
  Would willingly exchange a quiet life
  Within the ruling family, for the wear and tear,
  The gruelling responsibility of government?
  It has never crossed my mind. I have no ambition
  To be king in name, or in fact.
  I live like a king. Sometimes, I hope,
  I act like one. And that's enough.
  No sensible man would want more than that.
  If I had your job, there'd be too many things
  I wouldn't like doing: and no more satisfaction
  From the kingship itself, than I get now
  From royal rank, without royal obligation.
  I'm not so drunk with the prospect of power
  As to envy a position that yields no profit.
  Look at me now. Everyone knows me,
  Everyone loves me, I think. Anyone who hopes

To get your attention, first tries for mine,
Because my influence guarantees success.
Why should I change such a favourable situation?
Is it likely that I'd be such a fool
As to break with you in such conditions,
As far as to commit treason? As a political policy
It has nothing to recommend it. It's not mine,
Nor the policy of any of my friends,
Not if I know them. If you want proof,
Send to the priestess at the oracle;
Check the message I brought, if it was true!
Produce some evidence of conspiracy
Between the blind man and me. Prove that,
And condemn me to death, out of hand.
My verdict, in those conditions,
Will be as merciless as any man's.
But to condemn me like this, on mere suspicion,
Without any evidence! I can't endure that!
It is unjust to condemn people with no good reason.
If mere supposition, unsupported,
Is all your evidence, you can call bad men honest
And decent citizens crooks and villains,
And justice will be done to none of them!
A reliable friend is a precious possession,
Worth a man's life. Throw friendship away,
You destroy something living and irreplaceable.
The truth of this will emerge in time.
Time is the one incorruptible judge.
One minute is long enough to accuse a man.
To prove his innocence takes longer.

CHORUS. If you weigh his words, they make good sense,
Well worth a prudent man's consideration.
Quick judgements are not always the wisest.

OEDIPUS. Conspiracies don't take their time,
They keep on the move! And counter-intelligence
Must move fast too, or be caught napping!
Shall I sit and do nothing while he takes power
And my own sluggishness destroys me?

CREON. What do you want then? To have me banished?

OEDIPUS. Banished? Oh no, I want you dead.

CREON. What have I done to provoke such jealousy?

OEDIPUS. Are you still so obstinate, still pretending?

CREON. Yes I am. Because you're not thinking straight.

OEDIPUS. I know where my best interests lie.

CREON. But what about mine?

OEDIPUS.   You are a traitor.

CREON. And you are mistaken.

OEDIPUS.   Kings must take decisions.

CREON. Not wrong decisions.

OEDIPUS.   O Thebes, my city –

CREON. Thebes is my city as well as yours!

CHORUS. Princes, stop this brawling. The queen, Jocasta,
Is coming from the palace, not a moment too soon.
She will help us to put an end to this quarrel.

Enter Jocasta, from the palace.

JOCASTA. What is all this shouting? From inside the palace
I heard angry voices, like a quarrel.
Aren't you ashamed, indulging yourselves
In private arguments, squabbling like boys
While the city dies all round you? Go inside,
My husband – and you too, Creon, go back
To your own house, before you make
A private row into a public spectacle.

CREON. Sister, we are blood relations! But your husband
Has condemned me, unheard, to the choice
Of death or exile!

OEDIPUS.   Certainly I have,
And that, dear wife, is the least I can do!

CREON. May all the gods curse me for ever
If I was even remotely guilty!

JOCASTA. Oedipus, You must believe him. An oath
Like that can't be taken lightly.
Believe him, for my sake, and for the sake
Of these reliable counsellors. They heard it all.

CHORUS. Great king, be prepared to change your mind.

OEDIPUS. Are you asking me to break my word?

CHORUS. No man ever questioned his integrity.
He confirms it by oath. Show some leniency.

OEDIPUS. Do you know what you're asking?

CHORUS.   Certainly we do.

OEDIPUS. Say it openly then. Let everyone know.

CHORUS. He's your long-trusted friend, above suspicion.
Don't condemn him by hearsay, and in spite of his oath.

OEDIPUS. Don't you understand your own implication?
Spare *him*, and you demand *my* banishment or death!

CHORUS. By the life-giving sun, that necessary power
By whose warmth we live, such a terrible thought
Never crossed my mind! I had far rather
Be an outcast, godless, friendless, distraught
And despised, than embrace that destiny.
Our city is in anguish. What greater blow
Could fall on us in our misery
Than anger and hatred between you two?

OEDIPUS. Then let him go.
Even if my death, exile and disgrace
Is the price of your mercy. Your voice buys his pardon,
Not his. Wherever he hides his face
Let my backbreaking hatred be his burden.

CREON. Your apology's as graceless as your anger's insane.
An unforgiving nature breeds misery
In its own heart, not that of its enemy

OEDIPUS. Leave me in peace! I want you gone!

CREON. Yes, I'll go. They respect my integrity.
I am misjudged by you alone.
Exit Creon.

CHORUS. Take the king inside, madam. Speak to him in private.

JOCASTA. What caused this quarrel? Who began it?

CHORUS. Rumours were mentioned, unfounded suspicions:
Then the anger that follows unjust accusations.

JOCASTA. Both men were at fault then?

CHORUS.   Yes, madam, they were.

JOCASTA. Tell me all the details. You can speak without fear.

CHORUS. We have troubles enough, best to keep silent.
  In all our interests, let sleeping dogs lie.
OEDIPUS. Your intentions are honourable, but your advice is

                                    pregnant

  With disaster. All the guilt falls on me!
CHORUS. Great king, believe me when I say again
  What I've said before: we would be stark-mad
  To counsel an action so insane
  As to cast you out without proof. We need
  Your help and guidance. We all remember
  How like a pilot in that desperate storm,
  Half-wrecked, you navigated us to harbour.
  You are our captain, in rough weather or calm.
JOCASTA. Please tell me. What harm
  Can Creon have done to provoke such fury
  So suddenly? I am worthy of your trust.
OEDIPUS. These old men mean well. But you matter to me
  Far more. It's Creon. I'm sickened with disgust
  At the scope of his conspiracy.
JOCASTA. What conspiracy? And why do you accuse my brother?
OEDIPUS. He says I'm responsible for Laius' murder.
JOCASTA. Has he any evidence? Or is it hearsay?
OEDIPUS. He says nothing himself. That corrupt fortune-teller
  Speaks for him, with his bird-talk and prophecy!

JOCASTA. And is that all? Set your mind at rest.
  No one can forecast the future. I know
  What I'm talking about, from personal experience.
  I have proof! When Laius was alive
  An oracle told him – I won't say the god spoke,
  But his mouthpiece did – that he would be killed
  By his own son – our own child.
  But it didn't happen. Laius was killed
  By persons unknown, foreign robbers –
  According to the story – at a place
  Where three roads meet. As for the child,
  It was abandoned on a deserted mountain
  Before it was three days old, by a servant.

To make doubly sure, its ankles were pierced
And strapped together with leather thongs.
So *that* prediction didn't come true,
In spite of Apollo. That prophecy of parricide
Wasn't fulfilled. Laius was murdered,
But not, as he feared, by his own son.
The oracle had been unambiguous,
Its meaning quite plain. So why take notice
Of these fortune-tellers and astrologers?
The gods always get their own way,
Without anyone's help, when they are ready.

OEDIPUS. Something you said Jocasta . . . I remember . . .
  My brain's a turmoil . . . feelings, memories . . .

JOCASTA. Why do you look at me so strangely? What's the matter?

OEDIPUS. You said, didn't you, that Laius was butchered
  At a place where three roads meet?

JOCASTA.   Yes,
  That was said at the time. It's still
  The common story.

OEDIPUS.   Where? What country?

JOCASTA. A place in Phocis, at the junction
  Where the road from Thebes forks to Daulia and Delphi.

OEDIPUS. And how long ago did all this happen?

JOCASTA. You hadn't arrived. The news became public
  A short while before you became king.

OEDIPUS. Oh Zeus . . . What will you do to me?

JOCASTA. Oedipus . . . you look terrified. What have I said?

OEDIPUS. Not yet. Don't ask me yet. How old
  Was Laius? What kind of man was he?

JOCASTA.   A big man.
  Hair greying. About your build.

OEDIPUS. Dear God. Without knowing it
  I may have damned myself. Just a moment ago.

JOCASTA. Don't look at me like that! What do you mean?

OEDIPUS. Maybe Teiresias could see after all:
  Terrifying, but possible. Tell me one more thing.

JOCASTA. Why are you frightening me? I'll tell you everything.

OEDIPUS. Who was with the king? A few attendants,

Or was he travelling in state, with servants and armed men?

JOCASTA. Five men, all told. One of them a herald.
Laius himself rode in a carriage.

OEDIPUS.   Ahh . . .
Nothing could be clearer than that. Every detail.
Where did you get this information?

JOCASTA. There was one survivor, a servant. Eventually
He got back to Thebes.

OEDIPUS.   Is he still here now?

JOCASTA. No he isn't. By the time he got back
Everything had changed in the city,
And you were king in Laius' place.
When he saw how things were, he came to me
And begged me on his knees to let him go
Away to the country, to be a shepherd.
He said he wanted to be done with Thebes,
Out of sight, out of mind. So I let him go.
He was a good servant and deserved better than that.

OEDIPUS. I want him here at once, today.
Can we find him?

JOCASTA.   Of course we can.
Why are you so anxious?

OEDIPUS.   My dear wife, I'm frightened,
Of what I've done – what I'm doing.
I've already said far too much.
I must see this shepherd. Ask him some questions.

JOCASTA. You will see him. We'll send for him.
But why are you so worried? You must tell me.
I do have a right to know.

OEDIPUS.   Yes, yes.
You have a right to know. If the truth
Of this is what I think it is,
No one has a better right to know
Than you. I'll tell you the whole story.
My father, Polybus, was Corinth-born,
And Merope, my mother, came from Doris.
I was an up-and-coming fellow,
Very much the man to watch, until one day

An odd thing happened: an astonishing thing
Which caused more trouble perhaps than it merited,
But which I took seriously. At a banquet one day,
A man who had drunk too much jeered at me,
And said I was not my father's son.
I was very hurt, angry and insulted,
But I kept it to myself for the rest of that day.
The next morning I went to my parents,
Father and mother together, and asked them
Question after question, almost compelling them
To tell me the truth. They were very angry
That anyone should dare say such a thing,
And put my mind at rest as best they could.
But a thing like that gets under your skin.
I couldn't forget it. And the story
Got around a good deal as these things do.
So, without telling my parents, I went
To the oracle at Delphi. I got no answer
To the question I asked: a catalogue
Of horrors and miseries instead – that I
Would marry my own mother, and father
Children on her, conceived incestuously,
And become a public outcast for it, notorious
Throughout the world. As if this weren't enough,
I would kill my own father. What could I do?
I ran, as fast and as far from Corinth
As any man could, always checking
My distance from that forbidden city
By the positions of the stars: so that those dreadful

                                      prophecies
Could not possibly come true. The route
I took brought me into that part of the country
Where, according to you, Laius was murdered.
Now listen Jocasta, this is the truth
In every detail. I reached a place
Where three roads meet. At the junction,
I was confronted by a herald, ahead of a carriage
Drawn by horses and carrying a passenger,

Just as you described, grey-haired, my build.
The man in front shouted at me
To clear the road, and the old man too
Rudely ordered me to get out of his way.
The driver barged into me, so I hit him
Hard. I was furious by now, uncontrollable.
The old man in the carriage was watching for his chance.
He waited till I passed him. And then, he struck me
Full on the head with his two-pronged stick –
The kind you use for goading the horses
To make them gallop. I paid him back
With interest, and double quick.
I whacked him, savagely, with my staff,
And knocked him out of the carriage. He fell
Flat in the road. The others attacked me,
Of course. And I killed them. Every one.
Now if that old man was remotely connected
With Laius – if the king's blood
Ran in his veins – is there any man
On earth more miserable than I am?
Every god will hate me, and all men.
No one will speak to me, friend or stranger,
No one will take me into his house.
I cursed the murderer. And the weight of that curse
Now falls on me. These same hands
That killed him have fondled his wife!
Was I cursed from the beginning then, a filthy
Corrupted thing infecting the city,
Deserving exile if anyone deserves it?
Now I am cast out from Thebes, denied
The sight of my wife and children, forbidden
Ever to return to my home in Corinth.
No. Never again can I go back there,
For fear that the oracle might be fulfilled,
And that I should somehow marry my mother
And kill my father Polybus, who nurtured me,
And gave me life. The immortals, I suppose,
Have devised this inhuman scenario

To amuse themselves. But listen, gods,
As you revel in the purity of your power
Over human affairs, I shall do my best
To deprive you of that pleasure. Never,
Never will that day come, if I can prevent it.
I'd rather die, with every memory
Of my existence blotted out
From the face of the earth, than live to see
Such dreadful things come true, and be shamed,
Branded and notorious before humanity.

CHORUS. Your story is terrifying, great king.
But don't give up hope. There was an eye-witness.
Until you've questioned him, say nothing.

OEDIPUS. The shepherd is my last chance.
I'll cling to that.

JOCASTA.   Even when he gets here,
What possible help can he be?

OEDIPUS.   One detail,
And it's crucial. If his story
Corroborates yours, I am proved innocent.

JOCASTA. What detail? Does it matter? What did I say?

OEDIPUS. In your version of the shepherd's evidence
The king was killed by robbers. Robbers,
Plural. If he says the same,
Still calls them robbers, I'm in the clear.
One man is not a group of men.
Plural is plural, not singular.
But if he describes a single traveller,
Walking alone, then quite obviously
All the evidence will point to me.

JOCASTA. Oh, but he did say that, I'm certain.
He can't change his story now, he spoke
In public, the whole city heard him!
And even if his evidence varies in detail,
By no stretch of the imagination can he pretend
That Laius died as predicted. A child
Of mine would kill him, the oracle said.
And it didn't happen. My poor little boy

Killed no one. He was the one who died
Years before any of this happened.
That's how much oracles are worth. In future
Whatever they say one way or the other
I won't waste my time with any of them!

OEDIPUS. That's the truth of the matter. But we'll speak to the
shepherd.
Send someone to fetch him. Now, this minute.

JOCASTA. At once, we'll get him at once! Come inside.
I'll do nothing without your approval. Nothing.
Exeunt Oedipus and Jocasta, into the palace.

CHORUS. I only ask for an honest life,
And justice, and belief in the moral law,
As the gods decree it
From the ancient summit
Of Olympus, the sacred mountain.
No man made those precepts, they never sleep
Nor decay with age, as men decay.
They run their courses
From immortal sources
Like a pure and eternal fountain.

Arrogant self-love breeds absolute rule,
The tyrant, who eats up money and men.
He seeks absolute power
And in one foolish hour
Overreaches himself, and ends in the gutter.
An ambitious man most honours the gods
When his demon drives him to serve the state.
He sets his store
By the moral law.
The gods love him, and his people prosper.

But what if a man should laugh at justice,
Grab what he wants and disregard,
By his words and actions, honesty and truth,
And plunder holy shrines?
Can he hope to escape

The consequences of his rape?
When the criminal makes off with his loot
And the murderer becomes king,
Why should I still cling
To the old wisdom and morality,
Or honour in song the sacred harmony?

And why should I make pilgrimages
To Delphi and Olympia,
Or any holy place, if these manifest truths
Are not made absolute for every man,
And the gods' warnings provoke laughter
With no thought of what comes after?
Oh Zeus universal, if you hear our song,
Show us again your immortal power
In this darkest hour,
When Laius' fate and Apollo's word
Are both forgotten, and your warnings unheard.

Enter Jocasta from the palace, attended by women, who carry incense and garlands of flowers.

Jocasta is disturbed, and moves towards a small stone altar.

JOCASTA. I have decided, senators of Thebes,
To visit the holiest temples of the city
To make sacrifices there, with incense and flowers,
To the all-powerful gods. The king is confused
At the moment, by his own nightmares and fantasies.
He can't make balanced judgements, or estimate
From past experience what is likely to happen.
Each new sensational revelation
He takes as truth, and is terrified the more.
I've tried to comfort him. But I failed.
So it seemed sensible to offer prayers,
And first to Apollo, whose altar stands nearest.

As she invokes the god, the women lay the offerings on the altar.

Brilliant god of sunlight and healing,
We live in the shadow of a curse. Shine
On our darkest corners, where there is sickness
And dirt, make us whole and clean.

38

Like desperate sailors, we lose our last hope
When we see our captain in despair.
Enter a Messenger from Corinth.

CORINTHIAN. Gentlemen! Can anyone show me the way
To the palace of King Oedipus? Or better still,
To the man himself, if you know where he is?

CHORUS. This is the palace, and the king is inside it.
This lady is his wife, and mother of his children.

CORINTHIAN. God bless her then, and all her family,
Bearing children to such a great man!

JOCASTA. God bless you too, sir, and thank you
For such a courteous greeting. Have you travelled here
For your own purposes, or to bring us news?

CORINTHIAN. News, dear lady, good news too
For your husband, and for his whole family.

JOCASTA. What news is it? Who sent you?

CORINTHIAN. I come from Corinth, and my message
Is bound to please you: though it's painful too,
And will make you sad to begin with.

JOCASTA.   One message
Causing two such opposite reactions? Tell me.

CORINTHIAN. The Corinthians will make Oedipus king
Of the whole isthmus. Everybody says so!

JOCASTA. But Polybus rules in Corinth, and has done
For years. Isn't he still king?

CORINTHIAN. Polybus is dead, My Lady, and buried.

JOCASTA. Polybus is dead? The father of Oedipus
Dead?

CORINTHIAN. Unless I'm a liar. In which case
Strike me dead on the spot!

JOCASTA.   You girl, quickly,
Go to the king, tell him the news!
Oh, oracles, dreamers of dreams,
Fortune-tellers, where are your predictions now?
The one man Oedipus has kept clear of
For all these years, for fear he should murder him!
And that man's dead, at long last,
Dead! And Oedipus had nothing to do with it!

Enter Oedipus from the palace.

OEDIPUS. Jocasta? My dearest. You called me out
From the palace again? What's going on?

JOCASTA. This man has news for you. Listen,
And then tell me what you think of oracles
With their mystification and mumbo-jumbo!

OEDIPUS. Who is he? What does he have to say?

JOCASTA. He comes from Corinth. Your father. He's dead.
Polybus. Do you understand? He's dead!

OEDIPUS. What! Tell me yourself! Get it quite clear.

CORINTHIAN. I can't put it any plainer. He's dead all right.
He's gone the way we all go.

OEDIPUS. How did he die? Was it murder, or sickness?

CORINTHIAN. Sleep comes easily to an old man's eyes.

OEDIPUS. He was ill, then, and gradually declined? Poor old man.

CORINTHIAN. He was old, and tired. He'd lived long enough.

OEDIPUS. Well then! Ha! What now, Jocasta?
That priestess at Delphi, and her oracle,
A whole skyful of screaming birds
Prophesying ruin! I was the man
Who would kill my father! And my sword
Has never left its scabbard! Maybe
He died of a broken heart, because I
Was in exile? Maybe I killed him that way!
But I don't think so. Polybus is dead.
And so is the oracle and its prophecies,
Dead and rotten!

JOCASTA. And that was my prophecy.
Didn't I say so, right from the beginning!

OEDIPUS. You said it, but I was confused and frightened.

JOCASTA. Forget it now. It's over.

OEDIPUS.   My mother.
While she's still alive, I can't be safe.
There's still that to fear.

JOCASTA.   Fear? Why fear?
We live our lives at the mercy of chance,
The purest coincidence. No one can predict
The future, so what is the point of fearing it?

Live! Enjoy life! Take each day as it comes!
As for marrying your mother, you're not the first
To have dreamed that dream; every son
Is his mother's lover in imagination
Or in day-dreams. It's commonplace.
If a man broods on his most private fantasies
His life won't be worth living, believe me!

OEDIPUS. All very well, your celebrations,
If the woman who brought me into the world
Happened to be dead too. But she isn't,
Not yet. She's alive. And while she lives
Somewhere inside me I'm still afraid.

JOCASTA. But much less afraid. Your father's dead.

OEDIPUS. Less afraid maybe. Still afraid of her.

CORINTHIAN. Don't mind me asking, sir. Who is this lady
Who scares you so much?

OEDIPUS.   The queen, Merope,
The dead king's wife.

CORINTHIAN.   What's she done? There's nothing
To scare you about her, surely.

OEDIPUS. My friend, there was an oracle once, from Delphi,
A dreadful prophecy.

CORINTHIAN.   Too dreadful
To tell a stranger? Or can anyone hear it?

OEDIPUS. It's no secret. Apollo's mouthpiece,
The Pythia herself, told me I was doomed
To marry my own mother, and kill
My father, bloodily, with my own hands.
It was for that reason I left Corinth,
And have stayed away so long. I've prospered,
As you see, abroad. But nothing can compensate
For the loss of my parents' love, the pleasure,
Denied me, of seeing them face to face.

CORINTHIAN. And that's the fear that's kept you in exile,
No other reason?

OEDIPUS.   It was enough.
I was determined not to kill my father.

CORINTHIAN. Well, I came to do you one good turn,

41

And now I can do you another.

OEDIPUS.   What other?
If you know more, you'll earn my gratitude.

CORINTHIAN. That was, partly, my motive in coming,
I will admit. And to do myself
A good turn later, when you come back home.

OEDIPUS. Home? You mean Corinth? I shall never go back.
I shall never see either of my parents again.

CORINTHIAN. My dear young fellow. You've got it all wrong.

OEDIPUS. What do you mean, old man, for god's sake tell me!
Tell me everything you know!

CORINTHIAN.   This fear
Of yours, that stops you coming home . . .

OEDIPUS. The fear that the god's prediction should come
                                                true . . .

CORINTHIAN. Is it all that about your parents
And the crime you're doomed to commit . . . ?

OEDIPUS. Of course it is. And from the very first moment
That fear has never left me.

CORINTHIAN.   Pointless
Sir, quite without basis. Nothing to be scared of
At all.

OEDIPUS. Why? I don't understand you.
If I'm their son . . . ?

CORINTHIAN.   Who says you're their son?
Polybus wasn't your father. No relation
At all.

OEDIPUS. What are you saying? Polybus
Was not my father?

CORINTHIAN.   No more your father
Than I am. Just the same relationship in fact.

OEDIPUS. The same relationship, my father and you?
How is that possible?

CORINTHIAN.   It's possible because
That man was not your father and neither
Am I.

OEDIPUS. Then why did he call me his son?

CORINTHIAN. I gave you to him. As a present.

42

OEDIPUS. Gave me to him? But he loved me
  Like a son, no father could have done more!
CORINTHIAN. He had no children: and wanted a child.
OEDIPUS. What was I then? A foundling? Or a slave-child,
  Bought somewhere?
CORINTHIAN.   Not a bit of it!
  You were found, on the mountain, in a hollow
  Under some trees. Up there, on Cithaeron!
OEDIPUS. And what were *you* doing up there?
CORINTHIAN. Looking after the sheep. That was my job.
OEDIPUS. What were you, a journeyman shepherd
  Taking whatever work came?
CORINTHIAN.   That's right.
  And a good job for you that I was, eh? Son?
  Because I saved your life. No question about that!
OEDIPUS. Was I in danger then? Or in pain?
CORINTHIAN. In pain! Look at your ankles! They're still
  Swollen up, more than normal.
OEDIPUS.   What's that
  To do with it? An old weakness
  I've had since a child.
CORINTHIAN.   I know you have!
  Your ankles were drilled through and tied together!
  I cut you free!
OEDIPUS.   That must be true.
  You can still see the scars. I had them as a boy.
CORINTHIAN. How else did you get your name? 'Oedipus.'
  'Swollen Foot'! That's what it means, doesn't it?
OEDIPUS. Dear gods, who would do such a thing to a child?
  My father, or my mother?
CORINTHIAN.   Don't ask me that!
  Ask the other chap, the one who gave you to me.
OEDIPUS. Gave me? You didn't find me yourself?
CORINTHIAN. I did not. There was another shepherd.
  He asked me to look after you.
OEDIPUS. And who was he? Could you identify him?
CORINTHIAN. He was always thought of as one of Laius' men.
OEDIPUS. Laius? The Laius who was king here before?

43

CORINTHIAN. King Laius, that's the one. This chap worked for
him

OEDIPUS. Is he still alive? Where can I see him?

CORINTHIAN. Ask your own people. They should know.

OEDIPUS. This shepherd . . . Good people, do any of you know
him,

  Has anyone seen him, here, or in the country?
  If you know this man, for god's sake, say!
  Speak out, now! The time has come
  To solve this mystery, once and for all!

CHORUS. I think this shepherd, and the other shepherd
  You've already sent for, must be identical.
  But ask the queen. She's sure to know.

OEDIPUS. Jocasta, you know this shepherd, the one
  We've sent for. Is it the same man?
  Jocasta is white with fear, hardly able to reply.

JOCASTA. What man . . . ? What does it matter . . . One shepherd
or another . . .

  What difference does it make? None of it matters.
  Forget it. The whole thing. Don't pursue it.

OEDIPUS. Forget it! Of course I can't forget it!
  What nonsense! My birth's a mystery,
  But with all these clues, I intend to solve it!

JOCASTA. Listen to me in heaven's name,
  Listen. If you want to stay alive
  This search must end. It's making me ill
  I'm sick with it already, isn't that enough?

OEDIPUS. There's no need for such gloom! Suppose it proved
  I was born a slave, from generations of slaves,
  Would that sicken you? Or affect your standing?

JOCASTA. Listen, I'm begging you! Don't go on!

OEDIPUS. I must go on! I must know the truth!

JOCASTA. I know! I know what I'm talking about.
  I'm telling you this for your own good.

OEDIPUS. And when did I ever put my own good,
  As you call it, before the service of the state?

JOCASTA. My god, you're doomed, you can't escape!
  I have one wish, and one wish only:

That you never discover who you really are.

OEDIPUS. Hurry, one of you! Get that shepherd here!
My wife is too proud of her blue blood.
She's scared she may have married a slave!

JOCASTA. It's finished. No chance now. You're doomed.
I've said all there is to say:
And my last word to you. Forever.
Jocasta goes into the palace.

CHORUS. Why has the queen left us so suddenly?
Why did she become so emotional?
I don't like it, this refusal to speak.
It's like the silence that hangs over a city
When a storm is about to break.

OEDIPUS. Storms, hurricanes, let them all come!
I've travelled this far, and now I'm determined
To discover my identity. If my birthplace
Was the gutter, I shall hunt it out!
My wife, like all women, is snobbish
About rank and upbringing. If I was the child
Of chance, with good luck for my godparents,
I wouldn't be ashamed. My true mother
Is fortunate coincidence, my brothers and sisters
The changing seasons, and I change with them
As naturally as the trees. If that's my background
Who could ask for better? I am what I am.
I have no wish to be otherwise. But who I am,
That I must know. And I will know it!
Oedipus remains on stage during the following chorus.

CHORUS. If I can foretell the future,
Either by prophecy, or common sense,
I predict that by tomorrow morning
This truth will be dawning:
That mysterious Cithaeron,
That magical mountain
Was father and mother and nurse
To Oedipus our king,
And our voices will sing
Praises for his outlandish birth,

A child of the earth,
And glory to Apollo, and thanksgiving.

Or perhaps some skyborn Olympian
Brought him to birth, an immortal mother?
Maybe Pan, who goes roaming
The slopes at evening
Seduced a wild goddess
Of woodland or scree?
Or Apollo, who relishes high pasture,
Bred a son from a spirit?
Or Hermes, in his summit
Of Cyllene, did the deed?
Or was Dionysus' passionate seed
Sown on Helicon, where a nymph lay dreaming?

OEDIPUS. Elder statesmen of Thebes, I think I can see
    The man we are waiting for: I'm making a guess,
    I've never set eyes on him. But my men
    Are bringing him, and he looks the same age
    As this man from Corinth. Is he the one?
    You should know him, you've seen him before.
CHORUS. I recognise him. This is the man.
    He was Laius' servant, and honest as the day.
    Enter the old Shepherd escorted by palace servants or guards.
OEDIPUS. Now, friend from Corinth, you speak first.
    Is this the man you mean?
CORINTHIAN.   It is.
OEDIPUS. And you, old shepherd. Look me in the eye,
    And answer my questions. Did you work
    For old King Laius?
SHEPHERD.   Yes sir, I did.
    I was born and bred in his service, not bought
    In the market.
OEDIPUS.   And what was your job here?
    How were you employed?
SHEPHERD.   For most of my life
    I've been a shepherd, sir.

OEDIPUS.   And where?
In what part of the country did you usually work?
SHEPHERD. Well . . . it would be . . . Cithaeron mostly,
All around there.
OEDIPUS.   And this fellow here,
Have you ever seen him before?
SHEPHERD.   What man
Do you mean, sir? How would I know him?
OEDIPUS. This man, standing here! Did you have any dealings
With him ever, that you remember?
SHEPHERD.   I can't say . . .
Not just this minute. I can't remember . . .
CORINTHIAN. Of course, he's forgotten. But I'll soon remind
                                                          him!
The days when us two were neighbours, up there
On Cithaeron, he won't forget that, will you?
He had two flocks, and I had one.
Three seasons altogether we were up there, the two of us,
From spring right through to autumn. Then I
Drove my lot down to Corinth, and he
Took his lot down to Thebes, to Laius' place.
Now, is that true, or isn't it?
SHEPHERD. Well. True enough. It's a long time ago.
CORINTHIAN. In that case, you won't have forgotten that boy,
The baby you gave me . . . You told me to look after it
And bring it up as my own.
SHEPHERD.   Why
Are you asking about that? It's years ago.
CORINTHIAN. And he's a grown man! My dear old mate!
This is that baby!
SHEPHERD.   God damn you, be quiet!
Keep your mouth shut!
OEDIPUS.   Now now, old fellow,
You deserve that sharp tone more than he does.
SHEPHERD. Why, great king? What have I done wrong?
OEDIPUS. Not giving a straight answer
To a straight question. He asked you
About the child.

47

SHEPHERD.   It's just talk. He knows nothing.
He doesn't understand.

OEDIPUS.   Now listen.
If you won't speak willingly, you'll be forced to speak.

SHEPHERD. I'm an old man, sir. For god's sake don't hurt me.

OEDIPUS. You two, twist his arms back: quickly!

SHEPHERD. Oh, god help me now, what have I done
Sir, what more do you want to know?

OEDIPUS. This man is asking you about a child.
Was it you who gave him that child? Was it?

SHEPHERD. It was me. I wish I'd died that day!

OEDIPUS. You'll die today, unless you tell the truth.

SHEPHERD. I'll die if I tell it, as well, that's for sure.

OEDIPUS. This fellow is still determined to prevaricate.

SHEPHERD. No, no, I'm not. I told you, I gave it to him.
What else?

OEDIPUS.   Where did it come from? Was it your child?
Or did someone give it to you?

SHEPHERD.   Not mine.
Would I give my own child away?
It came from someone else.

OEDIPUS.   Who else?
From Thebes? From one of the citizens here?
What kind of house did that baby come from?

SHEPHERD. I beg you sir, by all the gods,
Don't ask me that!

OEDIPUS.   I am asking.
If I must ask again, you're as good as dead!

SHEPHERD. Well . . . you see . . . it was born in Laius' house.

OEDIPUS. A slave? Or was it a blood relation?

SHEPHERD. I'm on the edge, sir. Must I say it?

OEDIPUS. Yes, we're both on the edge. I must hear you say it.

SHEPHERD. They did say the child was his.
But the queen, in the palace, she could tell you!

OEDIPUS. Do you mean she gave it to you?

SHEPHERD.   Yes, sir.
She did.

OEDIPUS. Why? For what purpose?

SHEPHERD. To kill it, sir.

OEDIPUS. Her own child? Poor woman.

SHEPHERD. Yes, sir. There was some prophecy.
She was scared stiff.

OEDIPUS. What prophecy?

SHEPHERD. There was talk that the boy would kill his father.

OEDIPUS. And why, in the name of all the gods,
Did you give it to this man?

SHEPHERD. I couldn't
Kill it, master. I couldn't do it.
A little boy, only three days old.
I thought, 'he'll take it miles away
To his own country. It'll be all right.'
So he took it and saved its life. And now
It's all turned out like this. If you
Are that man, the boy my friend took to Corinth,
You were marked out for suffering, from the day you were
born.

OEDIPUS. All. All of it. I know it all now.
Nothing left to find. It all came true,
Every single word. Let the night come.
Daylight has no mercy.
It shows too much, too clearly. Yes.
My conception, a crime.
My marriage a crime.
And that murder, committed on my own father.
I see it all now.

*Exit Oedipus, into the palace, as the attendants lead the old Shepherd
and the Corinthian away.*

CHORUS. Like a shadow thrown in the dust
Is the short life of man:
The sunlit generations
Pass into the night,
And happiness, like a bird in flight,
Flutters, and is gone.
We have seen Oedipus the king
Brought down to misery.
Suffering, brief happiness, pain,

Is mortal man's destiny.

Like a champion marksman, he shot down
The Sphinx in full flight.
The master of the gods' reward
Was kingship, and power
Over men, the prize of one hour
Of brilliant insight.
From that day he was king
In Thebes, like a solid wall
His power surrounded us, and we sang
Of the benefits of his rule.

Was there ever a reversal of fortune
More terrible than this?
How can any man endure
Such merciless agony?
Who was ever marked out by destiny
For suffering like his?
Oedipus, world famous king,
When you sucked and fondled at the same breast
How could the flesh keep silent so long,
Where both son and father caressed?

Time is an all-seeing eye
That searches out hidden guilt
When it seems most secure,
Then brings down the knife
On the father and son who shared a wife.
And the blood that was spilt.
Son of our murdered king,
Why did you ever come here? Your destiny
Leaves me choking with tears: bringing
Salvation for us with your own misery.
*Enter the Messenger, running from the palace, terrified and
desperate.*
MESSENGER. Senators! Counsellors. Wise men of the city!
If you have any feeling at all

For the royal family of Thebes, those descendants of Labdacus,
You can't hold back your tears, not when you hear
What I have to tell you, and see yourself
The terrible scene in the palace! In there
Things have been done, deliberate things
Of such horror, such self-mutilations,
That rivers could not wash away the blood,
And the stain on the family will be everlasting!

CHORUS. Haven't we seen and suffered enough?
    What more is there to say?

MESSENGER.   First of all,
    In the plainest language: the queen is dead.

CHORUS. Dead? How can she be dead? Poor woman!

MESSENGER. I'll tell you. She killed herself!
    You haven't seen it, and count yourselves lucky!
    I shall never be able to forget it. That image
    Will always be with me now. I was there,
    And I'll tell you what happened, as accurately as I can.
    When she rushed into the palace, in anguish,
    She went straight into the bedroom, tearing
    Her hair out in handfuls, and muttering
    Like a madwoman. She slammed the door,
    And locked herself in: and we heard her shouting,
    Something about Laius, her first husband,
    Who's been dead for years, and the night
    They conceived the son who was to kill him
    And breed misbegotten children on his own mother.
    Then it became confused. She screamed,
    And beat upon the bed, where she had conceived
    A husband by a husband, and children by a child.
    I heard all that. Her actual death
    Was behind the locked door: and Oedipus
    Broke in at that point, raving up and down
    The hall and howling for a sword,
    So that all our eyes were fixed on him
    And we all forgot what she was doing.
    'That wife of mine, that wife and mother,'
    He shouted, 'her fertile belly,

51

Twice it's been harvested, me and my children!'
Then he suddenly made for the door –
None of us told him – as though some premonition
Suddenly told him she was there. He bellowed
And shouted and shoulder-charged the doors,
And kicked them, till the bolts and hinges
Shattered, and he stumbled in . . .
We saw her, slowly turning in the air,
Swinging slightly, like a pendulum,
Strung up by the neck. She'd hanged herself.
The king ran to her, loosed the rope
And lifted her down, all the while groaning
Heartbreakingly, like an animal.
He laid her gently on the floor,
And then – this was unbearable, the worst
Of all – there were two golden brooches,
Pinned on her dress. He opened them up,
Held them high in the air, at arm's length,
And plunged them down into his eyeballs,
Screaming and groaning that his own guilt
And suffering were too great for his eyes to see it
That now they would both be in darkness forever,
That he would never see again
Those he should never have seen, nor ever
Love those he should never have loved.
That's the way he went on, cursing himself
And stabbing his eyelids again and again,
Till his face was a mass of blood and tears,
Not drops of blood, but like a thunderstorm
Or cloudburst, gushing down his cheeks! . . .
So, they embraced in the crime and embraced
In the punishment too, man and wife together.
They were happy you know, for a long time.
The family was famous, and considered fortunate,
But from today, horror, pain and grief,
All the suffering men have a name for
Will make their names notorious, forver.
CHORUS. Has he any relief? Or is the pain getting worse?

MESSENGER. He's yelling for someone to unbolt the doors
    And drag him out, so that all Thebes will see
    The father-killer and mother- . . .
    I can't say that word in public. He's shouting
    Repeatedly that he must be kicked out of the city.
    He's exiled by his own decree, he mustn't
    Stay long enough to bring down the curse
    On his own family. But he's in pain,
    And half his strength has gone, poor man.
    He can't see, he needs someone to guide him,
    And the physical agony must be much worse
    Than any man can bear. You'll see yourself.
    The doors are opening. Sorrow and pity
    You must feel, when you see him with your own eyes.
    His worst enemy couldn't wish him this.
    Enter Oedipus, blinded.

CHORUS. Have any man's eyes ever seen
    Sufferings more terrible? Mine have not.
    What mania, what insanity has turned your brain,
    Man of all sorrows? Some demon of the night,
    Some destructive impulse in man, prowling
    Silently round you, waiting its chance,
    Has sprung with inhuman strength, howling
    At your throat. I'm fascinated and repelled, in a trance
    Of horror and pity. I want to watch your pain,
    And to turn from it. I want to learn from your torments,
    But I shudder at what that knowledge might mean.

OEDIPUS. Anguish, ah, agony . . .
    Pity, someone. I can't see
    Where my legs are taking me. Is that my voice,
    Floating like a ghost in front of my face?
    The punishment begins here. Where will the end be?

CHORUS. A place unspeakable to men's ears:
    Horrors too dreadful for human eyes to see.

OEDIPUS. Dark now, all dark.
    This nightmarish blackness surrounds me. I shall never
    See daylight again. A black cloud, a thick fog, forever

Enfolds me like a cloak.
The pain in my eyes, ah gods, grinds sharper,
But the pain in my memory cuts deeper.
CHORUS. This is his life now: to suffer twice over:
The body's sharp pain, and the mind's dull ache.

OEDIPUS. My friends, are you there?
You don't desert me, still loyal, still kind:
You stay with me, although I am blind,
You give me your care.
I have no eyes now to see your face,
But I know you're here, by the sound of your voice.
CHORUS. Your mutilated eyes! What darkness in your mind,
What demon, could bring you to such despair?

OEDIPUS. Apollo, my friends, Apollo the god,
His power determined my agony!
But these eyes were blinded by my own hand.
Why have eyes to see
My own degradation and misery?
CHORUS. This is the truth: simple and hard.
OEDIPUS. Can the earth's loveliness, or all its beauty
Comfort eyes like mine? What music could I hear
To soothe such pain? What could I ever see
Or hope to see, to bring relief or cure?
Waste no more time. Take me from this city.
No one has ever been more damned. No pity
For the man all men curse and the gods abhor.
CHORUS. The pain in the flesh is doubled in the mind:
Ignorance made you happy. The truth has made you blind.

OEDIPUS. Damn the man who saw my ankles bleed
And cut me free from those straps! His mercy
Only made things worse. I should have died!
Did I live for this agony –
And for those that love me, a lifetime of misery?
CHORUS. Better a child's grave on the mountainside.
OEDIPUS. Now my name will be known forever:

54

My father's killer, my mother's lover,
Husband and child, father and brother:
Born to cause suffering, and to suffer.
Will there be any horror or shame
Not synonymous with Oedipus' name,
Or ever a man more damned? No, never!

CHORUS. You bring blindness and exile on your own head
By this action. You would have been better dead.

OEDIPUS. No! You must never say that, never!
What has happened here, has happened for the best,
Don't dare tell me otherwise! If I could see,
How could I look my father in the face
When I meet him in the underworld?
Or my mother? No death could be punishment enough
For the horror of what I have done to her.
And my children, whom I love: what pleasure
For me to see their faces again
Conceived as they were conceived? My eyes
Are a father's eyes. What would they see?
And this marvellous city, in which I was born
The greatest among men: if I had eyes
I would still see its palaces and temples
Which by my own edict, my own folly,
My own insane determination, are forbidden
The murderer of Laius, the unclean thing
All men turn away from and the gods hate.
I mean myself. With eyes in my head,
How could I look anyone in the face,
Even the Theban people in the streets?
My hearing too, these ears! If I'd known a way
To block up these receivers, or cut them off
From every sound the world makes,
I'd have done that too, with no regrets.
To make a prison cell of my own mind
In solitary confinement from the world.
No sight or sound of all these horrors
Could touch me there. That would be peace . . .

The wastelands of Cithaeron, like a nurse,
Cradled me, kept me alive. For this.
Trees, gulleys, naked rocks,
You should have let me die. You preserved me
To parade before the world the well-kept secret
Of who my father was, and who my mother.
And Corinth, my childhood home,
And Polybus and Merope, whom I loved
And thought my parents, how could you imagine
What a corrupt man your open-faced boy
Would become in his age? If ever a rosebud
Was soggy and rotten within, if ever an apple
Was filthy with maggots, let these images
Describe me in my youth, born damned, among the damned.
And that triple junction under the trees,
That overgrown place where three roads meet,
Do the trees still remember, and the shady pathways,
What happened there, whose blood was spilt,
My father's, my own? On the way to Thebes
I was, that day, and what acts I did
When I got there, on the dead man's wife,
Entering so joyfully that same passage
That gave me exit into the world, sowing my seed
In the warm earth where I was germinated!
A marriage for a monster, father, brother,
Son, bride, wife, mother,
Children, sisters, all confused,
Horribly mingled in a liaison
Too filthy to give a name to, too corrupt
To be remembered with anything but loathing . . .
No more then, nothing, what should never
Have been done should never be spoken of . . .
Take me away quickly, for god's sake,
Hide me, as far from this city as a man
Can go, drown me, bury my body
Under the floor of the ocean!
The Chorus shrinks away from his groping hands.

                                        Where are you?

Is anyone there, or have you all gone?
For pity's sake, someone help me!
Don't leave me alone! Take me,
You need not draw back. It's not infectious,
This crime of mine! I'm the one
Who must bear the guilt and the punishment
And the shame. And I must bear it alone.
Enter Creon.

CHORUS. Creon is coming. It's up to him
Now, to deal with you. He will advise us,
And take action as provisional governor in your place.

OEDIPUS. Creon. Of course. There is nothing I can say
To him, and why should he listen to anything
I say? I treated him unjustly.

CREON. I haven't come to crow, Oedipus,
Now you are down, nor to accuse you
Of crimes, or misjudgements, committed in the past.
Creon turns to Oedipus' attendants.
But you people, if you have no respect
For the common decencies, the sympathy
Due to any man's sufferings, revere the sun
At least, whose warmth and brightness sustains us.
The open street, in broad daylight,
Is no place for a thing unclean,
Cursed and sentenced to be cast out.
Not even in the open air, on the common earth
Or under the rain from heaven, will he
Find welcome or shelter. Take him in. His sufferings
Are no business of the public. It's private,
A question of family grief and prayer,
A matter for his relations, not the whole city.

OEDIPUS. This is a kindness Creon, more
Than I expected in my degradation.
For your sake, not mine, let me ask one favour.

CREON. What favour? You need not go on your knees.

OEDIPUS. Get rid of me quickly. Deport me
To some empty wasteland, where the human voice
Is never heard.

CREON.　　　　I could have done that
　Already, of course. But it seems wiser
　As a matter of priority, to consult the oracle.

OEDIPUS. But the oracle has spoken, unambiguously!
　Kill the father-killer. Cast out
　The unclean thing. I am the man.

CREON. That's true, that's what was said. But in circumstances
　As extraordinary as these, it seems safer
　To consult the god again.

OEDIPUS.　　　　　　For what?
　I am the cause of all this pain,
　And the punishment is known. What is there to ask?

CREON. Haven't you, of all men, learned
　To trust the Gods?

OEDIPUS.　　　　Yes, I've learned that.
　One favour more I must ask
　Or beg. The woman who lies dead
　In the palace, let her be buried
　Decently, with whatever formalities
　You think appropriate. She is your sister,
　Your flesh and blood, and you owe her that.
　In my case . . . Thebes is my country,
　My homeland – though I never knew it
　Until today – and my presence, alive,
　Within her walls would be a curse
　On her. Let me leave, and go up
　Into my own mountains of Cithaeron.
　My mother and father left me there
　To die in the wilderness and I shall die now,
　In accordance with their wishes who wished me dead.
　My death, I know, will be mysterious.
　My life was saved miraculously, and not
　For the common death of old age or sickness,
　But for some other ending – awe-inspiring
　And full of terror. Let it come as it will.
　But now . . . my children. The boys, Creon,
　Polynices and Eteocles, they're almost men
　And can look after themselves, wherever they go.

But the girls . . . they're so small, such babies yet.
They have shared everything with me, food and drink
And company. I doubt if they've ever so much
As eaten a meal away from their father.
Look after them Creon, for my sake . . .
And if I could . . . just once more,
Touch them, and share my tears
With theirs, just once, kindness
And generosity could do no more.
Grasping their hands and remembering,
I could imagine I had eyes
To see them once again, before I go.
The two young children, Antigone and Ismene, little girls of perhaps
six and eight, have already been led in, and they stand before
Oedipus.
Shh! I heard something! Are they here already?
Are they crying? You have taken pity
Creon, and brought them to me unasked.
The dearest of my children . . . Am I right?
CREON. I know how much you loved them, and love
Them still, in spite of everything.
OEDIPUS. God bless you Creon. May you have better luck
Both as a king and as a man, than I've had.
Children, where are you, come here to me.
Embrace me! Antigone, Ismene!
These are your brother's hands, and your father's,
The hands that blinded me. I was blind already
If the truth be known. I saw nothing
As I fathered you on my own mother,
Only a wife! Was ever a man more blind!
My eyes can't see you now, but they can
Cry still, and they do, when I think
What hard lives you will lead in the world
When you are grown up, the vicious things
People will say. Festivals,
And public holidays, no fun for you
They will be, staying at home in tears
While the others enjoy themselves. And later,

When you're old enough to be married, where
Is the man who will be brave, or foolhardy enough
To take you on, and that scandalous reputation
That will stick to all my children, and
My children's children. 'Their father killed
His father, then ploughed up that same ground
Where he sprouted, gave his own mother
Children, those girls, yes, they're his sisters!'
That's the sort of thing people will say.
And who will marry you in those circumstances?
Nobody will, my poor girls, virginity
And barrenness are all you can look forward to.
Creon, Menoeceus was your father,
And you must be their father now,
As nearest kin. The two of us
Who brought them into the world, we are both dead,
Or dead to them. They are quite alone,
Apart from you. Don't let them wander
As orphans through the world, homeless,
As well as husbandless, and don't condemn them
To share the punishment that falls on me.
They are very young, very poor now,
And if you don't help them, quite without hope.
Promise me, and take my hand upon the promise.
The two men grasp hands.
Good brother, good . . .
Oedipus turns to the girls.
                If you were older
My girls, and could understand such things
I could tell you so much . . . but we'll leave that now.
When you say your prayers, ask for peace,
A place to call home, and a better life
Than your father has had.

CREON.   That's enough. No more tears
In public. You must go inside.

OEDIPUS. No, not yet, just a moment longer –
Even against your better judgement.

CREON. No, everything must be done correctly,

The proper thing at the proper time!

OEDIPUS. On one condition! That I have your promise.

CREON. My promise?

OEDIPUS.   To send me into exile.

CREON. That is the gods' decision not mine.
  I shall follow their instructions.

OEDIPUS. Don't force me in there, when the gods hate me.

CREON. If they hate you, they will cast you out.

OEDIPUS. But do you agree? Will you do what I ask?

CREON. No. I shall do what I say I will do.

OEDIPUS. Well. I'm in your hands.

CREON.   Then go in.
  But leave the children here.

OEDIPUS.   The children?
  Don't take them away from me! Don't do that!

CREON. Don't give me orders! Those days are over.
  Your orders have brought you to this.
  Now you must learn to obey.

*Creon gestures to the Attendants, who take Oedipus into the palace.
Creon follows them, leading the two children.*

CHORUS. People of Thebes, inheritors
  Of the ancient city of our ancestors,
  You have all seen Oedipus the king –
  Who solved the riddle the she-monster sang
  And by his genius saved the state,
  And whose fame for that deed was so great
  No man could but envy him –
  Overwhelmed by a tidal wave
  Of disasters that will sweep him to his grave.
  Judge no man's life until he is dead.
  There are no winners till the race is run.
  Call no man fortunate, or safe from pain,
  Till he lies in his last ever-lasting bed
  And the earth covers his head.

Exit the Chorus

OEDIPUS AT COLONUS

Characters

OEDIPUS, once King of Thebes, now exiled, stateless, a beggar

ANTIGONE
ISMENE } his daughters

LOCAL MAN of Colonus

CHORUS of elders of Colonus

THESEUS, King of Athens

CREON, Oedipus' brother-in-law, effective ruler of Thebes, though not yet king

POLYNICES, elder son of Oedipus

MESSENGER

SOLDIERS

ATTENDANTS

This translation was commissioned by BBC Television and first produced in the autumn of 1986, with the following cast:

OEDIPUS	Anthony Quayle
ANTIGONE	Juliet Stevenson
LOCAL MAN	Paul Copley
CHORUS	Frank Windsor, Trevor Peacock, Ian Hogg, Jerome Willis, Barry Stanton, Edward Jewesbury, Christopher Hancock, Morgan Sheppard, David Belcher, John Gabriel, Andrew Burt, Bryan Pringle
ISMENE	Gwen Taylor
THESEUS	Clive Francis
CREON	John Shrapnel
POLYNICES	Kenneth Haigh
MESSENGER	Michael N. Harbour
DIPLOMAT	Michael Shevelew
ISMENE'S SERVANT	Bernard Losh
THESEUS' SOLDIERS	David Fieldsend, Rick Fisher, Ian Johns, Laurie Goode, Rod Goodliffe, Billy Raymond, Derek Chessor
CREON'S SOLDIERS	Bernard Losh, Terry Bradford, Ross Murray, Derek Van Weenan, Mike Jefferies, Graham Sueddon, Robin Squiers, Billy Newcombe, Peter Gates Fleming, David Rogue

Directed by	Don Taylor
Produced by	Louis Marks
Designed by	David Myerscough-Jones
Music by	Derek Bourgeois
Costumes by	June Hudson

The scene is set in front of a grove sacred to the Furies, near to the village of Colonus, and within sight of Athens. There is an ancient statue of a mounted horseman, the entrance to the grove, and a seat of natural rock visible just within it. The grove is mysterious place, a rocky path leading away out of sight overhung with laurels, vines and olive trees. In front of the grove, at a lower level, is an open space with projecting ledges of rock.

Enter Oedipus, blind, white-haired, dressed in rags, led by Antigone.

OEDIPUS. Antigone, your father is old and blind.
    And here's another new place, eh daughter,
    For the outcast in his wanderings?
    Country is it, or town? Whose charity
    Do we ask for today? A few scraps,
    That's all, the bare necessities:
    And if it's less than that we're given,
    Still we're content. Time passes,
    Suffering must be endured, till we learn patience:
    And I was born a king . . . Can you see
    Some place where I can sit down: on the common
    Earth by the roadside, or a cool grove of trees
    Sacred to some local god or other?
    And while I'm resting, dear girl, find out
    Where we are today. It's always wiser
    For strangers like us to talk to the locals,
    Discover from them how the land lies
    And take their advice.
ANTIGONE.   My poor father,
    You have suffered enough . . . In the far distance
    I can see the city, towers and walls.
    But this seems to be a holy place.
    There are laurel bushes and olive trees
    And vines, all running wild. In the grove
    Birds singing everywhere, a whole choir of nightingales
    Making music together.
    She enters the grove.

ANTIGONE.   There's a naked rock
  Like a seat, but carved by the hand of nature,
  Not man. You can sit there, and rest your legs.
  It's been a long journey. You're an old man.

OEDIPUS. Sit me down then. I'm blind. I can't do it for myself.

ANTIGONE. I don't need to be told . . . after all this time.
  She leads him into the grove and sits him carefully on the rock seat.

OEDIPUS. So tell me. Where do you think we are?

ANTIGONE. Athens, for sure. This place . . . I don't know.

OEDIPUS. Yes. Everyone on the road told us that much.

ANTIGONE. Shall I find somebody, and ask where we are?

OEDIPUS. Yes, if there's anyone to ask.

ANTIGONE. People live here, certainly. But no need to go looking.
  I think I can see somebody coming.

OEDIPUS. This way Antigone? Is he coming this way?
  A local man of Colonus has seen them in the grove and is running
  towards them in an agitated manner.

ANTIGONE. Yes, he is. Be careful what you say!
  He's standing directly in front of you.

OEDIPUS. You can see, my friend, that my daughter's eyes
  Do service for us both: and she tells me
  We're in luck, and that you perhaps can answer
  Some of our questions.

LOCAL MAN.   Before you ask anything,
  Get up from that seat, and come away!
  That place is taboo. You're trespassing
  On holy ground!

OEDIPUS.   What place is this?
  What god is honoured here?

LOCAL MAN.   It's sacrilege
  Even to enter, let alone sit down,
  And no one can live there. Terrifying goddesses
  Have made it their sanctuary, nightmare creatures
  From the mind's darkness, and primeval earth!

OEDIPUS. I must pray to these guardians. What are their names?

LOCAL MAN. Here we call them 'The Kindly Ones'
  Whose eyes are merciless and see everything.
  In other countries they have other names.

OEDIPUS. The Furies . . .
    I hope they will see and be kindly to me
    And accept my prayers. Because I shall rest
    Here, and never leave this place.
LOCAL MAN. What do you mean?
OEDIPUS.   Things which were prophesied.
    Signs which I recognise.
LOCAL MAN.   In that case
    I'd better not touch you, not without permission
    From someone in authority in the city.
    I'll report back, let them decide . . .
OEDIPUS. But just a minute, good friend. I'm homeless
    As you see. Bear with me, and answer my questions.
LOCAL MAN. Well, I can afford to be courteous, I suppose.
    That never does any harm.
OEDIPUS.   This place,
    What is it? Does it have a name?
LOCAL MAN. Everything I know, I'll willingly tell you.
    It's holy ground, first of all, all of it!
    Poseidon, the Sea God, is worshipped near by,
    And Prometheus the Giant, who brought fire from heaven
    And blessed mankind. The Brass Gateway
    That part is called, where you are now,
    The cornerstone of Athens. The stone horseman
    Is Colonus himself! Everyone round here
    Claims him as their chief and ancestor,
    And the place is called Colonus, after him.
    So that's where you are. Not a famous place,
    But much loved by everyone
    Who lives here, and calls it home.
OEDIPUS. There are people here then, some kind of settlement?
LOCAL MAN. Yes, descended from this hero, and bearing his name.
OEDIPUS. And are they ruled by a king, or elected leaders?
LOCAL MAN. There's a king in Athens, and he rules here too.
OEDIPUS. And who is this respected and powerful king?
LOCAL MAN. His name is Theseus. King Aegeus was his father.
OEDIPUS. Can one of your people take a message to the king?
LOCAL MAN. To ask him something, or to get him to come?

OEDIPUS. To tell him a small kindness might bring great blessings.

LOCAL MAN. What great blessings can a blind man bring?

OEDIPUS. Insight. Vision. My words are not blind.

LOCAL MAN. Listen to me then. You seem friendly,
And I don't want to see you in any trouble.
You've got troubles enough, by the look of you,
And I'd guess you'd seen better days, been among
The well born and powerful, I shouldn't wonder.
Just stay where you are, just there, where I found you,
And I'll tell everyone what you just said –
The locals, I mean, not the people from the city –
Then it's up to them. They'll decide what's best:
To let you stay here, or to move you on.
Exit the Local Man. Oedipus waits for a moment, listening.

OEDIPUS. Has he gone yet Antigone? The stranger?

ANTIGONE. Yes, he's gone now. We're alone again,
Father, the two of us. You can say what you like.
Oedipus, still seated, prays, Antigone standing a little apart by the entrance to the grove.

OEDIPUS. Goddesses of darkness, whose faces are too terrible
For living men to look on without fear,
This place is your sanctuary,
And this stone the spot where I first found rest
In a new land. Look kindly now
Upon me, and remember the god, Apollo,
Who, when he foretold all the horrors
And miseries of my life, also prophesied
That my long journey would come to an end
And I would find rest in an alien country
In a holy place sacred to the Furies,
Goddesses of punishment and absolution.
'In that place,' the god promised,
'Your painful life will come to an end,
With good luck and blessings on the fortunate people
Who give you shelter, and a lasting curse
On the others, who cast you out.' Confirmation
Of the gods' intentions will be given me
In thunder, and lightning, and by shaking of the earth.

And now I feel certain, great goddesses,
Daughters of darkness and the night's terrors,
That you have guided me to your sacred place
With unseen hands, led me to sit
Here, on this sacred stone, a man
Who never drinks wine, among you
To whom wine is sacrilege. Queens of the darkness,
Inhabitants of all our nightmares, what was foretold
So long ago, bring to consummation.
Let my life end in peace and serenity –
Unless you think that I, who have suffered
More than any man living has suffered,
Am beyond all redemption. You were born
With the original darkness of the world, children
Of the first creation. Hear my prayer . . .
Now may the city of Athens protect me,
The queen of cities, with the wisest of gods
As her patron. May she look with pity
On the shrunken carcass, the pale shadow
Of the man who was Oedipus, King of Thebes.

ANTIGONE. Shh, Father. I can see some old men coming.
    They're searching everywhere. They're looking for you!

OEDIPUS. Then I shall keep silent. Take my hand
    And lead me further into the trees,
    Where we can hear without being seen.
    It will be safer and wiser to know
    What they intend, before we meet them.

Antigone leads him into the grove and out of sight. Enter the Chorus.

CHORUS. Where is he? Who is this man?
    Where does he come from? What's his home?
    He's slipped away! Where is he hiding?
    He'll stop at nothing – look everywhere, comb
    Every bush and thicket, leave nothing undone!
    He must be a tramp, or a wandering
    Beggar of some sort – and he's old,
    A foreigner too, not one of us, I'm certain
    Of that! None of us would be so bold
    As to approach that holy place, where living

Goddesses have their habitation,
The awesome Furies! The very word
Makes me shiver! With eyes
Averted we pass by, heads bowed,
Muttering silent prayers of devotion
In a reverent stillness. But now the word goes
This tramp is in there! But whatever direction
I look, there's no sign of him, or his blasphemies.

OEDIPUS. I am the man! As the proverb says
  My ears are my eyes!
CHORUS.   This is a disgrace!
  Horrifying to see you, or hear such words.
OEDIPUS. I mean no disrespect to the spirits of the place.
CHORUS. Who is this old man? Zeus guard us now!
OEDIPUS. Not one, gentlemen, whom young or old
  Would call blessed with good luck – and for proof, look how
  I see through another's eyes, and hold
  My anchor to this slim cable, my guide
  And guardian through the dangerous world.

CHORUS. Dear gods! Look at his eyes! He's blind!
  Were you born to this misery? Your face
  Is scarred with long life and deep suffering.
  But now you are courting a deeper disgrace!
  Don't bring down a greater curse on your head
  By your sacrilegious trespassing!
  Not one step more! Further within
  There is a silent grassy glade
  Most secret, most sacred, a green
  Sanctuary, where the clear waters spring
  And the ritual offerings are poured,
  Honey and water from that pure stream.
  Never, old man, must you enter there,
  However exhausted, however far from home
  You may have wandered. Can my voice be heard
  At this distance? You can speak without fear,
  We'll listen – but not from forbidden ground.

Keep silent, or else come down to us here.

OEDIPUS. Well child, what's wisest? What shall we do?
ANTIGONE. This place is holy. It's best to conform
　To local custom – pay respect where it's due.
OEDIPUS. Take my hand then.
ANTIGONE. 　　　　　　　　　I have it already. Firm!
OEDIPUS. I'm at your mercy Gentlemen, if I must
　Come from this sanctuary. Don't betray my trust!

CHORUS. No one will stop you from resting here
　Old man, or drive you away by force.
OEDIPUS. Is it further?
CHORUS. 　　　　　　Yes, further!
OEDIPUS. 　　　　　　　　　　　　Further still?
CHORUS. Show him the way, girl. You have eyes
　And can see quite well what we require.
ANTIGONE. Not for the first time. Be careful! Don't fall.
OEDIPUS. Further into darkness with every step.
ANTIGONE. But my eyes are open. There's nothing to fear
　If we respect their feelings. We can hope
　They'll treat us kindly, if anyone will.
OEDIPUS. I have trusted you always, everywhere.
CHORUS. You are a stranger. Take our advice.
　Learn to respect what our state respects.
　In your situation it would be wise
　To revere the things that we revere.

OEDIPUS. Then lead me, Antigone, to some safe place
　Where I can speak without offence
　To these good people. It makes sense
　To do what they ask with good grace.

CHORUS. That's far enough! Not one step more
　Beyond that slab of bare rock!
OEDIPUS. Here?
CHORUS. 　　　　No further!
OEDIPUS. 　　　　　　　　　　Shall I sit, or stand up?

CHORUS. You can sit! To your left there's a naked block
  Of stone, low down, like a bench. Sit there.
ANTIGONE. I'll lead you father. Step by step.
OEDIPUS. My humiliation is complete.
ANTIGONE. Move as I move, and keep tight hold
  Of my arm. I can take the weight.
  I'm young and strong enought to cope.
OEDIPUS. I can do nothing. Helpless. Like a child.
CHORUS. Poor old man! Now you can relax
  And tell us your story. Where were you born?
  Who are you, tramping these stony tracks
  So far from home, so ravaged, and so old?

OEDIPUS. I have no home. Don't ask me that.
CHORUS. Don't ask you what? What are you hiding?
OEDIPUS. I beg you! Don't ask me who or what
  I am! You don't know what you're asking.
CHORUS. Why not?
OEDIPUS.   The story of my family . . .
CHORUS.   Go on!
OEDIPUS. Dear child, what now? What shall I say?
CHORUS. Who was your father? You must be some man's son.
OEDIPUS. Must I relive this suffering, every day?
ANTIGONE. You've led them to the edge. You'll have to speak.
OEDIPUS. You're right, I can't hide it. There's no other way.
CHORUS. Tell us now! We're agog! What a time you take!
OEDIPUS. Does the name Laius mean anything?
CHORUS.   Oh no!
OEDIPUS. And the line of Labdacus in Thebes?
CHORUS.   Dear God!
OEDIPUS. The damnation of a man called Oedipus?
CHORUS.   Is it you?
OEDIPUS. Does the mere name frighten you? It's only a word!
CHORUS. Get out!
OEDIPUS.   And again, and again . . .
CHORUS.   Get away!
OEDIPUS. Antigone what's happening? What are they doing?
CHORUS. Be off with you, quickly! Get out of our country!

OEDIPUS. But you promised me safety! Did your word mean
nothing?

CHORUS. We didn't know who you were then!
  No one will blame us if we pay you back
  In your own coin.
  You deceived us, and if we choose to break
  A promise, that's what you deserve!
  So now, get out of our territory, take
  Yourself back where you came from, don't deprave
  Our air with your breath, or pollute the soil we love!

ANTIGONE. Gentlemen, listen! I know you are just,
  And not without conscience. You have some moral sense,
  You know right from wrong. If you feel you must
  Refuse to listen to my father, whose offence
  Was committed in ignorance, and who endures
  Old age and blindness, and the terrible story
  Blasting his name for ever, pity my tears,
  I beg you, my share of his misery!
  He lives in darkness, alone. Let my eyes
  Speak to yours, and plead for his agony,
  As your own daughters' eyes would, with an intense
  Compassion for a father's degradation.
  You are gods to us, our destinies
  Are in your hands. Think of your wives,
  Your children, your homes, everything in your lives
  That matters, and pity our pain. The least
  Of mortal men is the gods' concern. Our innocence
  Or guilt will bring us all to the same dust.

CHORUS. You are Oedipus' daughter: and we pity you
  As much for that as we pity him
  For all his sufferings. But we fear the gods
  And obey their laws. What else can we do?

OEDIPUS. So much, then, for a good name
  And a reputation for honourable dealing!
  All worth nothing, when it comes to the point!
  Athens, of all cities, is famous for it –
  Her godlike hospitality: – any refugee

On the run from his homeland, here, if anywhere,
He'll find a welcome! But not in my case
Apparently. In my case
You lure me from the rock where I found sanctuary
And now you will drive me with curses to your frontier
And kick me out. And why is this?
Because you are afraid of my name!
Or are you afraid of my strength,
The power of my arm? I don't think so!
My greatest deeds brought the greatest suffering
On my own head, not on others,
My greatest power was the power of endurance:
As I could prove, if I were to tell you
What my father did, and my mother's part
In my life, because it's that you're afraid of,
I know! What do you find terrible
In me, or evil, or to be feared?
I struck a man who struck me, in self-defence.
Was that a crime? Even if I had known
All the convoluted circumstances, was that wrong?
Was I morally guilty? In fact I knew nothing
Of what I was doing, or the implications
Of what I did. But the ones who were cruel
The vindictive ones who deceived me,
They knew exactly what they were doing.
You made me leave the sacred grove
Out of reverence for the gods. By those same gods,
By that same reverence, I beg you to protect me!
Reverence must mean more than lip-service,
It means action, in the spirit of the moral law!
The Immortals have sharp eyes. They see
The just man and the unjust man
With equal clarity. They never miss
The trickster or criminal who dishonours them,
Later or sooner they run him down!
We all live under that unblinking stare,
You as nakedly as I.
Don't blacken the good name of Athens

With actions unworthy of her reputation.
I came as a refugee, I asked
For rest and protection, which you promised me.
Will you break that promise because of ugly scars
On my eyes, and an uglier history?
The gods see my sufferings, some of their holiness
Lingers about my wounds: and in my wretchedness
I come to bring your people a blessing.
When your king or some person in authority
Arrives, you will hear and understand
The whole story. Till then, don't deceive me,
And don't betray me by breaking your word.

CHORUS. What you say is worth hearing old man,
Full of spiritual meaning, wisely argued,
In well-chosen words, and must be taken seriously.
Our leader must hear you. He will decide.

OEDIPUS. And where is he, this man who takes the decisions?

CHORUS. In the city of our ancestors: but the local man
Who found you and alerted us
Has gone to fetch him.

OEDIPUS.   Will he bother to come
Himself, to see an old blind foreigner?

CHORUS. There'll be no stopping him, when he hears your name.

OEDIPUS. And who will tell him that?

CHORUS.   The road
To Athens is long, but rumour travels faster
Than an Olympic champion. He'll hear,
And when he hears, post-haste, he'll be with us.
Your name is notorious, world wide.
If he's in bed, fast asleep, your name
Will bring him, the quickest possible way.

OEDIPUS. May his coming here bring a blessing
For himself and his city, and to me:
An act of kindness brings its own reward.

ANTIGONE. Dear gods! Am I seeing things? I can't be certain.

OEDIPUS. Antigone? What's happening?

ANTIGONE.   I can see a woman
Riding a horse – Sicilian I think –

77

She's wearing a hat with a broad brim
To protect her from the sun – so her face is in shadow
And I can't be sure, but I think it's her.
But it can't be, can it? I must be dreaming.
But I think it is. It is! She's smiling!
Yes, I can see her now, it is,
Ismene, she's waving to us, Ismene!

OEDIPUS. What are you talking about?

ANTIGONE.   It's your daughter, my sister:
Here, before our eyes. Now listen – you'll know that voice.
Enter Ismene, attended by one male servant.

ISMENE. I've come a long way dearest Father, dear sister!
And now that I've found you, I can hardly see you,
My eyes are so full of tears!

OEDIPUS. My child. Are you here?

ISMENE.   You're so old Father, so tired.

OEDIPUS. You've managed to find me.

ISMENE.   So difficult to find.

OEDIPUS. Touch me, dear girl!

ISMENE.   There's a hand for both.

OEDIPUS. My children . . . My sisters.

ISMENE.   These dreadful sufferings!

OEDIPUS. Hers and mine.

ISMENE.   Mine too, we all suffer.

OEDIPUS. And why have you come, girl?

ISMENE.   I'm worried for you.

OEDIPUS. Because you missed me . . . ?

ISMENE.   That too. But the main
Reason was to bring you news. I've travelled
With this one servant I can still trust.

OEDIPUS. Where are your brothers. Couldn't they help?

ISMENE. They are . . . where they are. They have terrifying
                                                    problems.

OEDIPUS. Hum. I can imagine. They behave no better
Than Egyptians, the pair of them. The Egyptian fashion
Is for the men to sit at home sewing
While the women go out and break their backs
And earn the living. So your two brothers

Laze about at home, gossiping by the fire
Like a couple of housewives, leaving you two girls
To cope with all the problems, and carry the burdens
Of my miseries, and share my hard life.
This one, Antigone, ever since she grew up
And became a woman instead of a girl
Has been on the road with me, my nurse,
My guide, my governess. In wastelands
And forests, often without shoes, and hungry,
Drenched by the rain, sunburned, exhausted,
It has never crossed her mind to go home
And live comfortably. To look after her father,
To get bread between his teeth has been her first concern.
And you, my other daughter, more than once
You've slipped secretly out of Thebes
To bring me news of the latest prophecies
And predictions about me, when they threw me out
From my native city after so many years.
You were my contact with Theban affairs,
My ears in the market-place. Well Ismene, what's the news?
Why have you left home, and travelled such a distance
To speak to your father? It must be serious
I know that. Nothing frivolous could bring you so far.

ISMENE. My own troubles, dear Father, finding where you were
And how you were living, I'd rather forget.
Living through it was bad enough. The telling
Would be no easier. More to the point
Is the disastrous story of your unlucky sons.
That's what I've come to tell you. At first,
Well aware of the curse that for so long
Has plagued our family, they were more than keen
That Creon should take the throne, hoping
By that that the city would not be defiled
And that our family's long-lived guilt
Would finally be purged. But now some god
Of motiveless destruction, an unprincipled
Criminality, seems to possess them both.
The mania, the lust for power has infected them,

And they compete against each other to seize
Control, and rule in Thebes. Eteocles
Acted first, our mad-headed younger brother.
He outmanoeuvred Polynices,
Deposed him, and kicked him out of the city:
And the word is that Polynices is in exile
In Argos, raising mercenary troops
And making diplomatic alliances, to invade
Thebes and subdue the Theban people,
So that Argos will either destroy them completely
Or make Polynices master of the city!
Father, this is no fabrication of mine,
It's the dreadful truth. How long must we wait
Before the gods will stop punishing you?

OEDIPUS. They will stop some day then? You hope
For some deliverance, some pity at the end?

ISMENE. Oh yes! These latest oracles, if I understand them
correctly . . .

OEDIPUS. What oracles? What do they say about me?

ISMENE. That Thebes' safety will one day depend on you,
And they must get you back, dead or alive.

OEDIPUS. What can they want from a man like me?

ISMENE. Their power, they say, draws its energy from you.

OEDIPUS. Power? When I am dead? Is that the idea?

ISMENE. The same gods who humiliated you support you now.

OEDIPUS. A bad bargain, for an old man destroyed in his youth.

ISMENE. Be that as it may. Creon is coming
And for those very reasons. He'll be here today!

OEDIPUS. To do what? Don't mince matters.

ISMENE. To get you settled as close as possible
To the borders of Thebes. To keep you handy,
Without actually setting foot on Theban soil.

OEDIPUS. What use am I, outside the border?

ISMENE. They must honour your grave, or face the consequences.

OEDIPUS. Native wit should have told them that not oracles.

ISMENE. And that's why they want to keep you under observation
Just across the frontier. In effect, a prisoner.

OEDIPUS. And will they bury me on Theban soil?

80

ISMENE. Never. Your guilt for your father's death forbids it.

OEDIPUS. Then they will never have me at all.

ISMENE. If they don't, it will be a curse upon them one day!

OEDIPUS. But how my child? In what circumstances?

ISMENE. When they feel your anger risen from the grave
    Striking them when they're most vulnerable – in battle.

OEDIPUS. And where did you get all this information?

ISMENE. We sent envoys to Delphi. One of them told me.

OEDIPUS. And these predictions about me were made by the oracle?

ISMENE. My informer said so when he got back to Thebes.

OEDIPUS. And do either of my sons know this?

ISMENE. They both know it. And they know what it means.

OEDIPUS. They know it! The swine! They'd rather keep
    Power in their own hands than bring their father home!

ISMENE. That's a dreadful thing to say – but I'm afraid it's true.

OEDIPUS. Then it's my hope that no god will step in
    To put out the fire between them, or prevent
    This fratricidal battle. Let me be their judge
    In the bloody business they are preparing now
    And I will sentence them both, the one in power
    To lose it for ever, the other never
    To return from exile. Neither one of them
    Raised a finger when I was banished
    And thrown out of the city. Did they even care
    When the anathema was pronounced and the gate shut behind
                              me?
    They said nothing, did nothing. Some people have said
    That I myself requested exile
    And the State mercifully granted my wish.
    Not true! On the day of catastrophe,
    I wanted death, I asked for it,
    My soul was burning, I begged for it then,
    Even death by stoning, to be buried half alive
    Under a mountain of flint and rubble.
    What I longed for then no one would give me.
    And as time passed the pain lessened,
    And I began to realise that I had been excessive
    In my rage and self-punishment, more than I deserved.

81

And that, of course, was the time when my city,
After so many years, finally decided
To kick me out! And my two sons,
Who had a responsibility to help their father
Simply by being sons, did nothing.
They said not one single word. And out
I went, a pariah, a beggar, to tramp
The roads forever, until I dropped:
My only help, my two girls,
Who have done everything women could do
To ease my suffering. Food and shelter
And love they have given me, while their brothers
Sold out their father for the chance of power,
The sniff of kingship! If they want me
For an ally, they'll wait a long time.
I wouldn't lift my little finger
For either of them. And power in Thebes
Won't do them any good either, not
If these new oracles are to be believed,
And all the old prophecies too
Clinging so long to my name, which Apollo,
After so many years, is slowly fulfilling.
Let Creon come. Let them all come,
All the great ones of Thebes! If you good people
And the powerful presences which dwell in this place
Combine to protect me, this land of Athens
Will win a great champion to its side,
And those who persecute me, will be punished for it.

CHORUS. We have great sympathy Oedipus, for you
    And for your daughters. And your assertion
    That you will bring mysterious good fortune
    Persuades me to offer you some positive advice.

OEDIPUS. Please help me! I'll do what you say.

CHORUS. Make expiation at once to the goddesses
    Whose holy sanctuary you violated.

OEDIPUS. If you will instruct me. Tell me the ritual.

CHORUS. Cleanse your hands. Then fill the cup you will find there
    With water from the pure spring that never runs dry.

OEDIPUS. I understand. And when I have this water?
CHORUS. There are chalices there, marvellously carved:
  You must decorate them, handles and rims.
OEDIPUS. With fresh leaves, or fringes of wool?
CHORUS. With raw lamb's wool freshly shorn.
OEDIPUS. I see. And the sacrifice itself?
CHORUS. You must face the dawn and pour an offering.
OEDIPUS. Using the decorated chalices?
CHORUS. Three times you must pour – emptying them with the last.
OEDIPUS. And in these chalices just water?
CHORUS. Water and honey. No wine must be added.
OEDIPUS. On the shadowed earth under the trees. What then?
CHORUS. Spread sprays of olive branches and pray.
OEDIPUS. What prayers? That's the most important thing.
CHORUS. That these goddesses, the Furies,
  Whom we know to be kindly spirits,
  Will be merciful towards you, a beggar.
  Pray quietly, and reverently –
  You, or someone else standing in for you –
  Then come away, and don't turn back.
  If you do this, we will gladly stand by you.
  If you don't, there's nothing we can do.
OEDIPUS. Girls. Did you hear these old men's advice.
ANTIGONE. We were listening. What do you want us to do?
OEDIPUS. I can't do it. I'm too weak,
  And my blindness makes it impossible.
  One of you must pray for me.
  A prayer is a prayer. And one honest heart
  Can speak for thousands. Do it now,
  As quickly as you can. But one of you
  Must stay outside. I'm helpless alone.
  I dare not move without some sort of guidance.
ISMENE. I can perform the ritual and the prayers.
  But where is this place? Can somebody show me?
CHORUS. Go into the grove. Beyond the trees
  You'll find the acolyte who guards the spring.
  He'll tell you everything.
ISMENE.   Antigone,

Look after our father, while I undertake
The sacrifice. Nothing is too much trouble
When a parent's well-being is at stake.

Ismene goes into the grove and the Chorus watches her.
Then they turn to Oedipus.

CHORUS. It's a terrible thing, Stranger, I know
To disturb long-sleeping memories of pain
But I'm longing to hear you tell . . .

OEDIPUS.   What now?

CHORUS. The whole dreadful story! Those horrors that chain
You down to incurable suffering for ever!

OEDIPUS. For friendship's sake, let that tale remain
Untold, the shame I have suffered, and suffer.

CHORUS. But everyone knows it! So much better to hear
The authentic version instead of the rumour!

OEDIPUS. I can't . . .

CHORUS.   But we're begging you to tell us . . .

OEDIPUS.   Too much to bear!

CHORUS. Grant it as a favour to us, for giving you sanctuary here!

OEDIPUS. What can I say? My agonies are unique,
My punishments unparalleled: the gods well know
I suffer for my ignorance.

CHORUS.   But what caused this? Bad luck?

OEDIPUS. My infamous marriage. I never knew
The truth. Thebes enmeshed me in that horror.

CHORUS. And are those lurid rumours true,
That you shared your mother's bed, as a lover?

OEDIPUS. It's like death to hear it. But there's more to tell . . .
These girls, they're mine. My blood . . . but closer . . .

CHORUS. Do you mean . . . ?

OEDIPUS.   These daughters, these curses . . .

CHORUS.   Darkness of hell!

OEDIPUS. Were nursed by the woman who nursed me, and gave
                                        birth to us all!

CHORUS. Then these daughters must have another name.

OEDIPUS. Sisters. Sisters to their own father.

CHORUS. Unbelievable!

OEDIPUS. This never-ending horror!

CHORUS. Such suffering!

OEDIPUS. This unendurable shame!

CHORUS. But the crime . . .

OEDIPUS. What crime?

CHORUS. You committed?

OEDIPUS. Never!
    I took my reward for saving the city. The Queen came
    As my greatest prize, and my greatest misery for ever!

CHORUS. But that was not all. The blood you shed . . .

OEDIPUS. Must you have all the details, every drop that was spilled?

CHORUS. Your father?

OEDIPUS. New wounds, before the old have healed.

CHORUS. You killed him!

OEDIPUS. I killed him. But there's more to be said!

CHORUS. What?

OEDIPUS. Justice of a kind.

CHORUS. What justice?

OEDIPUS. I killed
    In ignorance, a man who would have killed me. That blood
    I admit. But by the laws of gods and men, my innocence is revealed!

CHORUS. Here is our king, the Son of Aegeus,
    Theseus. You asked for him, and he came,
    Enter Theseus with a small group of Soldiers and Servants. There is
    a pause as he looks at Oedipus.

THESEUS. I have heard the story, over and over again,
    Of the bloody mutilation of your eyes:
    And that alone would identify you
    As the son of Laius. All the details
    They told me while I was coming here
    Simply confirm the fact. And these
    Scars on your face, and beggarly clothes
    Make your identity quite certain.
    So let me call you long-suffering Oedipus,
    And ask you what favour you would beg of Athens,

Or of me, you and your companion,
Who endures what you endure. You can ask
Without fear. No story, however appalling,
Will frighten me, or make me ignore
Your request for help. I was brought up
In exile too, and I never forget it.
I had my struggles and dangerous times
In foreign countries – no man has had more.
For that reason alone, no wanderer or refugee
Ever comes here, seeking our help
And is turned away empty handed.
I am a man, like you. I know
I am not immortal, and the day will come
When I shall be what you are.

OEDIPUS. Theseus, you have spoken your mind briefly, and revealed
A generous heart and honourable nature.
I too can be brief. My own name,
My country and my family, you have correctly
Guessed. Now I need only ask
My favour, and then all is said.

THESEUS. What favour is it? Ask it now.

OEDIPUS. I come to offer you a precious gift:
My scarred, battered and exhausted body.
Not much to look at. But worth much more.

THESEUS. What is it worth? Why is it precious?

OEDIPUS. Time will teach you its value. Not now but later.

THESEUS. Later? How much later? When will we know?

OEDIPUS. When I am dead, and you have buried me.

THESEUS. Is that all you ask? A decent burial?
Does the rest of your life not matter at all?

OEDIPUS. If I am buried as I wish to be buried, no.

THESEUS. It's a small favour you ask of me.

OEDIPUS. No, it isn't! It's crucial! – and difficult to perform.

THESEUS. I can guess the difficulty – between your sons and me.

OEDIPUS. They will want to take me back to Thebes.

THESEUS. If they want you back, why not go with them?
There's no honour in exile for a man like you.

OEDIPUS. When I wanted to go they would not have me.

86

THESEUS. That seems childish to be resentful in your situation.

OEDIPUS. Listen to me, before you criticise.

THESEUS. Certainly. I should make no judgements before I know the facts.

OEDIPUS. I've been wronged so often I've lost count of my troubles.

THESEUS. That never-ending curse on your family, you mean?

OEDIPUS. No! They tell that story all over Greece.

THESEUS. Could any man suffer worse punishment than that?

OEDIPUS. That I can endure. My own sons
  Had me thrown out from my native city,
  And I am a parricide: my return is forbidden.

THESEUS. Then, why bring you back? If you can't live there . . . ?

OEDIPUS. An oracle has spoken and forced them to act.

THESEUS. What forces them? Some threat of punishment?

OEDIPUS. Yes, punishment here, in this country.

THESEUS. You mean in battle? There's no quarrel between us.

OEDIPUS. Dear son of Aegeus, only the gods
  Escape the penalties of age and death.
  Time undermines everything, nothing
  Can stop the inevitable process of decay.
  The earth itself is eroded, the bodies
  Of men wither, shrink, and die.
  Good faith dies too, and lies bear fruit
  And flourish. Between friend and friend
  Feelings slowly change, and between cities too
  Distrust grows, love turns to hate,
  Hate to love, and all joy
  In the passing of time becomes sorrow.
  It's fair weather now between you and Thebes,
  Not a cloud in sight. But time has an infinity
  Of days and nights to live through yet.
  And the slightest pretext, one day,
  Will be more than enough to cut down friendship,
  With whole regiments of swords. I shall be long
  In my grave, sleeping, a forgotten corpse.
  But it will be then that my cold body
  Will drink their hot blood. If Zeus
  Still rules, and Apollo, his son, keeps his word.

But enough of that. These things are mysteries
Not to be spoken of here. Let me say again
What I said at first. Keep your promise
To protect me. And you will never complain
That your hospitality to Oedipus was not paid back with interest.
Unless the gods and their oracles are determined to cheat me.

CHORUS. Before you arrived, my Lord, this man
    Swore he had this power to bless our land.

THESEUS. He offers us friendship. Who in his right mind
    Would reject that? In addition, as a friend
    And citizen of a city allied to us
    He has a right to our hospitality:
    And in coming to ask favour of our goddesses –
    He honours the city, and me, and speaks
    Of blessings in return. I respect all these things
    And think highly of him. Our city's protection
    Is his for the asking. You will be responsible
    For his well-being. Unless he would rather
    Return to Athens with me? Choose, Oedipus,
    Which of these two courses you prefer.
    We will be guided by your wishes.

OEDIPUS. Gods, these men are worth a blessing.

THESEUS. What is your decision? Will you come with me?

OEDIPUS. I would. But this is the place, I must stay.

THESEUS. Why here particularly? Speak freely. I won't stop you.

OEDIPUS. The people who banished me must be defeated.

THESEUS. And your being here? That will bring us the blessing?

OEDIPUS. You will see the proof. If you stand by your promise.

THESEUS. That's the least of your worries. I won't betray you.

OEDIPUS. No need to swear it. You're an honest man.

THESEUS. My word can be relied on, as much as any oath.

OEDIPUS. But if you leave me . . . ?

THESEUS.   What are you afraid of?

OEDIPUS. My enemies are coming.

THESEUS.   These fellows will protect you.

OEDIPUS. But if you go . . . ?

THESEUS.   I know what I must do.

OEDIPUS. It's my fear makes me speak.

THESEUS.   But I am not frightened.

OEDIPUS. But you don't know the threats.

THESEUS.   I know one thing,
For certain, that no one will take you from here,
Or anywhere, against my will.
I've heard threats before. Noisemakers and bullies
Are always very free with them. Very rarely
Do they come to anything, when people calm down
And assess the situation rationally.
These people may have spoken grandly
Of taking you away. Any voyage of that kind
Will be across very stormy seas,
I can promise them that. Don't be afraid.
Apollo is your protector, as much as I am.
Besides, you will find my name is enough,
Even when I'm not here, to keep you safe.
Exit Theseus, with his Soldiers and Attendants.

CHORUS. Your long journey has brought you here
Stranger, to Colonus of the white rocks,
Whose very name invokes
All beauty, all loveliness, as if the air
Breathed poetry. The horses we breed
Here are world famous, and nightingales sing
Their incomparable song
Endlessly in the leaf-shrouded glade,
Amid wine-dark ivy, where the luscious vine
Dangles its fat bunches – and untrodden within,
Hidden from the sun
Where no breezes breathe or winds tear, the shrine
Of the nymphs who nurse and caress the drunken God of Wine.

There, like star-clusters, the narcissus shines
Watered each dawn by the dew, and close by
The crocus' golden eye
Glitters like an ancient garland that twines
Flowers for jewels in the goddesses' hair.
There the pure and gushing spring
Flows ever unsleeping

To the river Cephisus, and its fertile valley floor
Is always watered and always green,
And the dark soil swells and brings to birth
All the fruits of the earth:
The song of the Muses can be heard in these trees, and the Queen
Of Love comes riding in her dove-drawn chariot with the golden
rein.

There the grey-leaved olive grows,
Self-sufficient, self-engendered,
Superior to anything that Asia knows
Or the Dorian farmer ever tended,
A terror to all our foes.
For its rich oil breeds up our sturdy youth
So that no brash young general or experienced commander
Can ever uproot, pillage or plunder
Our silver grey groves.
For Zeus the unsleeping guards this precious earth,
With his vigilant thunder,
And grey-eyed Athene herself protects the land that she loves.

But the greatest gift of all these
And the people of Athens' greatest boast
Is her skill at horsemanship and mastery of the seas.
Oh mighty Poseidon, son of Cronos, you first
Fathered our glories
In these quiet meadows, when you taught us to tame
Wild horses, and bring them under the bit,
And how to carve the slender oars to fit
The oarsman's strength that drives
The sweeping blade, and how to row like a team
Till the galley skims light
As the fifty Nereids who guide her, across the dangerous waves.
*Antigone, looking offstage, sees Creon approaching, accompanied by
a squadron of Soldiers.*

ANTIGONE. Yes, everyone in the world praises Athens,
But now you must live up to that reputation.
OEDIPUS. What's happening? Antigone?
ANTIGONE.   Creon is coming!

With a squad of soldiers. He's heading this way!

OEDIPUS. Good Counsellors, you have been generous to me.

Help me now to finish my journey in peace.

CHORUS. Don't be afraid. We may be old,

But our country is young, and full of energy.

Enter Creon, guarded by Soldiers, who immediately fan out to occupy the significant positions. Creon is an older man than Oedipus, but he has suffered less, is much more active, and very much in command.

CREON. Gentlemen. Good people of Colonus.

I can see from the look of panic in your eyes

That you are afraid of me. You need not be.

Nor need you shout at me, or be abusive.

I haven't come to make trouble. I'm too old

For that, and this is Athens, a city

Without equal in power and reputation

In Greece – as I know very well.

In fact, it was probably because of my age

That I was chosen to talk to your guest

To persuade him back to Thebes. I am here

Representing the whole city, you realise,

Not just one man. As his brother-in-law too,

I was the natural choice, sharing with him

The dreadful anguish of our unlucky family.

Oedipus. You have suffered enough. Listen

To me. Come home now. We want you back,

The whole city is asking for you, and it's right

That they should. And I, personally,

Even more than all the rest – indeed,

I would be an utter blackguard if I weren't –

Am heartbroken to see you in this condition,

On the road, like a tramp, with this one girl

As your companion and helper. And who would believe

That she could ever descend into poverty

As appalling as this. She's very young

To be condemned to beg for you and nurse your miseries.

She should be married, but has no chance

While she's on the road and penniless.

More likely, she'd be easy meat

91

For rape, unprotected, on the public highway!
We're all at fault. I am, you are,
It's a public scandal to our whole family,
And it's out in the open, it can't be covered up.
Oedipus, for the family's sake, listen,
And for all the gods our fathers have worshipped.
It's time to draw a veil across
The whole shameful business, remove it
From the public eye. Come home with me
To your father's house in your own city.
Thank these Athenians. They have been kind.
But Thebes bred you, and you belong with her.

OEDIPUS. You brazen hypocrite! Every decent motive,
Every kindly gesture, you manipulate
To serve your own advantage. Do you expect
The rabbit to be caught in the same snare twice
For a double dose of misery? Once upon a time
I was so horrified by what I had done
That I was desperate for exile. You said no,
Refused to allow it. But later on,
When time had soothed the pain, and the quietness
And comfort of my own home was some solace to me,
Then, you decided to kick me out, like a dog
At the back door, booted into exile!
Family feeling! Blood relationship!
You didn't give a damn for either! And now
Once again, you see me kindly treated
By all these decent people, welcomed by their city.
And so naturally, you want to drag me away,
And you disguise a hard-headed political tactic
With an appearance of generosity and concern.
But let me tell you, your friendly offers
Are not wanted here. Suppose you were to ask
A favour of someone, and that man
Refused it, point blank, and then, later,
When you didn't need it, grandly condescended
To grace you with his charity! Would you thank him?
Oh no, you would not! You would see his gifts

For what they are, hollow deceits
Serving his own ends, deceptively generous,
But vicious in fact. Let me make it clear
The real reason why you want me back.
Not to set me up in comfort in my old home,
But to plant me at your frontier, like a border fence,
To keep the peace for you with Athens!
Well. You'll never get that much from me.
What you will get, is my curse, condemning
Your country for ever. And as for my sons,
Their inheritance in my kingdom shall be
A square yard of earth to die on, no more.
I think I can predict the future
Of Thebes with greater skill than you can,
Having Apollo, and his father Zeus as my instructors.
You come here dishonestly, with diplomatic speeches
To sweeten a brutal exercise in realpolitik.
But carry on talking. All this eloquence,
Will do you more harm in the long run
Than it does me. But I don't suppose
You believe that. So go back where you came from
And leave us two here. We'll live our own lives
Together: if this is misery, we choose it,
And because we choose it, we'll be content.
CREON. Do you think this kind of talk does me
Any harm? You suffer for it, I don't.
OEDIPUS. As long as you make as little impression
On these people as you do on me, I'm satisfied.
CREON. You're a fool: and old age hasn't made you any wiser.
You bring shame on the whole of my generation.
OEDIPUS. You're a clever talker Creon, but can any honest man
Take as many sides as fluently as you do?
CREON. Clever talking is one thing. Talking sense another.
OEDIPUS. So you think yourself a man of few words, but well chosen!
CREON. Yes, and beyond your mental capacity!
OEDIPUS. Get out! I speak for these people. Call off
Your bully boys, I won't leave here. This is my last home.
CREON. Well. I've finished with you. Let these men bear witness

How you insult your own. But when I *do* get hold of you . . .

OEDIPUS. You won't. These friends of mine will protect me.

CREON. I can still make you suffer. Without touching you!

OEDIPUS. What does that mean? . . . What have you done?

CREON. You have two daughters. My men have arrested
One of them already. The other I'll take now . . .

OEDIPUS. No, no!

CREON.   Don't shout before you're hurt.

OEDIPUS. You've got my daughter!

CREON.   And I'll have this one too.

OEDIPUS. Good friends, don't betray me! The laws of the gods
Mean nothing to this man! Drive him from your country!

CHORUS. Away you go, foreigner! There is no justice
In what you've done, or what you're doing now.

CREON (*To one of the Soldiers*).
It's time to move. You, get hold of the girl.
If she won't come, drag her away by force.

ANTIGONE. Ah, God help me, where shall I run to?
Somebody help me!

CHORUS.   Stranger, what are you doing?

CREON. Keep him if you like, but the girl is mine!

OEDIPUS. Athens, do you have leaders!

CHORUS.   Sir, this is unjust!

CREON. Purest justice!

CHORUS.   How can it be?

CREON.   She's Theban therefore mine!

OEDIPUS. Athenians, help me!

CHORUS. Don't touch her stranger, let her go before
It comes to a fight!

CREON.   Get back!

CHORUS.   When she's free!

CREON. If you touch me, our cities will be at war!

OEDIPUS. I warned you.

CHORUS.   I tell you that girl must stay
Where she is!

CREON.   Words mean nothing without power!

CHORUS. I order you, let her go!

CREON. I order you, make way!

CHORUS. Help, people of Colonus, we're under attack,
Our homes are threatened, you dare not hold back
Defend your country!

ANTIGONE. Somebody, help me, they're dragging me away . . .

OEDIPUS. Antigone, where are you?

ANTIGONE. . . . by force, I can't stop them.

OEDIPUS. Give me your hand!

ANTIGONE. I can't, I can't move!

CREON. Get her out!

OEDIPUS. No end to this misery.

*The Soldiers drag Antigone away. Creon begins to follow, but can't
resist a last jibe at Oedipus. He turns back and walks across to the
blind man.*

CREON. And as for you, your two little walking-sticks
Are broken now. Stagger as best you can
Without them: and since it pleases you
To abuse your friends, and damn your country,
Whose representative I am honoured to be,
Although I'm of royal rank: carry on,
By all means, enjoy yourself. You'll learn
In time that you're your own worst enemy.
Your uncontrollable temper, and spite towards your friends
Has caused trouble enough for you in the past.
And now, once again, you'll live to regret it.

*Creon turns to go. But his own Soldiers have gone with Antigone by
now. He has been left on his own, and, unknown to him, the Chorus
has moved round to bar his escape.*

CHORUS. No further, stranger!

CREON. Don't you dare to touch me!

CHORUS. You won't leave here till you release those girls.

CREON. I see . . .

*Creon looks round towards Oedipus, who has moved back towards
the sacred grove.*

CREON. Then I shall claim the bigger prize,
Something worth more than two young women!

He begins to move deliberately towards Oedipus.

CHORUS. What are you doing?

CREON. I'll take the man.

CHORUS. Do you dare to say that?

CREON. I'll dare more than say it,
I'll do it!

CHORUS. Not if our king can stop you.

OEDIPUS. Are you shameless enough to lay hands on me?

CREON. Be quiet, all of you!

OEDIPUS. I won't be quiet!
Terrible goddesses who inhabit this place,
Let me say one more thing, one more
Curse in your presence. You, swine, listen!
Do you see my eyes? They've been dark for years.
And now you have taken the one person
Who replaced them, my daylight, from me.
May the god of daylight, the sun, who sees everything
Reward you, and all those you love
With misery, and suffering, and an old age like mine.

CREON. Well, men of Athens, can you hear all this?

OEDIPUS. They hear me, and they see your brutality!
They know the only strength I have left
Is the strength to curse!

CREON. I've had enough
Of all this. Old as I am,
And without my soldiers, I'll take you myself!
He takes hold of Oedipus, and prepares to drag him away.

OEDIPUS. God help me now!

CHORUS. How dare you! You won't get away with this!

CREON. I will.

CHORUS. Yes, if Athens and her laws are brought low.

CREON. Law fights for the weaker, when he fights for justice.

OEDIPUS. Do you hear his ravings?

CHORUS. It's all noise and no profit
The gods know that much!

CREON. And you know much less!

CHORUS. What insolent arrogance!

CREON. You must put up with it.

CHORUS. Citizens, leaders, get weapons in your hands,

Our sovereignty's flouted, block the roads,
Don't let them go!
Re-enter Theseus, with his Soldiers and Attendants.
THESEUS. What's all the shouting? What's going on?
  I was making my sacrifice at the altar of Poseidon,
  The most powerful local god, when this noise
  Interrupted me, and brought me here
  Faster than I intended. Tell me, what's happening?
OEDIPUS. My good friend, never was a man's voice
  More welcome. This man has attacked me.
THESEUS. What man do you mean? What has he done?
OEDIPUS. This man, Creon! Is he still here?
  He's taken all I have left, my daughters!
THESEUS. He's done what?
OEDIPUS.   Every word I've said is true!
THESEUS. All right, one of you, as fast as you can
  Go to the altar, tell them to cut short
  The sacrifice and make their best speed, both horse
  And foot, to the place where the main road forks:
  The cavalry at full gallop. The two girls
  And their captors must not pass that point.
  I must wipe the smile off this foreigner's face,
  If he thinks that he can make a fool of me
  With an arrogant show of force. Get a move on, man,
  An order is an order. This man can thank his stars
  That I have learned to control my anger.
  If I were to treat him as he deserves
  He'd leave here in a sorry state. However,
  He shall have law, or as much of it
  As he acknowledges in his own actions.
  (To Creon) You, sir, will stay exactly where you are
  Until those two girls are brought back here
  And stand in front of me. Your behaviour
  Is insulting to me and a disgrace to yourself,
  Your own people, and your country. Justice
  Is the ruling principle of Athens,
  We live by the rule of law, not force.
  And you come barging in, ignoring

Everything we stand for here, for all the world
Like a robber baron, plundering everyone
And everything, at your own whim.
Perhaps you think there are no men
In this city, or only cringing lackeys,
And that I myself am nobody to consider?
Did you learn this sort of behaviour in Thebes?
I don't think so. The Thebans are civilised,
Not savages. They would be ashamed to hear
Of your violence towards me, and towards the gods –
Invading sanctuary to arrest two young girls
And an old man! If I were in Thebes,
Even with the best possible arguments
To support me, would I ever be likely
To promote my cause by violence
Against the state, or it rulers, or its people?
Visitors, foreigners, don't behave like that.
You have brought shame and ignominy
On a city that doesn't deserve it, your own.
You've lived a long time. But old age
Hasn't brought you wisdom. Indeed,
The older you get, it seems, the stupider.
I've said it once, and I'll say it again:
You'll stay here, and like a prisoner,
Under close guard, until those girls
Are brought back safely. They had better return
Soon, and uninjured: for your sake.
This isn't just talk, my friend. I mean it.

CHORUS. You're in trouble now; by breeding and family
    You should be just. But you have acted wrongly.

CREON. No Theseus, you are wrong. It wasn't
    Because I thought the men of this city
    Lacked guts, or good sense, that I acted
    The way I did. It's very simple.
    I didn't expect you to take such a liking
    To one of my relations as to keep him here
    Against my wishes: and I felt absolutely certain
    That no one would want to protect

The despicable criminal who killed his own father
And incestuously married his mother, fathering
Children of incest! The Hill of Ares,
And the shrewd counsellors who meet there – symbol of Athens
In its justice and wisdom, and world famous
As such – would hardly give political asylum
To an old wandering reprobate,
I felt sure of that, and therefore entitled
To arrest him. It was my business, not yours.
In fact, I would have been easier on him
Even then, if he hadn't cursed me,
And all my family, and my people.
That was an act that deserved punishment,
And from me. Anger, you know, doesn't age,
Or grow senile, and only death
Finally cools it. Dead men
Are the only ones who can't be roused
By insult or injustice. You, of course,
Will do as you please with me. I'm old
And unprotected, however just my cause.
Don't assume, however, that because I'm old
I won't answer your actions with my own.

OEDIPUS. Doesn't that sort of abuse make you ashamed
Of yourself? Whose old age do you think
Is more degraded, mine, or yours,
By this sewer of vile accusations
You so much delight in, the murder and incest
And all the rest of it. I didn't intend
Any of those actions, I endured them.
The gods took their pleasure of me, paying back,
I suppose, some old sin of my ancestors.
Because you won't find anything
In me, no guilt, no sin, however
Obsessively you search, for which these crimes
I unwittingly committed, damning myself
And all my family, could be just punishment!
Answer me this. If my father
Was predestined by an oracle

99

To be killed by his own son, how can you
Blame me for it, when I was not born,
Not even conceived, nor even imagined
By my father and mother when the oracle spoke?
And if, being born under that curse,
As I was, I met my father by accident,
By accident killed him, having no idea
Either who he was, or what I was doing,
Can you reasonably condemn me of the crime of parricide?
As for my mother – what a swine you are,
How utterly without shame, in forcing me to speak
Of your own sister like this, and our marriage!
But all decent reticence means nothing
To you, and I must speak . . . She was,
Yes, she was my mother: she didn't know it,
Neither did I. We were both quite ignorant
Of what we were doing: and she bore me
Children, the children of her own son,
Shameful as it is to say it.
One thing I know for certain. You slander us,
Both of us, quite consciously. I married her
In innocent ignorance, and speak of it now
Unwillingly, only because I must.
I am not guilty, and I will not be condemned,
Neither for my marriage, nor my father's murder,
Which you delight in, and make so much of
Over and over again. Listen,
Here's a question for you. Suppose someone
Came up to you and threatened to kill you,
Would you mildly ask him, you paragon of justice,
If he could possibly be your father,
Or would you vigorously defend yourself?
You, I assume, love life as much
As the next man, and would fight for it,
Not stand there arguing the rights and wrongs.
Well, that was my situation, my danger,
The neat trap the gods had devised for me.
Even my father, if we could bring him back,

Wouldn't disagree with that. But you, Creon,
You are a scoundrel, you will say anything
In front of anybody, even things
Better left unsaid. You shame me
In public, in front of these decent people,
To degrade me in their eyes. But then,
When Theseus' name is mentioned, you grovel,
You sing fulsome praises of Athenian wisdom
And Athenian government, not realising
That flattery means nothing to a city like this
That knows how to honour the gods. And then,
In the same breath, you try to kidnap me,
An old man, in the middle of my prayers,
In a sacred place, having already
Seized and dragged away my daughters.
That was an insult to these goddesses,
And I call upon them to help and defend me,
And the people of this country, who will soon
Teach you that they are men to be reckoned with.

CHORUS. Theseus, this man is innocent, a helpless
  Victim of terrible punishments. We must help.

THESEUS. We've made enough speeches. While we stand here
  Discussing the matter, these villains are making off.

CREON. What can I do? I'm defenceless in your power!

THESEUS. You can come with me and show me the way.
  If you're hiding the girls somewhere here,
  You can point out the place yourself. If your henchmen
  Have galloped off with them already,
  We can relax. My men are after them,
  And will catch them long before they can get home
  To thank their gods for a safe journey.
  All right. Move out! The man who came here
  To arrest innocent people has been
  Himself arrested. The hunter is caught
  In his own net. Profits craftily made
  And without sound backing, are the soonest lost.
  I suppose you had allies. You would hardly have planned
  Such a daring raid without some support.

But here they can't help you. I shall see to that.
We cannot allow the State to be threatened
By one man's arrogance. Do you understand me?
Or do you think my words as worthless
As good sense always is to a man plotting mischief!

CREON. I have no quarrel with you, not here.
When I get back to Thebes I shall know what to do.

THESEUS. Threaten me by all means, but quick march!
Oedipus. Stay here. And be confident
That I shall bring your daughters back.
Nothing but my own death will stop me.

OEDIPUS. The gods give you good luck Theseus,
For your generosity, and your kindness.
Exit Theseus, with Creon and the Soldiers.

CHORUS. Who would wish to be anywhere
But where our enemies turn to fight,
And the voice of bronze is heard in the air,
And the clash of shields, as the swords bite!
Perhaps their vanguards meet
Where the Pythia guards Apollo's shrine
By the shore? Or where the sacred torch light
Brightens the bay of Eleusis, and divine
Demeter, the fertile queen,
And her dark daughter enact their mysterious rites
Beneficial to men, and the vow of secrecy is sworn
Like a golden seal on the lips of their acolytes.
And there I'd see Theseus, denying these raiders escape from our
land,
And rescuing Oedipus' daughters, with his own invincible hand!

Or maybe their clattering chariot wheels
Or their straining horses' speed and stamina
Have swept them past snowy ridges and fells
And reached the uttermost western pasture?
But they'll get no further!
Have you seen the War God's bloody face
As his terrible chariot thunders nearer?
Awesome that sight! And Theseus no less

As his brilliant squadrons pass.
Their harness glitters, on easy rein
Each horseman sweeps by in a gleam of brass
To prove himself best of Theseus' men.
Athene's praises they sing, and the mysterious birth
Of Poseidon, bursting like a living earthquake from his mother
the earth.

Is it now, the fighting,
Or will they soon fight?
Something tells me that before tonight
We'll come face to face with these girls who've endured such
suffering
At their own family's hands! Zeus will bring
All the anguish we endure to a mysterious conclusion,
And victory, and peace, out of all this destruction.
Oh to be free as a bird in flight,
To look down like a god on this struggle, from the cloud-swept
Olympian height!

God-King, immortal,
All-seeing Zeus,
Grant this much to us:
That our local militia should distinguish themselves in this
battle,
In ambush, or cavalry charge. And may subtle
Athene, Zeus' grey-eyed daughter,
Apollo, the hunter, and his deer-slaying sister
Artemis, combine their powers to bring peace
With the guarantee of the gods, to the land and people of
Colonus!

One member of the Chorus detaches himself, and speaks to Oedipus.
CHORUS. Stranger. You have travelled far, but my instinct
    Didn't betray me, and now my eyes confirm it.
    Your daughters are coming, escorted by soldiers!
OEDIPUS. Where are they? Is it true?
Enter Antigone, Ismene, Theseus and Soldiers.
ANTIGONE.   Father, dear Father!

If only some god could give you eyes again
To see this great man who has rescued us!

OEDIPUS. My girls, are you really here?

ANTIGONE.   Both of us.
Rescued by Theseus and his cavalry men.

OEDIPUS. Come to my arms girls. I thought you were gone
For ever, that I would never embrace you again!

ANTIGONE. You couldn't long for that more than we do.

OEDIPUS. Where then, where are you?

ANTIGONE.   Here, both of us here.

OEDIPUS. My two precious girls!

ANTIGONE.   Even daughters are precious!

OEDIPUS. My life depends on you.

ANTIGONE.   One sadness supports another.

OEDIPUS. I could die now, without complaining –
No bitterness, with you two here.
Stay close, one each side, embrace me
As I embrace you. This is rest.
After all my many years' wandering
This is peace. Now. Tell me what happened.
Keep it brief and to the point. The simplest words
Are most suitable for young women.

ANTIGONE. This man saved us. Let him tell the story.
Is that brief and womanly enough!

OEDIPUS. My good friend, bear with us in all
These tears and laughter, this long drawn-out
Reunion. I thought I'd lost them for good.
I understand very well that you are the man
I should thank: their safety and my own unexpected happiness,
I owe entirely to you. I'll pray
To the gods to reward you, and your country.
I have found here, among these people,
And nowhere else, honesty, a sense of reverence,
And a concern for truth and justice. And you,
Above all men, great king, personify these virtues.
Let me publicly thank you for that, and the courtesy
I have been shown, which is all your doing . . .
Let me shake your hand in gratitude,

And exchange the kiss of fellowship . . .
He moves towards Theseus, and then draws back suddenly in horror.

OEDIPUS. Dear heavens, what am I saying! I forgot
For a moment who I am: a man infectious
With every misery, rancid with sin.
He keeps Theseus at a distance.
I can't let you touch me. No you must not!
Only these two, who know my miseries
And have learned to live with them, can share the pain.
Stay where you are, we'll speak at a distance:
And I hope your friendship, which has been so vital
To me already, will still protect me!

THESEUS. You don't need to apologise to me
For your affection to your children, or for talking to them
For a long time, rather than to me.
I assure you, I'm not at all offended.
What matters to me is what a man does,
Not what he says. And my own actions
I hope have proved that. I made a promise,
Old friend, and I have kept it, to the letter.
They're back alive, and none the worse for their abduction.
As for the skirmish? Well, why waste words
On that? Your daughters will tell you. And they
Will boast for me more effectively than I can.
There is one thing, though, I'd like to ask –
A small detail, but rather surprising –
Which came to my notice on the way back here.
I'd value your opinion. I never think it wise
To ignore odd or inexplicable occurrences.

OEDIPUS. Well, son of Aegeus, tell me about it.
We know nothing at all of the matter here.

THESEUS. A man, so they tell me, claiming to be
A relative of yours, but not from Thebes,
Has been found seeking sanctuary at Poseidon's altar,
Where I was praying myself, before I was called here.

OEDIPUS. Where does he come from? What favour does he ask?

THESEUS. Only one thing they've told me. He asks, apparently,
To speak with you: a brief word. Nothing more.

OEDIPUS. About what? Sanctuary is a serious business.

THESEUS. Simply to speak with you, they say.
  Then go back the same way he came unharmed.

OEDIPUS. Who would go to such lengths to speak to me?

THESEUS. Some relative of yours who comes from Argos,
  Or thereabouts, and needs a favour.

OEDIPUS. Not another word my friend!

THESEUS.   What's the matter?

OEDIPUS. Don't ask me.

THESEUS.   Don't ask you what? Tell me!

OEDIPUS. Argos gave the game away. I know who it is!

THESEUS. What has he done to provoke such antipathy?

OEDIPUS. He is my son, and I hate him! More than any other man
  The very sound of his voice would be loathsome to me.

THESEUS. But surely you can give him a hearing? You need not
  Do what he asks. What's so painful in that?

OEDIPUS. Sir. I am his father, but the mere sound of his voice
  Stirs up feelings of hatred. Don't force me to hear him.

THESEUS. But the man is praying. There are questions of religious
  Custom involved. I think you must hear him.

ANTIGONE. Father, listen. I know I'm young
  To give you advice. But let the king
  Have his way, and satisfy his conscience
  By giving the gods their due. For our sakes
  Too, as his sisters – let our brother come.
  There's no need to be afraid of him.
  What can he say that can injure you,
  Or weaken your resolve? There can be no harm
  In merely hearing him, surely? In fact,
  Questionable motives, if he has any,
  Will be quite obvious in what he says.
  He is your son, and whatever wrongs
  He has done you, however unfilial
  He may have been, it can hardly be right
  For you, as his father, to pay him back
  By treating him equally badly. Let him speak to you
  At least. Other fathers have ungrateful sons,
  And uncontrollable tempers. But most men accept

The good advice of friends and family.
Forget today. Remember the past,
Your own father and mother, your undeserved punishment,
And the resentment you felt towards them. Anger
Uncontrolled is evil in itself and leads
To terrible consequences. How can you forget that?
Every day your blinded eyes remind you.
Say yes, Father, to please us.
We shouldn't have to beg for him,
When what we ask, and he asks, is just.
You've been well treated here. Treat him
With similar consideration at least.

OEDIPUS. Yes, yes, you must have your way. However painful
The outcome for me. I can refuse you nothing.
But if he must come, Theseus, my friend,
Be sure I am well guarded. Don't leave me in his power.

THESEUS. One word is enough sir. I need not boast
About it, but you need have no fear.
While I'm safe in the gods' hands, you're safe in mine.

*Exit Theseus, with some of his Soldiers, leaving the rest to guard
Oedipus.*

CHORUS. A man who is desperate for long life
And will willingly prolong his grief
For more than a man's span of years
Is a fool to his last breath.
For what does old age bring
But biting pains and bitter tears
And pleasures few, and decreasing?
Later or sooner the same death,
Not with marriage songs, but funeral weeping,
Delivers us all to the earth.

Not to be born is best:
Or being born, to waste
No time in lingering, but return to the dark,
Our beginning and end. Youth soon passes
Like a carnival of frivolity: horror and pain
Follow behind, realities bleak

And inescapable, greed, envy, rapine
Civil war and carnage. Old age only increases
The torment. Short of friends and breath, you stagger on
Towards the last crisis.

And I know I am not unique. Everyone
In the end must learn to suffer alone,
As Oedipus does, our long-persecuted guest.
Like an exposed rock in a savage waste
Of northern seas, pounded by the waves,
Sucked and torn by remorseless tides,
He endures elemental forces of destruction,
Blasting him like the four winds, from the blood-red west
And the silver dawn, from where the sun rides
Like a burning ship in mid heaven, and the frozen midnight
                                                        ocean.

ANTIGONE. Father, our visitor is here, the stranger
    We spoke of. He's coming quite alone.
    And his eyes seem to be full of tears.
OEDIPUS. And who is he?
ANTIGONE.   We made a good guess,
    It is Polynices. And now he's here.
    Enter Polynices, Oedipus' elder son. There is a pause as he looks at
    his sisters and at his father.
POLYNICES. Sisters. My dear sisters . . . I don't know
    Where to begin . . . who to pity more,
    Myself, or my father – an old man
    Alone in a foreign country, with only
    You two to look after him. Filthy old clothes,
    All worn out and squalid, making him look
    Even worse than a beggar – a down-and-out.
    White hair, blowing across his forehead,
    Tangled and knotted with the wind; and stone blind.
    That dirty little bag, I suppose
    Carries what scraps he gets to eat.
    And it's all my fault. I see it now –
    Late in the day, admittedly.

And it's unforgivable of me, of course.
I don't need anyone else to tell me
That I have treated you abominably.
I know I have. I accuse myself.
You need call no witnesses. I'm guilty,
The verdict's given, the sentence passed. –
But mercy is the companion of the gods,
And sits in counsel with them. I hope
In your heart too there's room, Father,
For some compassion. What's past is past,
The wrongs done then can be put right now,
And certainly won't be made any worse . . .
Why won't you speak to me? Say something Father,
Don't turn me away without a word.
Will you send me back the way I came
With nothing but contempt and silence?
Without even telling me why you're angry?
Antigone, Ismene, you're his daughters,
My sisters. Persuade him to say something
At least. Not just this surly affectation
Of dumbness. I have prayed at the god's altar
With all due reverence and ceremony.
To ignore my prayer is an insult. He can't
Send me away without even speaking!

He pauses. Oedipus turns away and says nothing. Antigone goes to Polynices and speaks quietly to him.

ANTIGONE. My poor brother . . . Tell him yourself what you've come
for.

Keep talking. Something you say might please him,
Or provoke anger or pity; some response, not this silence.

POLYNICES (*To Antigone*). I take that point, and I'll tell him
everything.

Aloud, so all can hear.

But first I appeal to the god Poseidon,
At whose altar I was praying. The king of this country
Found me there and brought me here to speak with you,
And promised safe conduct for my departure:
A promise which I hope you, gentlemen,

And my sisters, and my father, will see fully honoured.
Well, Father, let me tell you why
I have come here. . . . I have been banished,
Driven out from the city of my birth,
Because I asserted my undoubted right,
As your elder son, to your sovereignty and throne.
My younger brother, Eteocles,
Was behind my banishment. There was no debate,
Not even any fighting. He seized power
Somehow, by persuading the people to support him.
He made good propaganda with the curse on your name,
Infecting me with the same disease.
I've spoken to soothsayers and they all say the same.
So I went down into Dorian territory,
To the city of Argos. There, I married
The daughter of Adrastus, and made good friends
With some of the best-known military men
In the Peloponnese. I planned an alliance
With them, a treaty with seven signatories
For a seven-pronged attack on Thebes.
Eteocles had taken what was mine by right,
And I promised myself to take it back
Or die honourably in the attempt.
So why am I here? I'll tell you. I've come
To ask a favour, for myself,
And on behalf of my allies, seven generals,
With seven private armies, who now,
At this moment, are making dispositions
With their troops across the whole plain of Thebes.
The most famous of these soldiers, Amphiaraus,
Is a brilliant swordsman, with a reputation
For predicting the outcome of a campaign
With great accuracy. Tydeus, the son
Of Oeneus, comes from Aetolia,
And the third man, Eteoclus, was born in Argos.
Hippomedon, our fourth general,
Represents his father, Talaos,
And the fifth commander, Capaneus,

110

Is a hard man, who promises to take out Thebes
Completely, and leave it a pile of ashes.
The sixth man, Parthenopaeus,
Was born in Arcadia, the son of Atalanta,
Who was a high-spirited woman, and ferociously chaste
In her youth, before she married late,
And he was born. I make up the number,
Your son in name, if not in affection –
The bastard son of an unjust destiny
I think myself more often – and I
Am the leader of the expedition
Of the bravest men of Argos against Thebes.
I speak for all of them, in coming to ask you
For the sake of your daughters, and for your own sake,
To put an end to your anger against me,
And support us, as we take the field
To punish my brother, who has seized the power
And position that are mine by right.
The oracles, if they can be trusted,
All say the same thing: the ones
Who have *you* on their side will win this battle.
Listen Father . . . listen . . . you love Thebes,
You remember those fountains, and the local gods
We were brought up with . . . Father, listen,
We're both in the same boat, both
Exiles and outcasts, both begging,
When it comes to the point, forced to crawl
Merely for the bread to live on: while he,
My brother, with no right to the throne,
Lives like an Emperor, and laughs at us both!
I can't bear to think of it! . . . But I'll show him.
With your help, I'll whip him out
Like a stinking dog, re-instate you
In the comfort you deserve, and finally,
When I've finished him off, establish myself
In the place that belongs to me. Your support
Will make my victory inevitable.
Without it, I don't see how I can survive.

CHORUS. Oedipus, you must answer him for the king's sake.
  He can't be dismissed without some reasonable reply.
OEDIPUS. Yes, gentlemen. What Theseus thinks
  Matters to me. If he hadn't sent him
  And asked me to speak to him, he would never
  Have heard one word from my lips. I shall grant
  His request, by giving him the sort of answer
  He deserves, in words he'll never forget
  Nor remember with any pleasure. You!
  You're contemptible! When you were in power,
  With that same sovereignty that your brother has seized
  Firmly in your hands, you kicked me out.
  Me! Your own father! You exiled me,
  Made me a stateless refugee,
  Forced me to wear these worn-out rags,
  This very same filthy coat you weep
  Such crocodile tears over now: being yourself
  In a predicament not unlike mine.
  Tears mean nothing, what are tears,
  They're a sentimental indulgence. This
  Must be borne, and will be borne
  By me, until my death. And you,
  As far as I'm concerned, are nothing
  More than my murderer! You threw me out,
  Opened up whole new worlds of pain
  For me, turned me into a beggar,
  Dependent on other men's charity
  Merely to stay alive. I would have died
  Too, if I hadn't had daughters, as well
  As sons. My sons cared nothing for me.
  These girls kept me alive, they
  Looked after me, they are my sons,
  Doing everything, and more, that men could do!
  And you two, you and your brother,
  You two are bastards, if ever men were,
  No sons of mine! There are eyes
  In heaven, looking down on you, seeing
  How you behave — not yet as severe

As they will be, when they see your armies marching
On Thebes! You will never take that city.
You'll die there, you and your brother,
In the same battle: your blood and his
Together staining – fouling – the earth!
I've cursed the two of you before now,
And now I call upon that curse
To fight on my side, and to teach you
The respect due to a father, and why
My blindness is not a fit subject
For your insults, degenerate as you are,
Making light of what you've done! These girls, you see
Have acted rather differently. You talk of 'favours'
And 'righteous claims'. To hell with them too!
If there is any justice, any moral laws
Instituted by Zeus, and like him eternal,
Then you're damned for sure, you and all your projects!
And now, get out, get right away
From here, I disown you, scum, no father
For you here, or anywhere! Just this curse,
My malediction echoing in your ears
For ever! You will never defeat
Your own people. You will die. Your brother will kill you
And you will kill him – the one who banished you
As you banished me – in a single moment
Of fraternal slaughter! My curse is upon you!
And I call on the gods of the dead to take both of you
To your true home in the most unrelieved darkness
Of the bottomless pit of Hell: and Ares,
The god of blood, who provoked this hatred
Between brothers, and the ferocious goddesses
On whose sacred ground we stand! Get out,
And shout it aloud on every street corner
In Thebes, and tell your famous friends
Oedipus' testament, the inheritance
He has divided between his loving sons!

CHORUS. I was suspicious of you, Polynices, and your motives
From the moment you got here. Now make yourself scarce!

POLYNICES. And is that all? After such a long journey,
So many high hopes, and friends who trust me?
Nothing. Less than nothing. We marched from Argos
Full of optimism. You reward us with curses.
I can't tell my friends that, can I,
Or turn back now. I must advance
Towards whatever the outcome is,
And keep my mouth shut. Well, sister,
You heard his curses. If they come true,
And if you manage to get back to Thebes,
For God's sake remember I'm your brother.
See that I'm properly buried, decently,
With the proper ceremonies. Everyone will praise you
For looking after him in exile.
But how much more famous you'll be for caring
For me too when I'm helpless – after I'm dead.

ANTIGONE. Polynices, you must do one thing for me. Listen!

POLYNICES. My sweet little Antigone, what one thing is that?

ANTIGONE. Turn back your army, back to Argos, now.
Stop the war! Don't destroy yourself and Thebes!

POLYNICES. That isn't possible! How could I ever
Lead an army again, if they see me flinch now?

ANTIGONE. Baby brother, why should you ever want to lead it?
What's the point of destroying your own city?

POLYNICES. The alternative is permanent exile,
Acquiescence in dishonour, and a younger brother's contempt.

ANTIGONE. But he forecasts death for both of you!
You're doing your best to make those prophecies come true!

POLYNICES. Well. That will please him. I can't turn back now.

ANTIGONE. Dear heavens! But your men will never follow.
Not when they hear the prophecy!

POLYNICES. But they won't hear it. I won't tell them. A good general
Is always optimistic. He keeps bad news to himself.

ANTIGONE. My love, will you go on as if nothing had happened?

POLYNICES. Yes. I'll go on. Don't try to stop me.
The way ahead is reasonably clear.
It's dark, and there are terrifying prospects
And ghastly images lurking in the shadows:

My father's curse, and the promise of death.
But I have no choice. Your road, sisters,
Will be better lit. The gods, I hope,
Will be kinder to you, particularly
If you carry out my last request
After I am dead: a decent burial.
For the present, there is nothing you can do,
So let me go, and say goodbye for ever.
Look into my eyes: you're seeing them
For the last time alive.

ANTIGONE.   God, brother, my brother . . . !

POLYNICES. Don't cry.

ANTIGONE.   How can you tell me not to cry?
You're going to your death. It's certain! You know it!

POLYNICES. If it's certain, I must endure it.

ANTIGONE.   For God's sake, listen!

POLYNICES. I can't listen! So be quiet!

ANTIGONE.   I can't bear it, how can I?
Knowing you won't come back.

POLYNICES.   Knowing
Is the prerogative of gods, not men.
Who knows anything? Good luck to you both.
And may those who control our destinies
Give you some chance in life. You're innocent,
And that much is the least you deserve.
Exit Polynices.

CHORUS. More suffering, more pain
From the blind man's anger:
That, or the unseen power
Of Fate, which is always a mystery,
And the gods' wishes, never in vain.
Time is the eye of mortality,
Watching some men rise, and some go under
On the wheel of destiny.
Thunder.

CHORUS. Zeus is speaking! Listen to the thunder!

OEDIPUS. Antigone, Ismene, send a messenger

For Theseus, my friend. I need him now!

ANTIGONE. Why do you need him? What's happening father?

OEDIPUS. The thunder is the voice of Zeus speaking
In the hour of my death. There isn't much time!
Louder thunder.

CHORUS. More thunder, louder, nearer!
Will the lightning strike here?
My hair's on end with fear,
My skin's goosepimples!
Lightning.

CHORUS.   And now the lightning!
Could the message be any plainer?
The Thunder God speaks, and brandishes his frightening
Firebrands! Gods only appear
Like this when something tremendous is happening.
Louder thunder.

CHORUS. Save us, Zeus, from these terrors of the air!

OEDIPUS. Daughters, this is the end of my life,
As the oracles promised! No avoiding it now!

ANTIGONE. How can you tell? Is the thunder a sign?

OEDIPUS. I know, and it is. Fetch the king, quickly!
Get him here, there isn't a moment to lose.
Loud thunder.

CHORUS. Again, thunder, like the heavens breaking,
Shatters the bowl of the sky!
Gods, as your thunderbolts fly
In the darkness, if by pitying
This old man, we share in his guilt, take pity
On us too, Lord Zeus, spare us your terrible lightning!
Thunder, lightning.

OEDIPUS. Where is the prince? Is he coming yet?
He must get here while I'm still conscious.

ANTIGONE. Is there something important you have to tell him?

OEDIPUS. I promised a blessing for him and his country
In return for kindness. I must make it good!

CHORUS. Even, son of Athens, if you stand in prayer

At Poseidon's secluded sanctuary,
Don't linger! The stranger will bless you and your city,
His blessing for your kindness, as he stands here
On the threshold of eternity!
Thunder.

CHORUS. Theseus, come quickly! His last moment is near!
There is more thunder, as Theseus enters: it rumbles away into the distance.

THESEUS. For the second time I hear desperate shouting,
Both from my own people and our foreign guest
Calling me back. Is it this terrible storm,
The sky on fire with lightning, all the weaponry
Of the heavens in action? All men are nervous
To see the gods' power so nakedly demonstrated.

OEDIPUS. I needed you Prince, and now you are here
To take the good luck the gods have given you.

THESEUS. What's happening, son of Laius, something new and
strange?

OEDIPUS. My time has come. I made a promise
To you, and your city: and now I must fulfil it.

THESEUS. No man can foretell his death. How do you know?

OEDIPUS. The gods themselves forewarned me, by signs
And omens which they taught me to recognise.

THESEUS. What signs? Do you recognise them now?

OEDIPUS. These repeated thunderclaps and flashes of lightning
The whole arsenal of the Immortals exploding over my head!

THESEUS. I've good reason to believe you. You make prophecies
And the events follow. What must I do?

OEDIPUS. What I am about to reveal to you,
Son of Aegeus, is treasure beyond price,
Knowledge your city must keep secret,
And living, till the end of time.
In a moment I shall lead you,
Myself, and without anyone to guide me,
To the place where my life will come to an end.
That place must remain your secret. No one
Must ever be told where it is,
Nor even what neighbourhood.

And that secret will give your city strength
Greater than regiments of Athenian infantry
Or powerful allies. What will happen
Is a sacred mystery, unspeakable,
And never to be spoken of. You will understand
When you reach the place, alone, and see it.
I can tell no other man of Athens,
Nor these people, nor any other living being,
Not even my own children, though
I love them with all my heart. You
Alone are the man to learn the secret,
And you must keep it to yourself, and bequeath it
At the moment of your own death, to your heir,
And so, from heir to heir, for ever.
This secret power will give you an advantage
Over the people of Thebes, that nation
Sprung from the harvest of the Dragon's teeth,
For all time. Disputes arise
Between neighbouring states, however justly
They are ruled, and men go to war
For the sake of insult or interest,
And even the most frivolous of motives. The gods
Are always watching, they see wickedness
And injustice when it occurs,
When rational men become lunatics
And mankind suffers for it. The gods repay
All such tyrannies in their own good time.
Never, Theseus, give them cause to repay
You in that manner. I need not say it,
I know, you understand these things as well
As I do, and could teach me . . .
And now, I think, it is time to go.
Some instinct tells me the way, as though
A god's hand were in mine, and leading me.
My two girls, follow, follow me!
You have guided my footsteps for so long,
Now it is my turn. No, don't touch me.
I shall find my own way, quite unaided

To my mysterious grave, the earth of Athens
That will hide my bones like a shroud for ever.
Ah, yes. This way. This way.
The Angel of Death is here, Hermes
Himself, I feel his chilly finger.
And I can see Persephone, in a black veil
Beckoning me into her silent kingdom.
Sun, daylight which has been no light
To me, for years, I saw you once,
I remember how good you were. And now
I can still feel you, your life-giving warmth
On my face, here, for the last time.
Now I go down with faltering steps
To the last darkness, the blindness of eternity.
Theseus, you have been my best friend.
My blessing on you, your land, and your people.
Be famous, and prosper. And in your prosperity,
Remember me, among the dead.
*Oedipus leads Theseus, Antigone, Ismene and Attendants into the
sacred grove. The Chorus watches in silence, until the procession is
out of sight.*

CHORUS. Can you hear our prayers in your dark country,
Queen invisible to human eyes,
And Hades, master of the dead?
Let there be no pain as the old man dies,
Nor any tears as he goes to his bed
In the earth, and enters eternity.
Let him take his place on the dark plain
Walking the endless fields of night.
Unjust persecution, pain
And suffering were his destiny.
Justice, at the end, is his right.

Take pity on him, powers of darkness,
And you, many-headed dog of Hell
Slobbering in your chains at the gate
That's always open, snarling at all
Who pass to their last everlasting state:

Let him pass in peace and quietness
Into the grey fields of silence.
Born of earth and horror, master of the deep,
Lead him down in reverence,
Muzzle the beast, and bless
His passing with eternal sleep.

There is a pause: then the Messenger appears at the entrance to the sacred grove.

MESSENGER. People of Colonus, in the plainest words
    Oedipus is dead. But it isn't possible
    To do any justice to what happened in there
    As briefly as that. I must tell the whole story.

CHORUS. He's dead at last then, that long-suffering man?

MESSENGER. Be quite sure about that. He's crossed over into death.

CHORUS. Did he suffer much? Or did a god come for him?

MESSENGER. It was strange, and marvellous.
    You all saw how he left us, moving with difficulty
    In his age, but leading the way himself
    Instead of being guided by one of his friends.
    He walked as far as that great crack
    In the earth, the bottomless cave
    Where the rocks seem like a stairway of bronze
    Leading down into the dark. Nearby
    There's a natural basin of rock, at a place
    Where many paths meet, where the celebrated pact
    Between Theseus and Peirithous
    To raid the underworld and kidnap Persephone
    Is commemorated: everything there
    Is sacred, the great chasm itself, the basin,
    The rock of Thoricus, the hollow pear tree
    And the ancient stone tomb. Surrounded
    By these mysteries, he sat down, and quietly removed
    All his filthy and worn-out clothes.
    Then he spoke to his daughters, and asked them
    To fetch some pure running water
    From a stream somewhere, so that he could wash himself
    And pour an offering to the spirits of the dead.
    Just nearby, there's a small hill

Sacred to Demeter, goddess of growing things,
Which is always fresh and well watered.
So they did as he asked, and soon brought the water,
And washed him with it, and dressed him
Reverently, and with all the ritual
Customary when a man is dying.
When he was satisfied that everything was done
As it should be – he had his way in everything,
They attended to his slightest whim –
There was a low rumbling, like thunder
From the bowels of the earth. The girls were frightened,
And they cried, and fell on their knees, trembling,
And with their arms clasped round *his* knees.
And they went on like that for some time,
Crying out loud, and hugging themselves
And swaying from side to side, as if
They were heartbroken. And when he heard them,
And saw how upset they were, he lifted them up,
And put his arms round them, and soothed them,
And said, 'My dear daughters, today
I must leave you, as all fathers must leave
Their children. Today is the end of me,
My life is over: and your long penance
Is over too, the never-ending task
Of looking after me, which you performed
Without a complaint, although I know
How irksome and tiring it was. One word,
Though, makes every burden lighter
To bear, and that word is love.
I have loved you as no man has ever
Loved his children. You must carry on living
Your own lives, without me now,
And you must live them to the full.'
So that's how it was. They all cried,
And they all embraced each other, clinging
So hard, it seemed they could never be parted:
But eventually they were, the crying stopped,
And there was silence. And suddenly,

There was an unearthly voice, a stomach-turning sound,
So that you could see everyone trembling,
And everyone's hair was standing on end.
This voice, which was low and deep,
And must have been the voice of a god,
Kept repeating, like a terrifying whisper,
'Oedipus, Oedipus, your life is over,
To the very hour, and now you linger
Too long, too long. . . .'
And when Oedipus heard this unearthly summons,
He asked for Theseus to come close to him,
And when Theseus was by his side, he said,
'My good friend, listen, I want you to promise –
And give your right hand on it, and my two daughters,
You give him yours – that you'll never leave them
To their own devices, and the world's mercy,
But do whatever seems best for them
In the uncertain circumstances of the future.'
And Theseus, like the generous man he is,
Held back his tears, and gave his oath
To do everything the old man had asked.
When this promise had been given, Oedipus
Groped for his girls, with his blind hands,
And when he had got them, he held them tight
And said, 'Now, my girls, you must be brave,
As you were born to be. You must go away now,
And make no attempt to see things
Which are mysteries, and forbidden to you.
Go quickly now. Theseus alone must stay
To see what happens.' We all heard that,
And we were all in tears at his words.
Then his daughters turned from him, and we turned with them,
And followed them away, leaving him there.
But after a few moments, as we were walking,
We looked round, and – I can hardly believe it –
The man was gone – he'd disappeared
From the face of the earth. The king was there,
Standing on his own, and holding his hand

In front of his eyes, as if he had seen
Something appalling, which no living man
Could bear to see. And then, formally,
He made short prayers to earth and to heaven,
Stooping, and raising his hand – and that
Was the end of it. How Oedipus died,
And by what strange rites of passage
He passed from this world into the dark
No man living can say, except Theseus.
There was no lightning from heaven struck him,
And no tidal wave swept him out to sea:
But he was taken for sure. Perhaps
Some kindly ghost from the dark regions
Came to show him the way. Or the earth
Silently opened, and silently took him
With love, like a child to its bosom.
One thing is certain. There were no tears,
No cries of pain, or sound of suffering
Of any kind. A stranger and more wonderful
Death than any man has experienced before.
Some of you won't believe me, I know.
You'll say this is fantasy, or a bad dream
In broad daylight, straining all credibility.
If that's what you think, that's your privilege.
I saw what I saw. There's nothing more I can say.

CHORUS. But where are the girls, and the others who were with you?

MESSENGER. They were following me, not far behind.
   Yes, I can hear them crying. They're here.
   Enter Antigone and Ismene from the grove.

ANTIGONE. Howl then! Weep! Time for tears
   For us two. Nothing good
   Can ever happen to Oedipus' daughters,
   Cursed in our corrupted blood!
   We travelled and suffered with him, so many years
   On his journey, to this unforgettable ending
   Mysterious beyond all human understanding.

CHORUS. Tell us what happened.

ANTIGONE.   We can only guess.

CHORUS. He's dead.

ANTIGONE.   As most men would wish to die:
    Not cut down in the pain and stress
    Of battle, or drowned at sea:
    But lifted by invisible hands
    To the sightless fields of eternity.
    And a night sufficiently deathlike descends
    On our eyes too, forced to beg our bread
    From strangers, without friends,
    In alien lands across dangerous seas. What bed
    Or board for us, among the outcast and rejected?

ISMENE. None that I can see. Let the god of the dead
    Lead us down with our long-suffering father to rest.
    Why live for a life of pain, among the persecuted?

CHORUS. What the gods decree must be endured by the best
    Of daughters. When grief blazes up like a firebrand
    It leaves only ashes. Your sufferings are not the worst.

ANTIGONE. All the pain I endured! How strange to discover
    That I long for those days of agony to return!
    Any anguish was bearable, while I held my father
    In my arms. I would welcome such agony again.
    But now the dark cloak of death for ever
    Enfolds him with its mantle of earth. My love survives
    Even there, in that darkness. Among the dead, it lives!

CHORUS. So now it is ended.

ANTIGONE.   And his hopes are fulfilled.

CHORUS. Fulfilled? How can that be?

ANTIGONE.   He wanted to die
    In a foreign land, among strangers. He is satisfied
    Now. In this shaded earth let him lie
    At peace. He has left grief behind
    With us, who mourn his tragic destiny.
    My dear, dead Father, my eyes are blind
    With tears, my voice choked with singing
    Your bitter threnody, and that song will never end.
    You died as you wished to die, among strangers, leaving
    Me alone, to mourn your mysterious passing.

ISMENE. A bleak future for us. Never-ending
   Misery. He had daughters to ease his pain.
   Fatherless, unprotected, who will care for our suffering?
CHORUS. The gods blessed his dying. Now he is gone,
   And you must make an end of weeping.
   Pain is the inheritance of every man.

ANTIGONE. We must go back there.
ISMENE.   Go back? Why?
ANTIGONE. I have to. I must!
ISMENE.   Why must you? Tell me.
ANTIGONE. To see that yard of earth, his sanctuary.
ISMENE. His grave?
ANTIGONE.   Our father's . . . the word chokes me!
ISMENE. You can't! It's forbidden for anyone to go
   To that holy place!
ANTIGONE.   Don't be angry with me.
ISMENE. But you must understand . . .
ANTIGONE.   Why must I? What now?
ISMENE. There is no grave: and he sleeps the sounder.
ANTIGONE. Take me to the place! And I'll die there too!
ISMENE. And God help me then! Bereaved twice over,
   Homeless and unloved! What will I do,
   Condemned to the misery of solitude for ever?

CHORUS. You need not be frightened.
ANTIGONE.   We're exiles, outcast.
CHORUS. You came to no harm today.
ANTIGONE.   That's true.
CHORUS. And you're quite safe here, for a time, at least.
ANTIGONE. I know that.
CHORUS.   Then tell us what's troubling you?
ANTIGONE. That this exile may be permanent. That I will never
   Go home to Thebes.
CHORUS.   Don't try to go!
ANTIGONE. From one trouble to the next.
CHORUS.   No one's sufferings have been greate~
ANTIGONE. And is this the worst? No, the worst is to come.

CHORUS. On your sea of troubles, the storm blows fiercer.

ANTIGONE. We were born to this.

CHORUS. Born to suffer.

ANTIGONE. Which way, Zeus, shall we go now? Are you dumb
   To our pleading? No word, no ray of hope for us, ever?
   Is there any road that leads to home?
   Enter Theseus from the grove.

THESEUS. Antigone, Ismene, dry your tears.
   Death came gently, and we, who are alive
   Share the blessing which the Dark Lords
   Of the Underworld granted to him.
   Over-indulgence in grief, when miraculous
   Favours have been granted, will make them angry.

ANTIGONE. Son of Aegeus, we must ask a favour.

THESEUS. Ask it then. You are my children now.

ANTIGONE. With our own eyes, we must see the place
   Where our father lies.

THESEUS. That is forbidden.

ANTIGONE. Why? You are the king. Your word is law.

THESEUS. His last request, dear daughters, was that no mortal
   Should ever approach the place, nor any hymns
   Nor sacred ceremonies be sung there
   Above the hidden patch of earth
   Which covers him, and ensures his rest.
   He laid that responsibility upon me,
   Promising good fortune to this city
   If I carried it out, in spirit, and to the letter.
   I swore I would do it, and there were gods
   Listening, who take note of men's promises.

ANTIGONE. Then I won't ask again. It is enough
   If he wished it so. But may I ask
   For you to conduct us back in safety
   To our ancient city of Thebes. A war
   Is brewing between our brothers, which I
   Must prevent, if I can, before a river
   Of blood flows, and drowns both of them together.

THESEUS. Certainly I will. I'll do anything
   I can to help you, for your sake,

And for my new, and newly-lost friend,
To please him, in his secret grave.
Exit Theseus with his Attendants and Antigone and Ismene.
CHORUS. Now sorrow has run its course
And tears must end.
These events have come to a just close
On holy ground.
The gods are eternal, and the life of man
A speck of dust on a great plain.
Exit the Chorus.

ANTIGONE

Characters

ANTIGONE ⎫
ISMENE ⎬ the daughters of Oedipus

CREON, King of Thebes

HAEMON, his son

TEIRESIAS, a prophet, blind

A SOLDIER

A MESSENGER

EURYDICE, wife of Creon

CHORUS of Senators of Thebes

GUARDS

SOLDIERS

ATTENDANTS

TEIRESIAS' BOY

This translation was commissioned by BBC Television and first produced in the autumn of 1986, with the following cast:

ANTIGONE	Juliet Stevenson
ISMENE	Gwen Taylor
CREON	John Shrapnel
HAEMON	Mike Gwilym
TEIRESIAS	John Gielgud
SOLDIER	Tony Selby
MESSENGER	Bernard Hill
EURYDICE	Rosalie Crutchley
CHORUS	Patrick Barr, Paul Daneman, Donald Eccles, Robert Eddison, Patrick Godfrey, Ewan Hooper, Peter Jeffrey, Noel Johnson, Robert Lang, John Ringham, Frederick Treves, John Woodnutt
TEIRESIAS' BOY	Paul Russell
GUARDS	Chris Andrews, Steve Ausden, Leon Ferguson, Stephen Epressieux, Steve Ismay, Paul LeFevre, David Rogue, Steve Roxton
ATTENDANTS TO EURYDICE	Jeannie Downs, Vanessa Linstone
ATTENDANTS	Michael Eriera, David Fieldsend, William Franklyn-Pool, Paul Holmes, Jack Lonsdale, Bernard Losh, Graeme Sneddon

Directed by	Don Taylor
Produced by	Louis Marks
Designed by	David Myerscough-Jones
Music by	Derek Bourgeois
Costumes by	June Hudson

The scene is set outside the royal palace of Thebes.[1]
*Enter Antigone and Ismene. They are both nervous and troubled.
Antigone looks round to be sure they cannot be overheard before
speaking.*

ANTIGONE. Ismene listen. The same blood
  Flows in both our veins, doesn't it, my sister,
  The blood of Oedipus. And suffering,
  Which was his destiny, is our punishment too,
  The sentence passed on all his children.
  Physical pain, contempt, insults,
  Every kind of dishonour: we've seen them all,
  And endured them all, the two of us.
  But there's more to come. Now, today . . .
  Have you heard it, this new proclamation,
  Which the king has made to the whole city?
  Have you heard how those nearest to us
  Are to be treated, with the contempt
  We reserve for traitors? People we love!
ISMENE. No one has told me anything, Antigone,
  I have heard nothing, neither good nor bad
  About anyone we love – not since the battle
  I mean, and the terrible news
  That both our brothers were dead: one day,
  One battle, and fratricide twice over,
  Each brother cutting down his own flesh . . .
  But the army from Argos retreated last night,
  I have heard that. Nothing else
  To cheer me up, or depress me further.
ANTIGONE. I thought you hadn't. That's why I asked you

---

[1] The first production of this translation was set inside the royal palace
as though in a council chamber or senate house. Translation and production
were conceived together so Antigone's second speech reads '. . .That's
why I asked you/To meet me *here*' rather than the literal *'outside the
palace'*.

To meet me here, where I can tell you everything
Without any risk of being overheard.

ISMENE. What is it then? More terrible news?
Something black and frightening, I can see that.

ANTIGONE. Well, what do you think, Ismene? Perhaps
You can guess. We have two brothers,
Both of them dead. And Creon has decreed
That a decent burial shall be given to one,
But not to the other. Eteocles, apparently,
Has already been buried, with full military honours,
And all the formalities due to the dead
Meticulously observed. So that *his* rest
In the underworld among the heroes is assured.
But Polynices, who died in agony
Just as certainly as his brother did,
Is not to be buried at all. The decree
Makes that quite plain. *He* is to be left
Lying where he fell, with no tears,
And no ceremonies of mourning, to stink
In the open: till the kites and vultures
Catch the scent, and tear him to pieces
And pick him to the bone. Left unburied
There is no rest for him in the underworld,
No more than here. What a great king
Our Creon is, eh Sister?
It's against us, you realise, and against me
In particular that he has published this decree.
And he'll soon be here himself, to make it public
To the senators, and anyone who may not have heard it.
He isn't bluffing. He means to act
To make it stick. The punishment
For anyone who disobeys the order
Is public stoning to death. So that's the news,
And you know it now. The time has come
For you too to stand up and be counted
With me: and to show whether you are worthy
Of the honour of being Oedipus' daughter.

ISMENE. Wait a minute Antigone, don't be so headstrong!

If all this is as you say it is,
What can I do, one way or the other?

ISMENE. Just say you will help me. Commit yourself.

ISMENE. To do what? Something dangerous?

ANTIGONE. Just to give me a hand to lift the body.
It's too heavy for me to move on my own.

ISMENE. To bury him you mean? In spite of the decree?

ANTIGONE. He is my brother. And like it or not
He's yours too. I won't betray him
Now that he's dead. No one will ever
Throw that in my face.

ISMENE.   You must be mad!
Creon has publicly forbidden it.

ANTIGONE. He can't forbid me to love my brother.
He has neither the right nor the power to do that.

ISMENE. Have you forgotten what happened to our father?
Contempt and loathing from everyone,
Even from himself, that was his reward.
And blinded too, by his own hand.
And his mother-wife, as ill matched with him
As those two words are with each other,
She knotted a rope, and hanged herself.
And now our two brothers, both in one day
Caught in the same trap, claiming
Blood for blood and death for death
Each one at the expense of the other.
We are the last ones left, Sister,
And what a death is promised for us,
More terrible than any, if we break the law
By defying the king, and the power of the State.
Think for a moment Antigone, please!
We are women, that's all. Physically weaker –
And barred from any political influence.
How can we fight against the institutionalised strength
Of the male sex? They are in power,
And we have to obey them – this time
And maybe in worse situations than this.
May God forgive me, and the spirits of the dead,

I have no choice! State power
Commands, and I must do as I am told.
When you are powerless, wild gestures
And heroic refusals are reserved for madmen!

ANTIGONE. Don't say any more. I won't ask again.
In fact, if you were to offer help now,
I would refuse it. Do as you please.
I intend to bury my brother,
And if I die in the attempt, I shall die
In the knowledge that I have acted justly.
What greater satisfaction than that,
For a loving sister to embrace a loving brother
Even in the grave: and to be condemned
For the criminal act of seeing him at peace!
Our lives are short. We have too little time
To waste it on men, and the laws they make.
The approval of the dead is everlasting,
And I shall bask in it, as I lie among them.
Do as you please. Live, by all means.
The laws *you* will break are not of man's making.

ISMENE. I reverence them. But how can I defy
The unlimited power of the State? What weapons
Of mine are strong enough for that?

ANTIGONE. Fine. That's a good excuse. I'll go
And shovel the earth on my brother's body.

ISMENE. I'm frightened, Antigone. I'm frightened for you.

ANTIGONE. Don't be frightened for me. Fear for yourself.

ISMENE. For God's sake, keep it quiet. Don't tell anyone.
I'll keep our meeting secret.

ANTIGONE.   Don't you dare!
You must tell everybody, shout it in the streets.
If you keep it secret, I shall begin to hate you.

ISMENE. There's a fire burning in you Antigone,
But it makes me go cold just to hear you!

ANTIGONE. I'm not doing it to please you. It's for him.

ISMENE. This obsession will destroy you! You're certain to fail!

ANTIGONE. I shall fail when I have failed. Not before.

ISMENE. But you know it's hopeless. Why begin

When you know you can't possibly succeed!
ANTIGONE. Be quiet, before I begin to despise you
  For talking so feebly! *He* will despise you
  Too, and justly. You can go now. Go!
  If I'm mad, you can leave me here with my madness
  Which will doubtless destroy me soon enough.
  Death is the worst thing that can happen,
  And some deaths are more honourable than others.
ISMENE. If you've made your mind up. . . Antigone, it's

                                   madness. . .

  Remember, I love you. . . whatever happens. . .
  Exit Antigone and Ismene in opposite directions.
  Enter the Chorus of the Senators of Thebes.
CHORUS. The life-giving sun has never shone
  More brightly on the seven gates of Thebes
  Than he shines this morning:
  Never a more glorious dawning
  Than this sunrise over Dirce's river,
  When the army of the foreign invader
  At first light
  Made its panic-stricken flight,
  And all its white shields and its bright weapons were gone.
  Like a snowy eagle from the mountain crest it came
  Shrieking down on our city,
  The army of Argos, with a spurious treaty
  To enforce Polynices' claim,
  All its horsehair plumes nodding together
  And a grinding of brass and a creaking of leather.

  By our seven shuttered gates it waited,
  Eyes glittering in dark helmets,
  Swords drawn, spears couching.
  But before the killing and burning,
  The metallic taste of blood
  And crashing stonework and blazing wood,
  They turned and fled, the music of death
  In their ears, at their backs, the dragon's breath.
  Zeus had seen them, he who hates inflated

Pride, and the empty boast
Of the windbag, he heard their singing
As if the victory were theirs for the taking,
And he brought down his thunder on their glittering host,
Struck them with lightning, and sent them flying,
Scorched them, and burned them, and left them dying.

Down like a rock from the mountain crest
He came thundering to earth, the flame
Dashed from his hand,
The son of Thebes whose best hope of fame
Was to conquer his native land
And who failed in his quest.
For the war god gave us his word of command,
Like a battle chariot his terrible name
Ran them down where they stood, and they died in the dust.
Now, at each of our seven gates
A Theban defender waits
As seven champions bring their fame and armour to the fight:
And before the coming of night
Six have put their fame to the test,
Six have laid both fame and armour to rest
As a tribute at great Zeus' feet.
At the seventh gate two brothers meet
Sharing their blood in death as in birth,
Each striking together,
Each laying the other
Dead on the earth.

There will be victory celebrations today
In this city of charioteers,
And singing in the streets.
There will be ceremonies of thanksgiving, and grateful tears
For the end of fighting, as the enemy retreats
And the time comes for relaxation and play.
Now, as all voices are raised, and the drum beats
The ecstatic god himself will appear,
Bacchus the drunkard, to take power for one day

In the city he calls his own. Time to dance all night,
To shake the foundations, till the faint light
Of dawn flushes the windows, and the lamps fade.
Now Creon is king. He made
The most of his fortune, and the gods' choice,
The son of Menoeceus. As the people rejoice
The new king enters to take his throne,
The responsibility his alone.
But why has he called us here, to debate
In emergency session
His public proclamation
So vital to the State?
Creon enters, well-guarded by soldiers.

CREON. Senators: our country, like a ship at sea,
Has survived the hurricane. The gods, who sent it,
Have navigated us into calmer waters now.
I have chosen to summon this assembly
Because I know I can trust you. Your predecessors
Were loyal and reliable in King Laius' time,
And when King Oedipus, in his exceptional wisdom,
Restored the fortunes of this city.
When tragedy struck him, and his rule was ended,
Your loyalty to the blood royal
Was never questioned, and you supported his sons:
Till they too were brought down,
In a single day, incestuously murdered,
Each brother shedding a brother's blood.
By that same bloodright, as next of kin,
I claim the throne, and all its power
Both city and kingdom. I claim it and hold it
From today, as mine by right.
There is no certain measure of a man's quality,
The depth of his intellect and the maturity of his judgement,
Until he is put to the supreme test
By the exercise of lawful power in the State.
My own opinion is well known:
The ruler who fears the consequences
Of his actions, or who is afraid to act openly,

Or take the good advice of his senators,
Is beneath contempt. Equally contemptible
Is the man who puts the interests of his friends,
Or his relations, before his country.
There is nothing good can be said of him.
Let me make it plain, before the gods,
Whose eyes are in every council chamber,
When I see any threat to this nation,
From whatever direction, I shall make it public.
No one who is an enemy of the State
Shall ever be any friend of mine.
The State, the Fatherland, is everything
To us, the ship we all sail in.
If she sinks, we all drown,
And friendship drowns with us. That's my policy:
A policy of service to the Commonwealth.
And in pursuance of that policy,
I have issued an official State decree
Concerning the sons of Oedipus.
Eteocles, who died fighting for his country,
And with exceptional bravery, we shall bury him
With all the honours and funeral ceremonies
Customary for a man who died a hero.
The other, the outcast, the exile –
His brother Polynices, who returned here
At the head of a foreign army, to destroy
His homeland, to burn down the city
And reduce the people to a condition of slavery,
Or kill them in the streets – I have ordered
That he is to have no grave at all.
No one is to bury him, or mourn for him.
His body is to be left in the open, uncovered,
A stinking feast for the scavengers,
Dogs and crows, a sight to inspire terror.
I intend to make it quite plain
That never, under my administration,
Will people who commit crimes against the State
Reap any benefit from their actions: and at the expense

Of honest decent citizens too.
But people who serve the State, alive
Or dead, that makes no difference –
I shall honour them for their patriotism.

CHORUS. Son of Menoeceus, you are king now.
You have delivered your verdict and sentence
Upon the man who defended the city
And the man who attacked it, unambiguously.
The full power of the law is in your hands,
And it binds the dead, as well as the living.
We are all at your disposal.

CREON.   Make sure
Then, that my orders are carried out.

CHORUS. Younger men than us should implement your policies.

CREON. I don't mean that. Polynices' body
Is already under guard.

CHORUS.   What else.
Must we do? What other responsibility
Do you lay upon us?

CREON.   Not to intrigue
With dissidents, or subversive elements.

CHORUS. We are not mad sir. We know the law,
And the penalty for breaking it.

CREON. Which will be death. And be in no doubt
I shall enforce it. Because there are always men
Who can be bought, who will risk anything,
Even death, if the bribe is large enough

*Enter a Soldier in a dusty uniform, struggling with the guards, who
bring him before Creon. He is very frightened.*

SOLDIER. My Lord Creon . . . sir! If I can hardly speak
For lack of breath . . . it's not 'cos I ran . . .
I kept on stopping, as a matter of fact,
Half a dozen times, and I hung about
As much as I dared. I haven't thought about anything
So much for a long time. 'Listen, don't hurry,'
I said to myself, 'the chances are,
Poor sod, you'll cop it when you get there.'
But then I said to myself, you see,

141

'Hang about,' I said, 'or rather, don't,
Because if Creon hears this from somebody else,
You're really in trouble.' So I hurried here
As slow as I could, going round and round
In circles, in my head, as well as with my feet!
It's funny how long a mile can take you
When you're thinking what I was thinking. However
Duty called in the end, and I reckoned
It would be safer to face it out.
It may be unimportant, but I've come here,
So now I'll tell you. If I'm punished for it
The gods'll be behind it, that's for sure.
So I wouldn't have escaped it anyway.

CREON. Talk sense man. Why are you frightened?

SOLDIER. Well, first of all sir, for myself, like,
My own point of view . . . I never done it,
And I didn't see who else done it neither.
So I shouldn't be punished for it, should I.

CREON. Is there any need for all this preamble?
You take great care to dissociate yourself
From what you say: it must be bad news.

SOLDIER. It is bad news sir: and I'm so scared.
I don't know how to put it for the best.

CREON. The plainest way. And then we can have done with you.

SOLDIER. Straight out with it then. The body's buried.
Someone or other. A handful of dust,
That's all, dry dust, but properly sprinkled,
You know, religiously – and then gone –
Whoever it was.

CREON.   Do you know what you're saying?
Who has dared to disobey my orders?

SOLDIER. No way of knowing sir, we've no idea!
There had been no digging, no spade marks or nothing.
The ground's rock hard. No wheel tracks either,
From a chariot, or cart, or anything.
In fact, no clues of any kind at all,
Nothing to tell you who might have done it.
When the sentry taking the early turn

Discovered what had happened, and reported back;
We were all shattered, and scared stiff.
It was as though the body had disappeared –
Not buried in a proper grave, I don't mean,
But lightly covered with a layer of earth.
Almost as though some passing stranger
With a religious turn of mind, knowing
That being left unburied means everlasting
Anguish, and wandering without rest,
Had scattered a few handfuls. There was no tracks
Of animals either, not of dogs or anything,
Who might have gnawed at it, and covered it over
With their front legs, like they do a bone.
A real row started then, I can tell you.
We shouted at each other, and it could have been a fight,
There was no one there to stop us. Any one of us
Could have done it, we all suspected each other:
But we all denied it, and there was no evidence
To prove one man guilty rather than another.
So we all dared each other to swear
To go through fire and water, to hold
Red hot pokers in our hands, and call all the gods
As witnesses that we hadn't done it,
And didn't know anyone who had,
Or would even think of it, let alone do it.
And none of any of it got us nowhere.
Then one of the fellers had his say, and he
Scared us all shitless, I can tell you.
He said – and we knew he was dead right –
There was no way out of it, we had to do it
And take our chances – this feller said
'One of us lot must tell the King,
Because we can't just hide it, can we!'
That's what he said. And we knew he was right.
So we decided we'd have to draw lots,
And, just my luck, I drew the short straw.
So here I am. And I don't like telling it
One little bit more than you like hearing it.

The bloke who brings bad news never gets a medal.
CHORUS. My Lord Creon, this policy of yours
  Has worried me from the start. My political instinct
  Tells me that this may be some sort of warning
  Or sign, and perhaps from the gods.
CREON.   How dare you!
  Shut your mouths, all of you, before I lose my temper!
  And you, if you are a superannuated fool,
  At least don't talk like one. Is it likely,
  Remotely likely, that the gods will think twice
  Over that pile of stinking meat?
  By God, it's blasphemy even to suggest
  That they would care a damn whether he was buried
  Or not! Let alone grant him an honourable funeral
  As though he were one of their principal supporters:
  The man who came to burn down their temples,
  Plunder their treasuries, pull down their statues
  And bring destruction and contempt for their land and its
                                  laws.

  Do the gods love criminals these days?
  Oh no! They do not! But, gentlemen, there are men
  In this city, and I have noted them,
  A subversive faction, enemies of the State,
  A cell of oppositionists, call them what you will,
  Who reject the law, and my leadership!
  They meet in secret, and nod and whisper
  Their seditious talk, and they are behind this,
  Any fool can see that. Their bribery
  Has suborned my soldiers, and paid for
  This demonstration against my authority!
  Money, gentlemen, money! The virus
  That infects mankind with every sickness
  We have a name for, no greater scourge
  Than that! Money it is that pounds
  Great cities to piles of rubble, turns people
  By the millions into homeless refugees,
  Takes homeless citizens and corrupts them
  Into doing things they would be ashamed to think of

Before the fee was mentioned, until there's no crime
That can't be bought – and in the end
Brings them into the execution chamber.
Well, whoever they are, these men
Who have sold themselves, they'll find the price
Considerably higher than they thought it was!
Creon speaks to the Soldier.
You! Come here! Get this into your head!
By Zeus, my God, whose power I revere,
I swear to you, soldier, that either you will find
The man who buried Polynices' body
In defiance of my express command
And bring him here – the actual man
Who sprinkled the earth, no other will do,
Standing here, in front of me – or you, soldier,
Will die for it. And death, I promise you,
Will be the least of your punishments.
You will be made a public example –
And interrogated by the security police,
Kept standing, beaten across the feet,
The whole repertoire of special techniques
At which we excel so much – until
You confess the full range of this conspiracy,
Who paid you, how much, and for what purpose.
The choice is yours: and perhaps that indicates
Where your own best interests lie. Crimes
Against the State and its laws, you'll find,
Are very unprofitable in the end.

SOLDIER. Am I allowed to speak sir?

CREON.   No!
Why should you speak! Every word you say
Is painful to me.

SOLDIER.   Well, it can't be earache,
Can it sir, not what I said!
It must stick in your gullet. Or further down
Maybe, a sort of pain in the conscience.

CREON. Do you dare to answer me back: and make jokes
About my conscience?

SOLDIER. Me sir? No sir!
I might give you earache, I can see that.
I talk too much, always have done.
But the other pain, the heartburn, as it were,
It's the criminal causing that sir, not me.

CREON. You're not short of a quick answer either.

SOLDIER. Maybe not. But I didn't bury the body.
Not guilty to that sir.

CREON. But maybe guilty
Of selling your eyes for money, eh sentry,
Of looking the other way for cash?

SOLDIER. I think it's a shame sir, that an intelligent man
And as well educated as you are
Should miss the point so completely.

CREON. I'm not interested in your opinions!
If you fail to find this enemy of the State
And bring him here to me, you'll learn
That money, from whatever source,
Will certainly not save *your* life!
Exit Creon.

SOLDIER. Let's hope they find him, whoever he is.
But one thing I'm sure of: they won't find me.
I never thought I'd get out of here
Alive. And when I do get out,
Nothing will bring me back again.
I've had an amazing stroke of luck,
And I won't chance my arm a second time!
Exit the Soldier.

CHORUS. Is there anything more wonderful on earth,
Our marvellous planet,
Than the miracle of man!
With what arrogant ease
He rides the dangerous seas,
From the waves' towering summit
To the yawning trough beneath.
The earth mother herself, before time began,
The oldest of the ageless gods,
Learned to endure his driving plough,

Turning the earth and breaking the clods
Till by the sweat of his brow
She yielded up her fruitfulness.

The quick-witted birds are no match for him,
Neither victim nor predator
Among the beasts of the plain
Nor the seas' seething masses.
His cunning surpasses
Their instinct, his skill is the greater,
His snares never fail, and his nets teem.
The wild bull of the savage mountain
And the magnificent stag who passes
Like a king through upland and glen,
The untamed horse with his matted tresses
Uncut on his neck, all submit to man,
And the yoke and the bit – and his power increases.

He has mastered the mysteries of language:
And thought, which moves faster than the wind,
He has tamed, and made rational.
Political wisdom too, all the knowledge
Of people and States, all the practical
Arts of government he has studied and refined,
Built cities to shelter his head
Against rain and danger and cold
And ordered all things in his mind.
There is no problem he cannot resolve
By the exercise of his brains or his breath,
And the only disease he cannot salve
Or cure, is death.

In action he is subtle beyond imagination,
Limitless in his skill, and these gifts
Are both enemies and friends,
As he applies them, with equal determination,
To good or to evil ends.
All men honour, and the State uplifts

That man to the heights of glory, whose powers
Uphold the constitution, and the gods, and their laws.
His city prospers. But if he shifts
His ground, and takes the wrong path,
Despising morality, and blown up with pride,
Indulges himself and his power, at my hearth
May he never warm himself, or sit at my side.

Antigone is brought in by the Guards, the Soldier is with her, a triumphant smile on his face.

CHORUS (*Severally*). But wait! I can't believe my eyes!
  Can this be true?
  This is Antigone. I recognise
  Her as clearly as I can see you.
  Her father's destiny
  Was suffering and pain
  And on all his progeny
  Misfortunes rain.
  Child, did you openly disobey
  The new king's order
  And bury your brother?
  Do you have to manhandle her this way?

SOLDIER. We saw it! Actually burying the body,
  Caught him in the act, as they say, red handed.
  Only it's not a him, it's a her. Where's the king?

CHORUS. Just returning now: when he's most needed.

Re-enter Creon.

CREON. What's all the noise? By the look of things
  I'm here not a moment too soon.

He sees Antigone and the Guards

                            What has happened?

SOLDIER. Lord Creon, I reckon it's always unwise
  To swear oaths and make promises,
  Even to yourself. Second thoughts,
  Nine times out of ten, will have their say
  And end up by calling you a liar.
  It's no time at all since I promised myself
  I wouldn't be seen dead here again:
  You were that angry with me the last time,

A right mouthful you gave me, more than enough
Thanks very much. But you can't beat
A real turn up for the book, can you,
There's nothing more enjoyable than a good win
When you're expecting a towsing. So here I am
Again, as the comic said, and my promises
Not worth the air they was spoken with!
This girl's your criminal. We caught her doing it,
Actually setting the grave to rights.
I brought her here, and there was no panic
This time, I can tell you, no recriminations
Or drawing lots! This job was all mine.
I caught her, and I claim the credit for it.
And now, she's all yours. Take her, and accuse her,
Stone her to death, if you like. By rights,
I'm free to go: and well shot of all of it.

CREON. Where did you arrest her? Tell me the details.

SOLDIER. She was burying him. What else is there to say?

CREON. Are you out of your mind? Do you realise
The implications of what you are saying?

SOLDIER. Sir, she was burying the body, I saw her:
The body you ordered not to be buried.
I can't speak plainer than that.

CREON.   Did you
Catch her in the act? Did you see her doing it?

SOLDIER. Well, gentlemen, it was like this.
As soon as I got back, remembering
All those threats, or promises you made me,
We brushed all the earth off the naked body,
Which was all wet and beginning to decay
By now, and we sat up on the ridge,
Well to the windward of the stink.
We all kept a sharp eye on each other,
Ready to nudge anyone who dropped off,
And tear him off a strip too. For hours
We sat there, till about midday.
The sun was smack overhead, blazing down,
And the heat was something terrible, I can tell you.

149

And then, it was as though a whirlwind blew up,
Definitely a twister it was, but localised, like,
And it raised up a dust storm, which swept across the plain,
Tore all the leaves off the trees, blotted out
The whole sky, and completely blinded us.
It seemed like some terrible manifestation
Of the gods, and you had to shut your eyes
To endure it at all. Then, suddenly it stopped,
And when the air cleared, we opened our eyes,
And saw this girl, standing there,
Beside the grave, and sort of wailing,
As though she were in pain, or maybe, anger:
Just like a bird who comes back to the nest
And finds the eggs smashed, or the fledgelings gone.
That's what it sounded like. She was standing there,
Looking at the naked body, and screaming,
And cursing the monsters who had done such a thing –
Us, of course. And then she crouched down,
And picked up a few handfuls of the dry dust
And scattered it on him. She carried an urn,
A small ceremonial bronze thing,
And she poured from it, three times, on the dead body –
Honey and wine and stuff in it, I suppose –
All the proper ritual for a funeral, anyway.
Soon as we saw that, we came charging down
And arrested her on the spot. She wasn't
Frightened or anything. She stood her ground.
So then we formally charged her with the crime,
This, and the one before. She admitted
She'd done them both, and we were relieved
To hear that, I can tell you. But sorry
Too, at the same time. It's very nice
To get out of trouble yourself. Not so nice
When you drop someone else up to the neck in it,
Someone you've got no quarrel with.
But still. Your own life comes first, I reckon.
You have to look after number one.
CREON. And you. You with your head down.

What do you say to this accusation?
Do you admit it? Are you guilty, or not?

ANTIGONE. Yes, I'm guilty. I don't pretend otherwise.

CREON. You, soldier, get out. You're cleared of all charges
Against you, and free to go back to your unit.

*The Soldier seems about to speak, thinks better of it, and goes, much
relieved.*

Now, tell me, a simple yes or no.
Did you hear of my order forbidding the burial?

ANTIGONE. Of course I heard it. How could I not?

CREON. And yet you dared to disobey the law?

ANTIGONE. Yes, I did. Because it's your law,
Not the law of God. Natural Justice,
Which is of all times and places, numinous,
Not material, a quality of Zeus,
Not of kings, recognises no such law.
You are merely a man, mortal,
Like me, and laws that you enact
Cannot overturn ancient moralities
Or common human decency.
They speak the language of eternity,
Are not written down, and never change.
They are for today, yesterday, and all time.
No one understands where they came from,
But everyone recognises their force:
And no man's arrogance or power
Can make me disobey them. I would rather
Suffer the disapproval and punishment
Of men, than dishonour such ancient truths.
I shall die, of course, some time,
Whether you make laws or not. If my death
Comes sooner rather than later, I shall welcome it.
My life has been misery – is misery now.
I shall be more than happy to leave it.
There will be no pain, and no despair
In that. But to leave my mother's son
Out there in the open, unburied,
That would have been unendurable,

I could not have borne it. Whereas this
I shall endure. By your judgement
Of course, I'm a fool. But by mine,
It's the judge, not the accused who's behaving foolishly.
CHORUS. This is her father speaking. Stubborn
Like him, she won't give way, not even
With the whole power of the State against her.
CREON. Well, we shall see. Any man can be broken,
And often the most committed and determined
Break soonest. Even iron, you know,
Left lying in the fire too long
Becomes over tempered, and will snap
As soon as a little pressure is applied.
You can break it in pieces. And the wildest horse
In the end submits to the bit and halter
Just like the rest. People without power,
Ordinary citizens, must necessarily obey
Those in authority over them.
This woman is very proud. That was obvious
In the first place when she broke the law,
And is even clearer now. She glories
In the crime she has committed, and insults me
To my face, as well as ignoring my decree.
If she is allowed to flout the law
In this way, all authority
In the State will collapse. I will not have that!
There will be no exchanging of roles here,
Me playing the woman while she plays the king!
She is my niece, my sister's child.
But I am the law. And that responsibility
Is above kinship. Were she even closer,
The closest, my own daughter, my duty
Would be plain. The law has its weapons,
And they will strike, at her,
And at her sister too – her accomplice,
I've no doubt, in this illegal act –
To the full extent of the punishment proscribed.
The other one, Ismene, bring her here.

I saw her in the corridor, talking to herself
And sobbing emotionally, like a madwoman!
Guilty consciences, you see, can never be hidden
Completely, the human face reveals
Conspiracies before they are enacted
Again and again. But there is nothing
More disgusting than the confessed criminal
Who tries to justify his actions,
As this woman has done here today.

ANTIGONE. What more do you want? Kill me, and have done
with it.

CREON. Nothing more than your death. That'll be enough.

ANTIGONE. Then what are you waiting for? Nothing you say
Will be of the slightest interest to me,
And my arguments you will not listen to.
I've done what I said I'd do. I've buried my brother.
I aspire to no greater honour, and if
I am to be famous, let it be for that.
All these, these senators of yours,
They all agree with me in their hearts.
But there is no gag like terror, is there
Gentlemen? And tyrants must have their way,
Both in word and action, that's their privilege!

CREON. You are quite mistaken. None of the Thebans
Anywhere in the city, thinks as you do.

ANTIGONE. They all do! But they keep their mouths shut when
you're here!

CREON. Not at all! And you should be ashamed
Setting yourself up against the majority,
Disregarding the will of the people!

ANTIGONE. I love my brother. I honour him dead
As I loved him living. There's no shame in that.

CREON. And the one he murdered? Wasn't he your brother?

ANTIGONE. My mother bore them both, and I loved them both.

CREON. If you honour one, you insult the other.

ANTIGONE. Neither of those dead men would say that.

CREON. Eteocles would. His brother was a traitor.
Does he merit no greater respect than that?

ANTIGONE. But he was not an animal. They both died
Together. And they were both men.

CREON. Yes, and the one died defending his country
While the other traitorously attacked it!

ANTIGONE. The dead have their rights, and we have our duties
Towards them, dictated by common decency!

CREON. And if good and bad are to be honoured equally,
Where are our values? Patriotism! Civic duty!

ANTIGONE. Death is another country. Such things
May not be valued there. May even be crimes.

CREON. An enemy is still an enemy. Dead or alive.

ANTIGONE. No, I was born with love enough
To share: no hate for anyone.

CREON. Very well. Share your love by all means,
Share it with the dead. I wish them well of it.
Women must learn to obey, as well as men.
They can have no special treatment. Law is law
And will remain so while I am alive –
And no woman will get the better of me . . .
*Ismene is brought in under guard. She has been crying, and looks
gaunt and worn.*

CHORUS (*Severally*). Look Senators, Ismene, weeping for her
sister!
Her face is raw with tears,
Flayed with misery!
Her loveliness is scarred now – this disaster
Darkens her fair skin with premonitions and fears
And flushes her cheeks with anguish, not beauty.
Ismene is dragged before Creon.

CREON. And you! Snake! Slithering silently
About my house, to drink my blood
In secret! Both of you the same!
I looked the other way: and like terrorists
You laid undercover plans to destroy me.
Well, do you too confess your complicity
In this crime? Or protest your innocence?

ISMENE. Yes, I confess. If she will allow me
To say so. I was fully involved,

And if she is guilty, so am I.

ANTIGONE. No! That isn't justice! When I asked
For help, you refused me: and so I told you
I didn't want you, I'd do it alone.

ISMENE. But now that you're in danger, Antigone,
I'm proud to stand beside you in the dock.

ANTIGONE. The dead man knows who buried him. What use
Are people who are all words and no action?

ISMENE. Please, my sister, don't despise me!
Let me share the honour and die with you.

ANTIGONE. You've no right to claim the honour for doing
What you were afraid to do. One death
Will be enough. Why should you die?

ISMENE. Because life without you won't be worth living.

ANTIGONE. Ask Creon to protect you. He is your uncle.

ISMENE. Do I deserve such contempt? Do you enjoy
Making fun of me, sneering at my misery.

ANTIGONE. You're right. It's a reflection of my own pain,
If such bitter pleasures are all I have left.

ISMENE. Let me help you then. It's not too late.

ANTIGONE. Save your own life. Do that for yourself
Without any criticism from me: or envy.

ISMENE. For God's sake, Antigone, will you not allow me
Even to share my death with my sister?

ANTIGONE. No. I won't. You chose to live
When I chose to die: and that's the end of it.

ISMENE. But I wasn't afraid to speak! I warned you
That this would happen. I knew how it would be!

ANTIGONE. And most, the majority, would agree with you.
But some would be of my opinion.

ISMENE. But we're both in the wrong, and both condemned!

ANTIGONE. No, you must live. I been dead
For a long time, inwardly. I am well suited
To pay honour to the dead, and die for it.

CREON. These women are neurotic, lunatics, both of them!
One of them going off her head before
Our eyes, the other one born unbalanced.

ISMENE. Well, are you surprised! Anyone would crack,

The most tough-minded person, under such treatment.

CREON. You lost your senses when you allowed yourself
   To be influenced by her lunacy.

ISMENE. There's no life for me here! Not without my sister!

CREON. Don't speak of her. She's as good as dead.

ISMENE. Will you kill the woman your son plans to marry?

CREON. There are other women: no lack of choice
   For a young man. Other fields to plough.

ISMENE. But they're devoted to each other. You can't
   Change love as you change your clothes!

CREON. No son of mine can marry a criminal.

ANTIGONE. Oh Haemon, when you hear how your father insults

you!

CREON. Let him hear. What does his mistress matter to me.

CHORUS. Lord Creon, you insult your own!
   They are formally betrothed. Will you tear
   The woman from your own son's arms?

CREON. Death parts all lovers, sooner or later.

CHORUS. If that's how the land lies, the poor child's doomed,
   Her death warrant sealed and delivered.

CREON. By you, gentlemen, if you remember,
   As well as by me. You heard the order,
   Agreed it with me, if only by your silence,
   Did you not, before the criminal was known?
   We'll have no more shilly shallying. Take them away,
   Lock them up, and keep them under close guard.
   It's time they understood they are women,
   And their proper place in this society.
   There's nothing like the immediate threat
   Of death to soften up their rhetoric,
   And make them look reality in the face.
   *Ismene and Antigone are dragged away by the Guards. Creon remains
   on stage during the following Chorus.*

CHORUS. They can call themselves lucky, the fortunate few
   Who live their lives through
   Never drinking from the bitter cup of pain.
   But when one unlucky family
   Incurs the gods' malignity

From generation to generation
They must swallow the bitter potion,
Again, and then again!
Just as rollers crash, and seaspray whips
On an exposed beach, and black clouds lower
And the gale from the north screams through frozen lips,
While the sea casts up from its depths a shower
Of pebbles on the shore, and black sand
From the chasms of ocean, darkens the strand.

On every descendant of the ancient line
Of Labdacus, divine
And merciless retribution falls.
In the unremembered past
Some unforgiving Olympian cast
The weight of his vengeance on the whole race,
So that agony, destruction, disgrace,
Destroys son and daughter, and darkens their halls
With tragedy. The cold hands of the dead
Reach out for the living, and no one is spared.
Another generation sheds its blood,
New light is snuffed out, the young root bared
For the same bloody axe. The characteristic sin
Of Oedipus, arrogance, brings its bleak harvest in.

For Zeus is all powerful, no man can match him,
He never sleeps, as man must sleep,
And time, which leaves its mark
On fair complexions and dark,
Can never engrave his face, or dim
The brightness of his palace, where the gods keep
Their ageless court, at the utmost peak
Of sublime Olympus. Zeus is master there,
And well did that wise man speak
Who said that past and future time
He holds in his hand by right,
And that those who climb
In their greatness or wickedness

Beyond the permitted height
He brings to destruction and despair.

But all men hope, and some have ambition,
Far-ranging birds that never tire.
Those wings bear some men steadily onward,
But some others aimlessly swoop and glide
Down to frivolous pastures, landscapes of obsession,
Pathways to disaster, and the merciless fire.
And no man can claim to have understood
Hope or ambition, till the flames burn
Under his feet, and the once solid wood
Of his life is reduced to its last condition,
Ashes, and dust. A wise man said
From out of the depths of his inspiration,
When a man commits crimes, and is proud of the action,
A flaming sword hangs over his head:
No future but the grave, and a funeral urn.
Haemon is seen approaching.
Creon, here comes your youngest son.
Is he desperate with grief
That his future bride
Should be so brutally denied,
And all his hopes of happiness gone?
For the last of your sons, what relief
From his consuming fears
And the bitter penance of tears?
Does he come to beg for mercy
For his beloved Antigone?

CREON. We shall know that from his own lips
Without any need of fortune-tellers.
*Haemon enters and the two men face each other. Both are aware
of the delicacy and magnitude of the situation.*
My dear son. I don't doubt you have heard
The news of our final decision, the condemnation
Of the woman you intended to marry. You come here,
I hope, not in any spirit of anger
Against your father, but understanding

That we are always comrades, and my love for you is unshaken.

HAEMON. I know I am your son, Father,
I understand the depth of your experience
In matters of State, and I try to follow
And benefit from it, whenever I can.
Any marriage would be worthless to me
That did not have your approval, and love.

CREON. Good fellow. Hang on to that! A father's opinion
Should always be influential with his son:
And fathers with young sons, when they pray for them,
Ask especially that they should grow up to be
Loyal, obedient, under pressure the first
To strike at their father's enemies,
Just as they are the first to support his friends.
A father whose sons yield no such profits
From the investment of his parenthood
Breeds grief and sorrow as his offspring,
And becomes himself a figure of fun,
Especially to his enemies. Don't be taken in
Boy. Don't let any woman ensnare you
By exploiting her sexuality, or any of the attractions
That lure infatuated men into submission.
God help the lovesick fool who marries
A dominating woman. Passion never lasts,
And a cold bedroom breeds cold hearts,
Anger, and bitterness, for there's no hatred
So violent as the hatred of two people
Who were once in love. Get rid of her,
My Boy, this girl's an enemy, no good
To you, or your best interests. Spit her out like poison!
Let her find herself a husband that suits her
Among the dead. Don't deceive yourself.
She has been openly apprehended
Performing a criminal act against the State.
She is a confessed traitor, and if I
Were to spare her life, I too would betray
The State, and its law, and everything I stand for.
I will not do it. And she must die.

Let her pray to Zeus till she drops,
Let her assert she stands for family love
And ancient virtues, and all the rest of it.
If I tolerate treachery in my own house,
Under my very nose, how can I crush subversion
Anywhere else in the city, or in the State
At large? A man who rules wisely
Within his own family, is more likely
To make sensible judgements in political matters
In his direction of the State. To pervert the law,
To twist it to serve one's own ends
Or the interests of one's relations –
That cannot be allowed, neither in States,
Nor in families: and will not be allowed
By me, in any circumstances.
Unquestioning obedience to whomsoever the State
Appoints to be its ruler is the law
As far as I'm concerned, and this applies
To small things as well as great ones,
Just or unjust, right or wrong.
The man who is firm in his dealings with his family
Will be equally firm in power, his wisdom
Will be equally remarkable, whether as king,
Or indeed as subject. In times of war
And national danger, he will be the man
You can rely on, the man you would feel safe with
Fighting beside you in the front rank
When the battle becomes critical. Indiscipline,
Anarchy, disobedience, what greater scourge
Than that for humankind? States collapse
From within, cities are blown to rubble,
Efficient armies are disorganised,
And potential victory turned to disaster
And carnage, and all by disobedience,
Anarchy, indiscipline. Whereas the well-drilled regiment
That asks no questions stands firm,
Knows nothing, and needs to know nothing, and wins,
Thus saving the lives of millions of honest people.

Authority is essential in any State,
And will be upheld in this one, by me.
There will be no yielding to female fantasies,
Not by so much as an inch. And if we must be deposed,
Let it be by a man's hand, eh son?
Not by a conspiracy of women!

CHORUS. If an old man is fit to judge, Lord Creon,
You have spoken rationally, sensibly, and with the wisdom
Gathered from long experience.

HAEMON. Father, the most enviable of a man's gifts
Is the ability to reason clearly,
And it's not for me to say you are wrong,
Even if I were clever enough, or experienced enough,
Which I'm not. But it's also true to say
That some men think differently about these things,
And as your son, my most useful function,
It seems to me, is to keep you in touch
With what other people are thinking,
What they say, and do, and approve or disapprove of,
And sometimes what they leave unsaid.
The prospect of your disapproval is a great
Silencer of most men's tongues, and some things
Are never said, for fear of the consequences.
But I can sometimes hear what people whisper
Behind their hands: and everywhere, I hear sympathy
Expressed for this unfortunate girl,
Condemned, as she is, to a horrifying death
That no woman has ever suffered before,
And unjustly, in most people's eyes.
In burying her brother, who was killed
In action, she did something most people consider
Decent and honourable – rather than leaving him
Naked on the battlefield, for the dogs to tear at
And kites and scavengers to pick to the bone.
She should be given a medal for it,
Those same people say, and her name inscribed
On the roll of honour. Such things are whispered
In secret, Father, and they have reached my ears.

Sir, your reputation matters to me
As much as your good health and happiness do,
Indeed, your good name matters more.
What can a loving son be more jealous of
Than his father's reputation, and what could please
A father more than to see his son's concern
That people will think well of him?
Then let me beg you to have second thoughts,
And not be certain that your own opinion
Is the only right one, and that all men share it.
A man who thinks he has the monopoly
Of wisdom, that only what *he* says
And what *he* thinks is of any relevance,
Reveals his own shallowness of mind
With every word he says. The man of judgement
Knows that it is a sign of strength,
Not weakness, to value other opinions,
And to learn from them: and when he is wrong,
To admit it openly and change his mind.
You see it when a river floods, the trees
That bend, survive, those whose trunks
Are inflexible, are snapped off short
By the weight of water. And a sailor in a storm
Who refuses to reef his sail, and run
With the wind, is likely to end up capsized.
I beg you Father, think twice about this.
Don't let your anger influence you. If a man
Of my age may lay some small claim
To common sense, let me say this:
Absolute certainty is fine, if a man
Can be certain that his wisdom is absolute.
But such certainty and such wisdom
Is rare among men: and that being so,
The next best, is to learn to listen,
And to take good advice when it is offered.
CHORUS. There's a lot of sense, my Lord Creon,
In what this young man has said: as indeed,
There was in everything that you said too.

162

The fact is, you are both in the right,
And there's a good deal to be said for either.

CREON. Is there indeed? Am I expected to listen
And take lessons in political tactics
At my age, from a mere boy?

HAEMON. I'm a man, Father, and my arguments are just.
They stand upon their merits, not my age.

CREON. Oh, they stand upon their merits do they? What merit
Is there, please tell me, in breaking the law?

HAEMON. If she'd done something shameful I wouldn't defend her.

CREON. She has brought the law into contempt! That's shameful!

HAEMON. Listen to the people in the street, Father,
The ordinary Thebans! They say she hasn't!

CREON. I have never based my political principles
On the opinions of people in the street!

HAEMON. Now you're the one who's speaking like a boy!

CREON. I'm speaking like a king. It's my responsibility,
And I will act according to my own convictions!

HAEMON. When the State becomes one man it ceases to be a State!

CREON. The State is the statesman who rules it, it reflects
His judgement, it belongs to him!

HAEMON. Go and rule in the desert then! There's nobody there
To argue with you! What a king you'll be there!

CREON. This boy of mine is on the woman's side!

HAEMON. Yes, if *you* are a woman, I am.
I'm on your side Father, I'm fighting for you.

CREON. You damned impertinent devil! Every word
You say is against me. Your own father!

HAEMON. When I know you are wrong, I have to speak.

CREON. How am I wrong? By maintaining my position
And the authority of the State? Is that wrong?

HAEMON. When position and authority
Ride roughshod over moral feeling. . .

CREON. You're weak, and uxorious, and contemptible,
With no will of your own. You're a woman's mouthpiece!

HAEMON. I'm not ashamed of what I'm saying.

CREON. Every word you have said pleads for her cause.

HAEMON. I plead for you, and for myself,

And for common humanity, respect for the dead!

CREON. You will never marry that woman, she won't
Live long enough to see that day!

HAEMON.   If she dies,
She won't die alone. There'll be two deaths, not one.

CREON. Are you threatening me? How dare you threaten. . .

HAEMON. No, that's not a threat. I'm telling you
Your policy was misbegotten from the beginning.

CREON. Misbegotten! Dear God, if anything's misbegotten
Here, it's my son. You'll regret this, I promise you.

HAEMON. If you weren't my father, I'd say you were demented.

CREON. Don't father me! You're a woman's plaything,
A tame lap dog!

HAEMON.   Is anyone else
Allowed to speak? Must you have the last word
In everything, must all the rest of us be gagged?

CREON. I must, and I will! And you, I promise you,
Will regret what you have spoken here
Today. I will not be sneered at or contradicted
By anyone. Sons can be punished too.
Bring her out, the bitch, let her die here and now,
In the open, with her bridegroom beside her
As a witness! You can watch the execution!

HAEMON. That's one sight I shall never see!
Nor from this moment, Father, will you
Ever see me again. Those that wish
To stay and watch this disgusting spectacle
In company with a madman, are welcome to it!
Exit Haemon.

CHORUS. Lord Creon, an uncontrollable fury
Has possessed your son, and swept him off like a whirlwind.
A young man's anger is a terrifying thing!

CREON. Let him go and shout his head off about moral this
And decent that, till he raves himself senseless!
The two women are sentenced. It will take more than bluster
To reprieve them, I promise you.

CHORUS. Both of them sir?
You mean to put both of the sisters to death?

CREON. No. You are right. I can take advice.
    The one who covered the body. Not the other.
CHORUS. And for the condemned one: what manner of death?
CREON. Take her to some lonely place, rocky,
    And unfrequented by anyone. Find a cave
    And wall her up in it. Bury her alive:
    But with just enough food so that no guilt
    For her death will fall either upon us or the State.
    She'll have plenty of time to honour the gods
    Of the dead there, since they receive
    So many of her prayers. They will release her.
    And she will learn that worshipping the dead
    Is not the business of the living.
    Exit Creon.[1]
CHORUS. When the god of unbridled passion makes war
    He always wins.
    No force on earth can withstand
    His powerful, merciless hand.
    When the first flowers appear
    In a young girl's cheek
    The remorseless magic begins:
    And then, from the deepest valley to the highest peak
    His traps are set,
    And no man's sins
    Or virtues can keep him from the net.
    The mania is universal. The gods themselves run mad.
    Men lose their wits, and no one is spared.

    When the madness strikes, no one is safe.
    The maturest of men
    Will commit follies and crimes
    Undreamed of in saner times.
    What else could provoke this strife

---

[1] Most scholars assume Creon remains on stage throughout the Chorus and Antigone's threnody. My production proved that Creon's next lines can be played quite as effectively as an entrance as they can as an interruption.

tween father and son, this family divided
And murderous anger between kin?
There is fire in a woman's eye, incited
By such consuming heat,
A man's mind can burn.
Aphrodite shares power with Zeus, her seat
Is at his right hand, her lightning
Strikes to the heart, and its power is frightening.

*The doors open and Antigone enters, heavily guarded. She is dressed
in a plain white gown.*

CHORUS. Yet how can we talk of justice
And the needs of the State
While we stand and watch this
Unendurable sight?
My eyes will have their way and weep,
Seeing Antigone, like a young bride
Going to her bedchamber, to marry the dead
And share their everlasting sleep.

ANTIGONE. In all my wanderings, gentlemen, this place
Has been my home. I was born in this city:
And now I begin my last journey.
I look up at the sun in its familiar sky
And feel its warmth on my face
Only to say goodbye.
In the daytime of my life, in mid-breath,
This security policeman, death,
Arrests me, as he arrests everyone, young and old
At home, or in the street. To the cold
Waters of darkness we come, never
To return across that silent river.
No wedding for me,
No music, no guests in the room:
My wedding gift is eternity
In a stone tomb,
My dowry, for ever not-to-be,
Death my bridegroom.

CHORUS. But your action is famous,

In every street
Mouths whisper 'Antigone'.
You go down to the dead
With the promise of glory ringing in your head
And nothing to devalue your beauty.
No sword has scarred you, plague visited:
Unmarked, untouched, you pass
From the dangerous light
Into the safety of eternal night,
Alive, alone, and free.

ANTIGONE. Do you remember the sad story
Of Tantalus' daughter? She was a stranger
From Phrygia, unmarried, like me, in danger
Like mine. She was sentenced to die on the rock
Of Sipylus, and there was no glory
For her, only the endless shock
Of the elements, and the terrible place
Where she was imprisoned: the mountain's embrace
Like fingers of ivy tying her down,
Enclosing, entombing her, and she all alone
While the snows blinded her, and the freezing rain
Whipped her to rags, and exposed her pain
To the naked sky.
What bitter tears she shed
As she slowly turned to stone, and the grey
Rock petrified her by inches, and she died.
Her story is mine. Today
I shall share her rocky bed.
CHORUS. But she was a goddess
Not born for death
Like the children of men
Whose desperate mortality
Is their only certainty.
Will it soothe your pain
To share her destiny,
Or soften your distress
As alive in the earth

ou draw your last breath,
To live on in legend and stone?

ANTIGONE. This is a mockery! By everything
The city of our fathers has ever held sacred
You landowners, you elder statesmen,
You rulers of Thebes, my dying
Is no joke! Am I a figure of fun
To be treated like a child, insulted and humiliated
As I leave you for ever?
Then, forests and meadows, and our Theban river,
Glittering pathway, ceaselessly flowing
From Dirce's death till now, flat lands
Thundering beneath our chariots, you
Must be my witnesses, my only friends
And mourners, as, victimised by an unjust law, I go
To my last home
In the living tomb,
To wait, while the slow darkness descends,
Cold and starving on my stony bed
Half way between the living and the dead.

CHORUS. No one has ever dared
To go so far before
As you have dared to go.
Now you have stumbled, and stubbed your toe
And will shortly shed your blood
On the marble staircase of the law.
You carry your father's crimes
Like a millstone on your back:
Small wonder, in such times,
If the bones bend, or break.

ANTIGONE. Nothing more painful than that, the remembrance
Of my father's long agony, and the curse
On my suffering family from the beginning.
So much grief from the unlucky chance
Of the son finding the mother's bed, and worse

168

Than anything, the benighted offspring
Of that unspeakable marriage: and I,
With the others, share that terrible destiny.
Conceived in incest, no repentance
Can soften the punishment: the years
Pass, the agonies increase
And there is no pity for our tears.
No marriage for me, for certain. I shall close
That book for ever,
As I meet my father
And mother in the shades. The weddings will cease.
Marriage to the woman of Argos finished my brother
And finished me too. One death breeds another.

CHORUS. To pay respect to the dead
   Is praiseworthy, an act of love,
   And religion must have its due:
   But no civilised State can eschew
   Authority. Laws must be obeyed,
   Whether we approve or disapprove.
   If you refuse to sanction
   The power of the State
   By indulging your obsession
   You connive at your own fate.

ANTIGONE. Spare me your sympathy,
   Weep no false tears,
   I know the path that I must follow,
   To the sunless country of eternal sorrow,
   The bleak waters of eternity,
   The unimaginable years.
   No grief where none is felt. I shall go alone
   And in silence to my house of stone.
   Enter Creon, with his Guards.
CREON. If death could be prevented by singing arias
   About it, or other self-indulgent displays
   Of grief, this performance would go on for ever,
   I've no doubt. But I've had enough of it.

Take her away, lock her up
In her stone vault, with half a mountain
For a roof, then brick up the door! Let her die
There, if she chooses. Or if she prefers,
Let her stay alive in her grave, why not!
Because the grave's the only fit place for her,
Solitary confinement among the dead!
Whatever she does, there will be no guilt
On me, or on the State. Her death's her own.
But there's no place for her among the living.

ANTIGONE. To my grave then. My honeymoon bed.
My prison. My crypt, under the mountain.
My home for the rest of time. I shall meet
So many of my relations there:
We shall all be guests of the sad-faced queen
Of the shadows, Persephone, in that bleak hotel
That is never short of a room. I am the last,
The unhappiest, I think, and the youngest,
Booking in too soon. But my father will be there
To meet me at the door: my mother will smile,
And hug me close, as she always did:
And my brother. He will be glad to see me,
More than all the rest. At each fresh grave
My hands sprinkled the earth, at each
I poured the purifying water,
And made offerings. And for my beloved Polynices,
Whose broken body I set to rest,
I am rewarded with a shameful death.
There are some, I know, more thoughtful people,
Who respect my action. They must justify me.
Not for a husband, you understand,
Not even for a son would I have done this.
If the law had forbidden it, I would have bowed
My head, and let them rot. Does that
Make sense? I could have married again,
Another husband, and had more children
By him, if the first had died. Do you see?
Do you understand me? But my mother and father

Are dead. There will be no more brothers,
Never again. My love had to speak
At Polynices' grave, or nowhere.
And for that terrible crime, my dearest brother,
Creon sentences me to death,
Drags me here, and will shut me away
In a cavern under the mountain, a living death,
In silence and darkness and solitude.
I shall die unmarried, all those pleasures
Denied me, and motherhood denied
Too, no children to love me, to love:
And now, no friends. What moral law
Have I broken? What eternal truths
Have I denied? Yet now, not even a god
Can help me, and there's no man who will,
I'm sure of that. No help, and no hope.
How can there be, when common decency
Has become a crime? If the gods in heaven
Have changed their minds, and this is the way
They order things now, I shall soon know it:
And I shall have learned my lesson the hard way.
But if some others are mistaken,
Let them be punished as I have been punished,
And suffer the injustice that I suffer!

CHORUS. She hasn't changed, even now. The anger
Inside her still blows like a hurricane.

CREON. The sooner she's got rid of, shut up
Out of harm's way, and forgotten, the better.
Tell those guards to get a move on, or they will regret it!

ANTIGONE. That word is my death.

CREON.   And now it is spoken.
Don't comfort yourself with hope. There's none.

ANTIGONE. This is the land of my fathers: Thebes,
Built by a god. You see, senators,
My time has run out, there is no more left.
I am the last of the royal blood,
A daughter of kings. And I die *his* victim,
Unjustly, for upholding justice

And the humanity of humankind.
Antigone is led away by the Guards. Creon remains on stage.
CHORUS. Others have suffered, my child, like you:
Upon Danaë too
The same dreadful sentence was passed.
Far from the light of day
In a tower of brass she was shut away,
And that one single room,
Both prison and tomb
Became her wedding chamber at last.
Like you, she was a child of kings,
Yet in her womb the semen of Zeus
Descending in a golden shower
Made a mockery of the brazen tower.
Fate has its own momentum: when things
Must be, they will be. What use
Is power in the State, or wealth,
Massive armies, an unsinkable fleet?
Gods make their entrances by strength or stealth,
And no tombs or towers can keep them out.

The arrogant King Lycurgus discovered
Wisdom, when he angered
The god Dionysus with his railing.
That proud Edonian king
Was punished with madness, and long
Imprisoned in a rocky cell
To endure the private and particular hell
Of lunacy: till the healing
Silence soothed and re-ordered his brain.
He learned there the terrible power
Of the god he had challenged. Ecstasy
Is beyond man's understanding, a mystery
Deeper than reason, which overcomes pain,
And seeks truth in intoxication and terror.
Only a fool would attempt to stop
The Maenads in full flight,
Or silence their ecstatic singing. The sleep

Of reason is not darkness, but another kind of light.

And where the gloomy rocks divide the seas
In Thrace, by the Bosporos,
The savage god Ares
Laughed to see the sons of Phineus
Blinded with a spindle. Nothing could placate
Their vengeful stepmother's hate.
Her bloody needle darkened their eyes for ever,
Blinding the children, as the gods had blinded the father.
From their mother's wedding day, their destiny
Was settled. Their wasted lives
They wept away in sightless misery.
Yet she was descended from the gods. In the echoing caves
Of the north wind she hallooed, as a child,
And on the open mountainside ran wild
With the horses. Man's fate is determined, will not be
                                     denied.

The child Antigone pays for the parents' pride.
*Enter the blind man Teiresias, accompanied by his Boy. He looks
exactly as he did in 'Oedipus the King'. Nothing has changed, either
in age or dress or manner.*

TEIRESIAS. Senators of Thebes – and your new king, Creon!
  We have travelled together, my boy and I,
  Sharing one pair of eyes between the two of us –
  Which is the way blind men must make their journeys.

CREON. Teiresias! What news brings an old man so far?

TEIRESIAS. Important news, that can't wait:
  And advice, which if you're wise, you'll listen to.

CREON. I've always listened: and acted upon it
  More than once!

TEIRESIAS.   And like a sensible captain
  Who values his pilot, you've avoided the rocks.

CREON. I admit it. We all do. We're in your debt.

TEIRESIAS. Then for God's sake, listen to me now.
  You're like a man balanced on a razor,
  Likely to fall – or cut himself to pieces.

CREON. Are you serious? Any man would shudder

Hearing such things from your lips
That have foretold so many horrors. . .
Tell me what you mean.

TEIRESIAS.   Oh yes, I intend to:
Everything my experience of forecasting the future
And understanding symbols has revealed to me,
I will make plain to you. I was sitting
In my usual seat, a place where I can hear
The singing and the secret language
Of the birds, and understand their meaning,
When I heard, quite unexpectedly,
A terrible new sound, like shrieking, or cries
Of anguish, hysterical twittering and whistling
Like the babble of a barbaric language
Only capable of expressing hatred
Or pain. By that, and the wild beating of wings,
I knew the birds were at war. Such sounds
Could mean nothing else. I could well imagine
Their bloodstained beaks and dripping claws,
And that thought disturbed me deeply. At once
I went to my altar to see what I could learn
From the sacrifice by fire. But nothing would burn.
A filthy liquid ran from the flesh
And dropped on the embers – and sizzled and bubbled
Among the ashes. Then the gall bladder burst,
Spurting stinking acid across the meat,
And all the fat melted, and was rendered down
Till the bone was left bare. I saw all this –
Or my boy saw it. He sees for me
What my eyes cannot, just as I see
Things to which other people are blind.
But in that filth I read nothing. The oracle
Was clogged with fat and decay –
And then . . . it was revealed. I understood
That you, King Creon, have decreed this filth
That chokes our altars. The blood and flesh
That decays and stinks there, is the blood and flesh
Vomited from the gullets of dogs

And carrion crows, the blood of Polynices,
The flesh of that unluckiest of the sons
Of Oedipus, still unburied,
And affronting more than our sense of smell.
The gods themselves are disgusted. They reject
Our prayers and sacrifices. How could they do otherwise?
How can the birds sing of anything
But horrors, blown out with this banquet
Of human blood, clogged and stinking,
Till their very beaks drip with it?
My son, listen to me. Any man
Can make a mistake, or commit a crime.
The man who can recognise what he has done,
See that he was mistaken, or morally wrong,
Admit it, and put it right, that man
Proves that it is never too late to become
Wise, and no one will condemn him.
But if he compounds his stupidity
With stubbornness, and an obstinate refusal
To face the facts, he is nothing but a fool.
Is there anyone more stupid than the stupid man
Who cannot see his own stupidity?
Polynices is dead. Don't revenge yourself
On his remains. You can kill a man once,
And once only. Is there any glory
To be gained by defeating a poor corpse?
This is good advice my son, sincerely offered
By someone who wishes you well . . . Take it . . .

CREON. So that's your news, is it, old man.
I am to be the target, am I,
For everyone to shoot at? Well. I am wise too:
Wise to the ways of fortune-tellers,
And the buying and selling you all go in for.
And I'm to be the latest bargain
I see, I'm to be bought and sold
Like silver from the exchequer at Sardis, or gold
From India, I'm to be part of the trade!
Let me tell you this. There is not enough gold

In the world to buy a grave for that man!
If golden eagles should carry him up
By joints and shreds to Zeus,
And spew him in gobbets on the marble floor
Of Olympus, not even that blasphemy
Would be enough to deflect me from my purpose:
Because I know that no single human act,
However much it may degrade the earth,
And the men who perpetrate or suffer it,
Can stain the purity of the ever-living gods!
But, let me tell you this, Teiresias,
A man can fall: he can fall like a stone,
Especially if he pretends to give good advice,
And wraps it up in a profound cloak
Of religiosity, when all the time
Naked self-interest, and the greed for profit
Are the only motives that matter to him!

TEIRESIAS. Are there any wise men left? Anywhere?

CREON. Goodness, how profound! Do you have any more
Thunderous platitudes to follow that one?

TEIRESIAS. Mature judgement cannot be bought.
No treasure is as valuable. And good advice
Is worth more than a fortune to any man.

CREON. And bad advice is worse than worthless,
A disease which infects the wisest of men!

TEIRESIAS. You describe your own symptoms exactly.

CREON. I refuse to become involved in a slanging match
Or quarrel with the recognised prophet of Thebes!

TEIRESIAS. And yet you insult me to my face. You say
My predictions are both false and dishonest.

CREON. That is because all fortune-tellers
Are money grubbers and charlatans.

TEIRESIAS. Kings too have been known to be acquisitive.

CREON. Do you realise the man you are talking to?
I am the king!

TEIRESIAS.   You are the king, yes.
My good advice helped to make you one.

CREON. You've had your successes, I know that,

176

You've been proved right on more than one occasion.
But honesty's another matter. I've never trusted you.
TEIRESIAS. Don't provoke me to tell you everything.
The dark waters of prophecy are better left undisturbed.
CREON. Disturb them, I don't care! Say anything at all,
But say it honestly, not for cash!
TERESIAS. Are you really foolish enough to believe
That money has ever been my motive?
CREON. Because my integrity is not for sale!
TEIRESIAS. Listen Creon. This is the truth!
Before many more days, before the sun has risen
– Well, shall we say a few more times –
You will have made your payment, corpse
For corpse, with a child of your own blood.
You have buried the one still living: the woman
Who moves and breathes, you have given to the grave:
And the dead man you have left, unwashed,
Unwept, and without the common courtesy
Of a decent covering of earth. So that both
Have been wronged, and the gods of the underworld,
To whom the body justly belongs,
Are denied it, and are insulted. Such matters
Are not for you to judge. You usurp
Ancient rights which even the gods
Themselves don't dare to question, powers
Which are not in the prerogative of kings.
Even now, implacable avengers
Are on their way, the Furies, who rise up
From Hell and swoop down from Heaven,
Fix their hooks into those who commit crimes,
And will never let go. The suffering
You inflicted upon others, will be inflicted
Upon you, you will suffer, as they did.
Have I been bribed, do you think? Am I speaking
For money now? Before very long,
Yes, it will be soon, there will be screaming
And bitter tears and hysterical crying
In this house. Men, as well as women.

Other cities too, other States,
Will turn upon you for the crime you have committed.
Dogs and vultures will swarm in their streets
Dropping fragments of the unburied man
At corners, on doorsteps, in the public squares.
They will smell the pollution, and turn to you,
Its author! That's all I have to say.
You made me angry, Creon, with
Your crude accusations. So I made you my target:
And like a good marksman, all my shots
Have hit the bull. You can feel them, can't you,
You can feel the pain, like an arrow, here!
Take me home now Boy. Leave him alone
To entertain some younger ears than mine
With his ridiculous outbursts. Either that
Or let him learn maturer judgement
And how a wise man controls his tongue.
*Exit Teresias led by the Boy. The Chorus is appalled, and Creon
is visibly shaken.*

CHORUS. My Lord, he's gone, promising nothing
But disasters to come . . .
My hair grew grey in this city:
I was dark haired here, and now I am white,
And in all that time I have never known
Any of his prophecies to be proved wrong.

CREON. Neither have I, man! . . . I know that much
As well as you . . . My mind's torn apart
Like a tug of war, one way, then the other . . .
How can I give way now? But how
Can I stand here like a fool, and wait
Stubbornly for whatever disaster may be coming?

CHORUS. Lord Creon . . . it's time to take good advice.

CREON. Give it then. Don't be afraid. I'll listen.

CHORUS. Release the woman from her underground prison:
And give honourable burial to the dead man.

CREON. Oh, so that's your advice! Total collapse,
Complete withdrawal! Do you all think that?

CHORUS. We do sir. And do it quickly, for heaven's sake!

178

The gods never move faster than when punishing men
With the consequences of their own actions.
CREON. How can I do it? It's unendurable
To deny every principle and every action
I have stood fast by. But I dare not stand
Against the iron laws of necessity.
CHORUS. Go on sir, do it now, and do it personally,
Not by proxy – with your own hands.
CREON. Yes . . . I'll go, myself, at once!
Somebody, everybody, bring spades and sledge-hammers
Out onto the mountain. I'm coming with you!
If I've changed my mind, I'll act upon it
With exactly the same determination.
I sentenced her, and I'll set her free,
Tear down the bricks with my own hands
If necessary. Perhaps it is wiser
To let the old laws stand. My fear
Tells me it is. And that's a voice
Every prudent man must listen to.
Creon rushes off in near panic with his Soldiers and Attendants.
CHORUS. Great god with many names,
Child of the thunder,
Whom Zeus conceived on Cadmus' daughter
Here in Thebes: Bacchus, Dionysus,
In Italy revered,
And in Demeter's mysterious Eleusis
Both praised and feared,
This is your native city, where the quiet river
Of Ismenus waters the meadows, where the fever
Of ecstasy possesses your womenfolk, your own
Thebes, where the dragon's teeth were sown.

The whole world worships you,
Wine god, intoxicator:
On the two-pronged mountain where the torches glitter
And the nymphs of Parnassus dance: by the pool
Where Castalia's suicide
Made the fountain magical, and the cool

Waters of prophecy reside.
From the impenetrable slopes of Nysa, where the ivy runs
wild
And the vines hang thick in your face, come home, Theban
child,
Let the world sing its hymns in vain. In the Theban streets
'Hail,' we shout, 'Bacchus, hail.' And the city waits.

Your mother Semele died here,
Incinerated by the fire of the Universe,
Zeus in his splendour. Now in your city
Another disaster threatens, fear
Locks up our tongues, and, like a plague sore on the face,
The State's disease is made public. We have done wrong.
Now the first necessity
Is for healing. From Parnassus' rocky screes,
Or over the sighing waters of the endless seas
Come to us, healer, and heal. We have suffered too long.

All the stars of the galaxy
Whose hearts are fire, throb to your music,
And the remote voices of measureless night
Speak from the depths of their mystery.
Come, with your crazed followers, your lunatic
Women, the wild Maenads, authentic son
Of Zeus. Bring delight,
And dancing till we drop, bring rest, bring peace,
Bring healing and rebirth, let our anguish cease,
Ecstatic God, whose many names are one.
Enter the Messenger.

MESSENGER. Senators, listen! Descendants of Cadmus
Who founded our city, and Amphion, who built it,
Good people of Thebes! No man's life
Ever moves smoothly, according to plan.
Who can make judgements, say this is praiseworthy
In human existence, and this is to be despised
When chance rules everything? One moment a man
Rides high on his fortune, and the same moment

He crashes to the depths. Luck, like the tide,
Is certain to ebb, after the flow,
And no man can tell what will happen tomorrow.
Everyone, surely, envied Creon!
He had saved his country from its enemies,
Taken power as king, and his position
In the State was unchallenged. What's more,
He ruled well, with a firm hand, and his son
Was at his side, to help and succeed him.
All that is over now. What life
Can there be, when the things that make life pleasant
Are all destroyed? A kind of death,
Moving and breathing, but not living.
That's how it is for him. Of course,
He's rich, beyond accounting, he's a king
Still, with all the pomp and circumstance
That rank implies. But what's it worth
When all the joy of life is gone?
A shadow, a mockery, a vulgar pageant.
Who can take pleasure in wealth or power
When all happiness is dead in his heart?

CHORUS. More tragedy for this family? Tell us your news.

MESSENGER. They're both dead. And the living must take the
blame.

CHORUS. Who killed them? Who's dead? What happened? Tell
us!

MESSENGER. The king's son, Haemon. The royal blood
    Shed by a royal hand.

CHORUS.   His father
    You mean? Or his own?

MESSENGER.   His own held the sword.
    But his father's actions drove it home.

CHORUS. The prophet warned us: and it all came true.

MESSENGER. That's how things are. It's in your hands now.

CHORUS. The doors are opening, look, here's Eurydice,
    Poor woman, Creon's wife. Does she know,
    Do you think? Has she come here by chance,
    Or because she has heard rumours about her son?

Enter Eurydice with her Women.

EURYDICE. Gentlemen . . . good friends. My ears caught

something

Of what you were saying, a few words
As I opened the door. I was on my way
To offer prayers to Pallas Athene:
We had just drawn back the bolt, when I heard
A few scraps of your conversation: enough
To make me fear what all mothers fear:
An accident, or some disaster to those we love.
I almost fainted. My ladies-in-waiting
Caught me in their arms. Please, speak it out
Plainly, whatever it is. I can bear it.
We are bred to stoicism in this family.

MESSENGER. Dear Queen, whom we all respect . . . I was there,
I saw it all, and I'll tell you
Exactly what happened. There's no point
In trying to soften the blow now
Only to be proved a liar later.
It's best to tell the truth. I went
With the king, your husband, to the edge of the battlefield,
Where we saw the body of Polynices
Still lying where he fell, and in a terrible state:
The dogs had been at him. So we prayed –
First to Hecate, who haunts crossroads
And tombs, and the scenes of crimes committed
But not atoned for, and then to Pluto,
King of the Dead. We asked them to have pity
On him, and on us, and not to be angry.
Then we washed him, or what was left of him,
With holy water, cut fresh branches
To make a pyre, and burned the remains.
Then we shovelled a mound of his own Theban earth
Over the ashes, and when we had finished
We hurried off as fast as we could
To the prison cell furnished with stones
That served as a bridal suite for the girl
Married to death. But before we arrived,

One of the soldiers, with the unenviable job
Of guarding that god-forsaken place
Came running back to tell the king
That he'd heard a terrible noise, like screaming,
From inside the mountain. And as Creon got nearer
He heard it too – faint, but audible,
A kind of weird sobbing, or moaning,
Low and unearthly, as though grief were speaking
Its own naked language. The king groaned
Aloud, and we all heard him say
'Oh, God, this is what I was afraid of.
Am I a prophet too? This path
Up to the tomb, these last few steps,
Are the most agonising journey I shall ever make.
I can hear my son's voice in there!
You, quickly, Guards, anybody,
Get inside, squeeze between the rocks.
Where somebody has already forced an entrance,
Get into the main chamber of the cave
And tell me if it is my son's voice
I recognised, or whether the gods
Are playing some brutal game with me!'
So, we went in and looked, as the half-crazed king
Had told us to. And in the darkest corner
We saw her, strung up by the neck, hanging
From an improvised rope of twisted linen
Strips, torn from her own dress. Haemon
Was right beside her, cuddling her body
As it dangled there, sobbing broken-heartedly
At his wife's death, and the marriage bad luck
And his father's cruelty had made certain
Would never take place. When Creon saw them,
He staggered into the cave, groaning
Like an animal, and sobbed aloud, 'My Boy,
My poor Boy, what have you done?' And then,
'Have you gone mad, coming here? There's nothing
Here for you but death and annihilation
And despair. Come away from there, my Son

Come out, for God's sake, I'm begging you,
Come away!' But the boy just looked at him,
And his eyes were terrifying, with an anger
Like I've never seen before. Without a word
He spat in his father's face, and drew
His sword, and lunged straight for the old man.
But Creon was quick, and skipped out of distance.
And the poor lad, hysterical with grief
And self-disgust, held his sword at arm's length
And plunged it between his own ribs.
And then, still conscious, he lifted the girl
Down into the crook of his arm
And cradled her there, in his own blood.
His breathing got harder and shorter, as his life
Flooded away before our eyes, like a fountain,
Soaking her body – so that her white cheeks
Flushed red again with the bloodstains.

*Eurydice turns and walks out, without hurry. Her Women look round,
uncertain, then follow her. Some of the Chorus see the exit, and
are disturbed. The Messenger does not see it, and continues telling
his story to the rest of the Chorus.*

So now they're together, two corpses,
Joined in death. He got his marriage,
Poor lad, but it was solemnised in the grave
Where there are no celebrations.
They look like honeymooners, quietly sleeping
Side by side in one bed: evidence
Of the havoc man can bring upon man
By his own pig-headedness and arrogance.

CHORUS. That's strange . . . What do you make of it? . . . His wife

Has gone without a word: giving no indication
Of her own feelings, one way or the other . . .

MESSENGER. It scares me a bit . . . but I'm quite sure
She has good reason. A public demonstration
Of grief would be unlike her. She'll suffer
Like any other mother, for her son's death,
But in private, with her women. She'd never

Do anything foolish or indiscreet,
I'm sure of that. She's far too sensible.

CHORUS. I don't know. Her silence was unnerving,
Dangerously unlike what one would expect.
That sort of silence is sometimes more threatening
Than screaming and tears.

MESSENGER.   I'll go in after her:
Just to make sure that grief doesn't tempt her
To anything silly, or excessive. You're right,
The silence was unnerving. She seemed to feel nothing:
And in my experience, that can be dangerous.

*The Messenger goes in after the Queen. As he does so, the doors
open, and servants enter carrying the dead body of Haemon on a
bier, closely followed by the distraught Creon.*

CHORUS. Look there! The King is coming:
But not alone.
A silent witness comes before him,[1]
Dead as stone,
Unspeaking evidence that the crime
Like the grief, is all his own.
He suffers now for his wrongdoing.

CREON. Pain . . .
There was hatred inside me, the urge to destroy
Drove me like a maniac, an insane
Plunge towards death – your death my Boy.
See here, the killer and his victim!
See here, the father and his son!
I was responsible. My actions killed him.
There is no blame for him, none.
Blasted in the morning of your life,
My hope, my joy,
My hand powered the knife,
My arrogance determined your fate.

[1] It is perfectly feasible, though not always practicable, for Creon to enter carrying
his dead son – in which case this line should be rendered: 'He carries a silent witness
with him.'

185

CHORUS. You see the truth now, but you see it too late.

CREON. Suffering
  Is the only schoolteacher.
  The gods have broken my back,
  Whipped me like a beast up this stony track
  And destroyed my self-respect.
  All pleasure, all rejoicing
  They have turned to anguish and weeping.
  Man is a naked mortal creature:
  Affliction is all he can expect.
  Re-enter the Messenger.
MESSENGER. My Lord, you have suffered enough. But more
  Suffering is marked to your name.
  One agony lies here in the open,
  Another is waiting, the same
  Anguish redoubled, behind the door.
CREON. There can be nothing worse. My heart is broken.
MESSENGER. Your wife is dead, the mother of this slaughtered son.
  Her wound is fresh, but the breath of life is gone.

CREON. Hades
  Is deep, bottomless the abyss of the dead.
  Will you kill me too, or bring me to my knees
  To suffer longer: beating my head
  Insensible with pain? What can you say,
  Messenger of death with the sad face
  More than you've said already? My way
  Is towards the darkness, my case
  Can be no worse than it is. Can you kill me again?
  I am dead already. Is there more blood,
  More savagery, more hacking of flesh, more pain,
  First the son, then the mother? No end to this grief?
CHORUS. There's no hiding it now. See for yourself.
  The doors open to reveal Eurydice dead.[1]
CREON. Unending

---

[1] See introduction.

Unendurable pain.
This is the second time I am forced to see
What no man's eyes should ever see,
Even once. Is this how it ends?
Or will there be more torture, more suffering?
A few moments ago my trembling
Arms embraced a dead son.
Now death has snatched the mother from my hands.

MESSENGER. It was there by the household shrine she collapsed,
Still holding the razor-sharp knife. And as darkness
Drew down its slow blinds, and her eyes closed,
She spoke of Megareus who died in the fulness
Of his youth, her elder boy. By his empty bed
She wept, and for the son whose life ended
Today, and with her last, dying breath,
Cursed you as his murderer, who drove him to this death.

CREON. I'm shaking! I shall go mad with this terror!
There must be a sword, somewhere,
A sharp, two-edged knife
To cut away my life.
Living is misery for me now, for ever.
When I look, I see blood everywhere.

MESSENGER. It's no more than the truth I've told.
Her last word
Was to blame you for both deaths, mother and son.

CREON. How did she die? Did she do it alone?

MESSENGER. She heard them weeping for Haemon, cried aloud,
And skewered herself under the heart with a sword.

CREON. She spoke the truth. All the guilt is mine!
I am the murderer. Make that plain.
Somebody, anybody, take me away:
I disgrace the decent light of day.
I am nothing now. I have become nothing.
Nothing can happen to a man who is nothing.

CHORUS. How can we judge for the best
In times like these?

Prompt action is safest.
What more is there to lose?

CREON. Where are you, my friend? Come you shadowy
Messenger who runs faster than the wind,
Wrap me in darkness, as a friend should!
Why waste another day? What good
Is daylight to me? Why should my misery
Darken the face of another dawn? Pull down the blind.
CHORUS. Tomorrow is a mystery. No man can say
What time will make plain. We live day by day.
The future is in greater hands than ours.
CREON. I am nothing. I want nothing. My last, simplest prayers.
CHORUS. No time for prayers now. Too late to pray.
What must come, will come, tomorrow, or today.

CREON. I am nothing. Take me then. The man
Who killed, without knowing it, his wife and son.
Where shall I go then? Left, or right?
All wrong turnings now. Into the night,
Darkness, hide me. There's blood on my hands. My head
Is split, my back is broken. I should be dead.
Exit Creon.
CHORUS. The key to human happiness
Is to nurture wisdom in your heart,
For man to attend to man's business
And let the gods play their part:
Above all, to stand in awe
Of the eternal, unalterable law.
The proud man may pretend
In his arrogance to despise
Everything but himself. In the end
The gods will bring him to grief.
Today it has happened here. With our own eyes
We have seen an old man, through suffering, become wise.
Exit the Chorus.

TRANSLATOR'S NOTE
Sophocles English'd

'Bless thee, Bottom, bless thee, thou art translated', cries the literary-minded Peter Quince, when he sees his noisy amateur actor friend's earnest bonce metamorphosed into a braying ass-head – and Shakespeare's pun is exact: translation – particularly the translation of poetry – involves a fundamental metamorphosis of form. A poem may be written in blank verse, rhyme royal or *terza rima*, but even closer to the heart of the matter is the language it is written in. The words themselves are the underlying form of a poem, because it is only in the actual and precise choice of words that meaning and association, and feeling and music and shape, and all the other elements that go to make up a poem – reside. That is why genuine translation, the lateral movement of something called a poem from one language across to another, is impossible. It can only be transformed, re-shaped in a quite new formal structure, ass-head instead of man-head: and then, if it is any good, it becomes pure ass, essentially asinine, with only the memory of the man remaining. A good poem translated, must become a good poem in its new language, not merely a memory of the old. When Brecht was up before the un-American activities committee, a committee-man solemnly read out a translation of one of Brecht's poems, as evidence of his Communist connections. 'Mr Brecht', accused the committee-man, 'Did you write this poem?' 'No', replied Brecht, 'I wrote a very similar poem, in German'.

In fact, it is this dilemma that makes the impossible art of translation so endlessly rewarding. If it were simply a matter of transferring blocks of meaning from one language to another, we would programme our computers, and leave them to get on with it. But good translations, because they must live in their new linguistic surroundings, express as much of the translator as of the translated. We read Pope's Homer and Dryden's Virgil for Pope and Dryden, not Homer and Virgil: and who could deny that Tony Harrison's *Oresteia*, controversial as it is in its individuality, is as much a part of Tony Harrison's struggle to bring the northern voice

189

into its own in modern English poetry, as it is a version of Aeschylus?

The truth of the matter is that translations serve as many different purposes as there are translators, and at least four major kinds can be identified. The first is the literal translation, or crib, staff and companion of generations of students, good old indispensable Loeb. These are usually written in an execrable alien English, never spoken or even written anywhere else by the inhabitants of this planet, and full of words like 'suppliant', 'filet' and 'hecatombs', precise enough renderings of Greek and Roman realities, but utterly incomprehensible as lived English.

The second kind is the most ambitious, and the most common: the attempt to render as much of the poem as possible in the new language, trying to reproduce meaning, verse form, style, and even the musical movement of the original. This was attempted on an heroic scale by Dorothy L. Sayers' version of *The Divine Comedy*, but it can easily collapse into a twisted unidiomatic mish-mash, a game for contortionists, tying an elegant human shape into ugly knots in the pursuit of the impossible.

In the third kind of translation, the translator allows himself a considerable amount of freedom, to express the spirit rather than the letter of the original text. His main concern is to recreate the feel and impact of the original as completely as he can, and he allows himself the freedom to travel quite far from the original writer's literal meaning and style: but his overall intention remains to get as close to that original writer as he can, and he still sees himself as servant rather than master. Pope and Dryden might reasonably be described as translators of this kind, and Erza Pound's aggressively slangy version of *The Women of Trachis* joins that company in kind if not achievement.

The fourth kind, imitation, or re-composition, is effectively the creation of a new work, based on or inspired by an original text in another language, and it is here perhaps that the finest poetry is to be found – many hundreds of Elizabethan love sonnets, Johnson's *London* and *The Vanity of Human Wishes*, imitated from Juvenal, Pope's *Imitation of Horace*, and more recently, Robert Lowell's *Imitations*. We can't go to such poems for anything resembling a version of the original text, more often a perceptive commentary on the nature of the two cultures and ages compared: in Johnson's case, with the insight of genius.

Where does my own translation of the Theban Plays stand? The answer is not quite in any of the four sections, though perhaps nearer to the third than any other. What differentiates it from that third section, creating, in effect a sub-section of its own, is that I have no Greek, and have worked from one specially-commissioned literal translation, and a consideration of the work of many of my distinguished predecessors.

Of course, I did not sit down one bright morning and say to myself, 'I don't read a word of classical Greek, I'll translate Sophocles.' Wearing my other hat as a director, I was discussing with the BBC producer Louis Marks, the possibility of presenting some Greek tragedy on television. My main interest at that time was in setting up a production of Euripides' *The Trojan Women*. It hadn't occurred to me to suggest a trilogy of plays, because as a freelance I knew it was unlikely that I would succeed in getting even one Greek play onto television, let alone three. A few days later, Louis Marks rang me with the totally unexpected suggestion that we should tackle the whole *Theban Trilogy*, and my first reaction was somewhere between awe, delight and disbelief: but I soon grasped the point he had perceived, that there would probably be a greater chance of selling a project on this grand scale to the decision-makers in the BBC than there would be of selling them what in television parlance we would call a one-off Greek play. Louis Marks' instinct proved right. Though we were originally given the go-ahead only for *Antigone* – which had an effect on the translation – Louis' careful political instinct managed eventually, over a period of more than two years, to guide the Sophoclean trireme through the dangerous waters of BBC politics, and bring her safely to port.

We then considered what translation to use, and immediately we were confronted with a huge problem, crucial to the success of the whole project. We were both determined to present these wonderful plays, one of the cornerstones of European culture, in such a way as to reveal at least something of their stature, and why they have been considered the yardstick by which drama is measured for 2,500 years. In television, we were both well aware, the problem is enormously magnified by the fact that the vast majority of our audience would know nothing at all of classical Greek drama, and those who did know something of it would probably be prejudiced by the vulgar notion that it is gloomy, boring and out of date. We were quite determined not to talk down or sell Sophocles short. Our productions would have to be convincing and a pleasure to Greek scholars who have spent a life studying the texts, and a thrillingly compelling new world opening up for viewers to whom Attic tragedy wasn't even a name.

Though television is a good medium for genuine dramatic poetry, it is merciless with any kind of stilted language, and it soon became clear to us that we could present none of the existing translations of the Sophoclean Trilogy with the faintest chance of the particular kind of success we hoped for.

At this point, I decided that I ought to do the job myself. The playwright-translator without the original language is a not uncommon figure now, and in poetic drama, where the quality of the language is of the greatest importance, he has even more justification for his existence than in more naturalistic forms. The idea had already been mooted in our earliest discussions about *The Trojan Women*. At that time I had had sixteen of my own original TV plays presented, as well as nine stage plays in theatres around the country, and I had already written and directed the first TV play to be written in verse, *The Testament of John*, though it had not yet been transmitted. Louis Marks had himself been the producer on several of these plays, including *The Testament of John*, and he was very happy to agree with the idea. We discovered, to our amazement, that as far as our researches could probe, the whole *Theban Trilogy* had never been translated complete by a working playwright. It had been left to Greek scholars and poets to do the job. But these great works were written for public performance in a well-established and highly competitive theatre, by men who were themselves poets, singers, actors, composers and dancers, as well as directors of their own plays. That fact convinced me. It was surely time for a playwright to get a look in, even if he did have no Greek.

Before I set a word on paper, I bumped into my friend the actor Patrick Stewart. I mentioned that I was just about to begin translating Sophocles, and I was very surprised when he made a wry face and said he didn't much like Greek tragedy. I was astounded at this in so distinguished an actor, and one, too, so eminently well suited to Greek roles, and I said so. He replied that he had been in many productions, but had always found that the plays were difficult to act well because the actor found himself again and again involved in tremendous dramatic situations which were expressed in the most banal language, and that he himself could never find a satisfactory way of marrying the power of the situations to the poverty of the words. No more useful comment could have been made to me as I began the huge project. I determined that whatever else I did, and however much of a limitation my lack of knowledge of the Sophoclean original was bound to be, I would at least make sure I gave the actors some decent English words to say.

About one thing I was quite clear from the beginning: that these plays are non-naturalistic poetic drama, at the very highest level of the art, certainly the equal of Shakespeare, and that the poverty-stricken speech of modern naturalism, particularly the film-based television variety, would have no place in my versions. That I would write in verse was not a matter of choice, but the point I started from.

When I wrote *The Testament of John*, I had already confronted the problem that faces every twentieth-century English writer attempting drama in verse, namely, what verse form to use. I was quite convinced that the standard iambic pentameter is no longer a possibility in drama. Shakespeare, Milton, Wordsworth and Keats have done all there is to be done with that particular music: for me, at least, their shadow is far too large. So I looked back at the last successful attempt to write verse drama in English, and saw T S Eliot. I find his drama very unsympathetic, nor do I see in it any evidence that he possessed those particular qualities which make a writer a playwright. He seems to me to be a part of that long tradition in English letters of major poets who were fascinated by the drama without having any aptitude for it, and the plays he wrote and had successfully performed, a triumph of sheer intellect, a great poet's attempt to do something for which he was fundamentally unsuited. But nevertheless, he had been the first poet-playwright to confront the problem of a suitable verse form for modern drama; he too had rejected the iambic pentameter, and whatever the limitations of his plays as plays, he had created many passages of fine dramatic verse: so I decided to try to use his form to serve my own purposes.

Eliot had created a verse line, loosely based on Anglo-Saxon poetry, but without the alliteration, a line consisting of four feet, in which each foot had to contain one strong beat, but could contain any number of weak ones. In doing so he created a verse movement close to the rhythms of natural speech, with something of the flexibility of prose, but which, with the regular beat of its four stresses, clearly defined a recognisable verse music. The problem this metre sets a writer, one which I have not overcome, is that many lines remain ambiguous in stress, clear enough in the poet's mind perhaps, but capable of more than one kind of scansion. In spite of my strictures, the reader will find plenty of iambic pentameters in the five thousand-odd lines of verse in this book. But the experience of directing these translations suggests to me that the problem is an abstract one, more apparent than real. In the mouths of actors, it tends to disappear. The skill involved, as in all dramatic verse, is for the playwright's instinct for natural stress in dramatic English to coincide naturally and without strain with the formal pattern of the verse: and the freer that pattern, the finer the poet's ear must be. This was the metre I had attempted with *The Testament of John*, so it was natural that I should use it for the dramatic trimeters of Sophoclean tragedy. I decided not to be absolutely strict with myself, and to allow the occasional two- or three-footed line if I wanted it. But I tried to make sure that I only used the shorter line for positive effect, not simply because I couldn't think of any way of filling up the odd feet!

The lyric verse in these plays confronts the translator with his biggest problem, but here my experience as a theatrical practitioner helped me. As a director, I had already decided how I intended to present the choral odes. They had to create a quite new lyrical dramatic experience, utterly differentiated from the dramatic episodes. So Sophocles' formal odes would not be broken up, shared out between the chorus actors and spoken as individual lines, to make them seem as naturalistic as possible. I would use a chorus of twelve (Sophocles himself increased the number of the chorus from twelve to fifteen, but I decided upon twelve because it is divisible by six, four, three, two and one, and would therefore make more interesting formal groupings) and the characters would speak to the accompaniment of live specially-composed music, in unison, as individuals, and in all the possible sub-groupings. My lyric verse had to be English lyric verse, with its own life and vitality, so this meant that my models had to be not the Greek originals, whose texture was beyond my comprehension anyway, but the masters of English lyric verse, Keats, Shelley, Marvell, Donne, Jonson, the Cavalier poets, the young Milton. I would try to write tightly rhyming verses, using metres and verse movements imitated from these masters, and I would strive most of all to make these odes convincing as dramatic lyrics in their own right. Where Sophocles in a chorus or choral dialogue repeated the metrical form of a strophe with an exactly similar antistrophe, so I would repeat my lyric verses with meticulous accuracy, strictly reflecting metrical form and rhyme scheme. I would be particularly careful to avoid the use of thunderous full rhymes all the time, using half-rhyme, and even quarter-rhyme – the matching of final consonants only – to ensure flexibility and avoid musical banality. This was not an original decision, I knew. Many translators have tried to rhyme their choruses, using these or similar techniques. But I knew of none that had attempted it with the thoroughgoing concern for form that I intended: nor, indeed, any that were really good enough as English lyric verse. Yeats, of course, made famous versions of choruses from *Antigone* and *Oedipus at Colonus*, but they are a long way from Sophocles, Yeatsian poems in their own right, based on Sophoclean ideas, rather than usable translations.

But that strategic decision left a whole series of tactical questions unanswered. Lyric metres are used in Greek tragedy in a whole series of different ways, in the entry song of the Chorus (*Parados*) in the Choral Odes (*Stasima*), the Choral Dialogues (*Kommoi*), in the *Exodos*, which often takes the form of a choral dialogue, and even, in moments of excitement, within the dramatic episodes themselves. As a point of principle, I decided that whenever Sophocles used lyric verse, I would use my English lyric form, but I very soon discovered that this decision had considerable implications. Most of the greatest moments – one might almost say all of them – in these three plays are written by Sophocles in the form of choral dialogues, an interaction, in lyric verse, between the Chorus and one or two of the main characters. Oedipus' re-entry blinded, his recital of his woes at Colonus, Antigone's farewell to the Chorus, Antigone and Ismene's threnody for the dead Oedipus, and Creon's dirge over his dead son and wife, are all cast by Sophocles in the form of *Kommoi*, or formal choral dialogues, often with the most sophisticated poetic skill, in the exact repetition of metrical patterns from verse to verse, and in the breaking up of single lines between several voices. But these sections are usually translated either into prose, or into a loose free verse, with scarcely any differentiation made between them and the normal dramatic episodes. It immediately became clear that these sections represent the moments of the most intense grief and sorrow in the plays, and it is here that the poet has chosen to stylise his work most completely, to remove it utterly from the prosaic world of daily speech – which had little enough part in the world of Greek tragedy anyway – into the world of music, poetry and dance, a world in which grief can be expressed in its purest, most essential form. The wrong kind of naturalism is the greatest danger for twentieth-century actors and directors when attempting the Greeks. That kind of thinking would require Oedipus simply to mutter 'Christ, my eyes hurt' and fall down the steps when he enters blinded. The very fact that he does not say that, but utters a lyric poem, to music, is the essence of the kind of play we are dealing with. Here, too, was the answer to the subversive question that Patrick Stewart had planted in my mind. A tremendous situation requires tremendous things to be said, requires a poem of despair or suffering, upon which the actor can launch himself, and take wing. So the choral dialogues too would have to be written in tightly rhyming lyric verse, and acted to music. The further I looked into this, the more interesting the idea became. It is not only moments of grief and sorrow that Sophocles renders in his *Kommoi*, but moments of high drama, like the climax of the row between Oedipus, Creon and Jocasta in *Oedipus the King*, and Creon's seizure of Oedipus in *Oedipus at Colonus*. These, too, most modern translations render in an informal, 'naturalistic' way, and these too I decided to translate into lyric verse, and act to music.

This decision had further implications. I had never intended to

196

attempt to reproduce anything of Sophocles' own verse movement, music or texture – indeed, as a non-Greek reader, it was impossible that I should. But the decision to render such a large part of the plays into lyric verse meant that the translation must necessarily become freer. In the irreconcilable conflict between a literal rendering of all the subtleties of Sophocles' original, and the severe demands of English rhyming lyric verse, the needs of the latter would have to come first, if I was to avoid desperate convolutions and unidiomatic phraseology. My version of the choral odes and dialogues, if it was to do any sort of justice to Sophocles' drama by creating passages of striking, and emotionally-moving English, might have to do less than justice to his words. In practice this has meant the occasional use of metaphors not in the original, and the pursuit of ideas or the completion of concepts which Sophocles has not pursued or completed. Simply, there were times when I let my pen have its way, to complete the poem as my instinct told me it had to be completed, and the reader must be left to judge to what degree this is acceptable. Transformation is required, not transliteration. We need a new English poem, full of its own energy and vitality, not a pale reflection of the old.

Style was an equally crucial consideration, though here it was easier to see the road that had to be followed. We had decided on a new translation in the first place because we couldn't find one that was written in direct, modern theatrical English, the language employed by the best practitioners on the modern stage. We wanted no archaisms, no inversions, no puffing up of the emotions by Victorian rhodomontade. The great moments had to be earned, through a simple, strong, concrete, metaphorical English, with no vulgar indulgence of modernity or affectation of the ancient. The ambition was to make the language and the ideas expressed within it, as simple, direct and powerful as it must have been to its original spectators, and if this meant a simplification of mythological nomenclature, and the insertion of a few words or lines to make clear an idea that has not survived the journey of 2,500 years, so be it. Two simple examples will suffice. The Greek gods are invoked by many different names, expressing different elements of the same deity, but I have tended to use only one. Apollo remains Apollo, not Phoebus, the Delian, the Archer King, Loxias, or whatever. More importantly, in *Antigone*, all the original spectators would have known the horrific significance of a body remaining unburied – namely, that there was no chance of peace in the underworld until the correct rites had been performed. Creon is damning Polynices' eternal soul, as Hamlet or Isabella might have put it, as well as his body. Sophocles nowhere says this, because all his audience knew it, but I have inserted a line or two in the earlier part of the play to make the tragic issue quite clear.

The actual usage of words is always the most personal matter in any writer's style, and in this way my own verbal personality must be reflected in every line of the play. One of the clearest indications of this is perhaps in the use of certain modern words which in the purest sense would be considered anachronisms. Rumour, in *Colonus*, travels 'faster than an Olympic champion,' and Eurydice in *Antigone* remarks that 'We are bred to stoicism in this family.' Zeno of Citium began to develop stoic philosophy a clear four generations after Sophocles' lifetime, and the Olympic Games began in the eighth-century BC, many hundreds of years after the Heroic age. But the word 'stoicism' in modern English has nothing at all to do with the philosophy of Zeno. The word has become a part of general modern usage, representing endurance of an intense and uncomplaining kind; just as the phrase 'Olympic champion' doesn't represent to us anything specifically Greek, nor even a specific modern champion, an Ovett or Coe, but the idea of world supremacy in sport: in this particular case, the fastest. People who object to such usages will probably also object to words like 'realpolitik', 'security police', and Antigone's description of Hades as 'that bleak hotel which is never short of a room': but I stand by my usages. In performance they work well, expressing in a vivid modern way an idea that does not seem un-Sophoclean. They are I suppose the standard-bearers or forlorn hope of my attack on the problem of style. My loyalty, as a translator of a text written for performance, must always be principally to the language being translated into, not the language being translated from. That is where my attempt will succeed or fail, not in the details of my treatment, or maltreatment, of the original.

One external factor had an effect on these translations. I was originally commissioned to translate all three plays, and I worked on them in story order, beginning with page one of *Oedipus the King*. Most of the problems of form and style were confronted within the process of translating the first play, but obviously I learned as I went along. I didn't feel that I had really learned how to translate the formal odes and choral dialogues until I was about half way through *Colonus*, and when I looked back on the completed first draft, it seemed to me that *Antigone* was, by a long way, the best of the three, as by that time I was confident in what I was doing. In these first drafts, I had made no attempt to reproduce exactly the formal patterns of the choruses and choral dialogues. I had allowed my own verse forms to emerge naturally, and simply repeated them where repetition was required. The passages of stichomythia likewise, I kept as sharp as I could, but did not attempt to reproduce the formal one-line or two-line patterns of the original. My translations came out quite a lot longer than the originals, of course, but I had expected that. Part of the greatness of any poet lies in his compression of language, and I knew that that was one of many areas where I couldn't hope to be in Sophocles' league.

It was decided to produce *Antigone* first. In the light of advice from Geoffrey Lewis, my classical mentor, I made several crucial retranslations, but *Antigone* went into production much as originally drafted. A year passed before the next two plays were scheduled for production, and during that time I did a great deal of revision and retranslation . I had always been dissatisfied with the first half of *Oedipus the King*, and while reworking it, I found that I was in fact capable of making versions of Sophocles' odes which were much closer to Sophocles' own length, and I soon discovered the delights of reproducing the stichomythia patterns exactly. When I moved onto *Oedipus at Colonus*, I was very conscious that I was courting disaster by letting the English play become too long. The original Greek text is the longest in the canon, and my first version sprawled to some two-and-a-half hours playing-time. So I took a deep breath and decided to attempt to do all the choruses, choral dialogues, and stichomythic passages in the same numbers and patterns of lines employed in the original Greek, which, although I could not read it, was always at my elbow, so that its formal patterns, or those of them that can be clearly seen on the page, were clear to me. My versions are still longer, of course, even when I employ exactly the same number of lines as the original Greek: but they are not so much longer as to threaten the plays' structure, and the formal patterns, in *Colonus* at least, are absolutely reproduced. In this formal respect, *Colonus* is the closest of the translations. *Oedipus the King* is almost as close, and *Antigone* is the freest of the three. The Greek text of the first choral dialogue in *Colonus* is mutilated, and several lines are missing. Because the lines are part of an exact strophe-antistrophe pattern, the number and length of the lines can be conjectured, and I have supplied lines of my own at that point, to complete the pattern.

'A poem', as Auden said, 'is never finished. You simply stop working on it.' The needs of production gave me an unavoidable deadline, but all three plays have been allowed the luxury of some degree of retranslation after the productions. In the first two plays only the odd line or phrase has been changed, but in *Antigone*, the degree of reworking has been considerable.

Sophocles is one of us, not one of a lost them, buried in centuries of dust in forgotten libraries. He is alive now, he lives in our world, and because he is alive, his ideas have changed subtly over the centuries, as mankind has acquired more experience against which to measure his work. Because he was one of the greatest of theatrical artists his work stands up to this scrutiny of the succeeding generations, and as we bring to it our own experience, it becomes richer and more revealing. So there must be nothing archaeological about the act of translation, nothing of the creation of vanished historical epochs. We owe him the best, most idiomatic, up to date language we can manage, so that the burning immediacy and power of his art can strike us as powerfully as they struck his contemporaries. My main aim in making this new version of these much-translated works has been to make them seem that they were written not 2,500 years ago, but the day before yesterday, today, and tomorrow.

Methuen World Classics

Aeschylus (two volumes)
Jean Anouilh
John Arden
Arden & D'Arcy
Aristophanes (two volumes)
Peter Barnes
Brendan Behan
Aphra Behn
Edward Bond (four volumes)
Bertolt Brecht (three volumes)
Howard Brenton (two volumes)
Büchner
Bulgakov
Calderón
Anton Chekhov
Caryl Churchill (two volumes)
Noël Coward (five volumes)
Sarah Daniels
Eduardo De Filippo
David Edgar (three volumes)
Euripides (three volumes)
Dario Fo
Michael Frayn (two volumes)
Max Frisch
Gorky
Harley Granville Barker
Henrik Ibsen (six volumes)
Lorca (three volumes)
Marivaux
Mustapha Matura
David Mercer
Arthur Miller (three volumes)
Anthony Minghella
Molière
Tom Murphy (two volumes)
Peter Nichols (two volumes)
Clifford Odets
Joe Orton
Louise Page
A. W. Pinero
Luigi Pirandello
Stephen Poliakoff
Terence Rattigan (two volumes)
Ntozake Shange
Sophocles (two volumes)
Wole Soyinka
David Storey
August Strindberg (three volumes)
J. M. Synge
Ramón del Valle-Inclán
Frank Wedekind
Oscar Wilde

Methuen Modern Plays

include work by

Jean Anouilh
John Arden
Margaretta D'Arcy
Peter Barnes
Brendan Behan
Edward Bond
Bertolt Brecht
Howard Brenton
Jim Cartwright
Caryl Churchill
Noël Coward
Sarah Daniels
Shelagh Delaney
David Edgar
Dario Fo
Michael Frayn
John Guare
Peter Handke
Terry Johnson
Kaufman & Hart
Barrie Keeffe
Larry Kramer
Stephen Lowe

Doug Lucie
John McGrath
David Mamet
Arthur Miller
Mtwa, Ngema & Simon
Tom Murphy
Peter Nichols
Joe Orton
Louise Page
Luigi Pirandello
Stephen Poliakoff
Franca Rame
David Rudkin
Willy Russell
Jean-Paul Sartre
Sam Shepard
Wole Soyinka
C. P. Taylor
Theatre Workshop
Sue Townsend
Timberlake Wertenbaker
Victoria Wood